QUANTITATIVE CRITERIA FOR
ACADEMIC RESEARCH LIBRARIES

A Report Submitted To
The National Center for Education Statistics
Under Contract 300-82-0284

March 20, 1984

K. L. Stubbs
University of Virginia Library
Charlottesville, Virginia 22901

Association of College and Research Libraries
American Library Association
Chicago

Additional copies of this book are available PREPAID from

ACRL/ALA
50 East Huron Street
Chicago, IL 60611

ACRL members $15.
Nonmembers $19.

ISBN 0-8389-6788-4

CONTENTS

I. WHAT IS AN ACADEMIC RESEARCH LIBRARY?

Classification problems, an eminent statistician says, arise in all fields of science and beyond.[1] Among academic libraries, a knowledgeable observer can fairly easily classify this or that library as a two-year or four-year college or university library. But it is not so simple to decide what a research library is. The category of research libraries overlaps other categories. A university library may be a research library; so may a special library or a public library or even a college library. In Kruskal's phrase, the category is marked by an ineluctable fuzziness.

A research library is "A reference library provided with specialized material, where exhaustive investigation can be carried on in a particular field (as in a technological library) or in several fields (as in a university library)."[2] But what does "exhaustive investigation" mean? To take two examples from non-academic libraries: The Albemarle County Historical Society in Virginia has several hundred volumes and can support exhaustive investigation on some aspects of Albemarle County history. But no doubt this is not what we mean when we speak of research libraries. On the other hand, a large urban public library may have thousands of volumes, but they may comprise mostly duplicates of popular fiction and non-fiction scattered among branches; and exhaustive investigation will not be possible there.

A fuller definition of research libraries (at least of academic research libraries) is offered in Title II, Part C, of the Higher Education Act (20 U.S.C. 1021, 1041-1042) and in the Regulations on II-C (47 FR 35454-35461). According to II-C, a research library is one that makes a significant contribution to education and research, is broadly based and has national or international significance for research, is in demand by researchers, and so on. Or in brief, a research library is a library that supports research. Since "research" is ambiguous, the category of research libraries, as a result, does not have well-defined boundaries. It is not evident in what the "research-ness" of research libraries consists.

Nevertheless, the term research libraries is not devoid of meaning. Librarians and scholars know that Harvard and Yale and Berkeley and Stanford are research libraries and are doing something that other types of academic libraries are not doing or are doing in lesser ways. If we can describe clearly what it is that characterizes Harvard and Yale and Berkeley and Stanford and similar research libraries then we shall be closer to criteria for academic research libraries.

In this report, therefore, we begin with the universe of approximately 3,000 U. S. academic libraries, as measured in the HEGIS library data file. Within this universe we find a cluster of libraries assumed to support research. We measure the quantitative characteristics of these libraries. We search out the ways in which they resemble one another and the ways in which they differ from other libraries. We ask which other libraries share the essential characteristics of this cluster. When we find other libraries quantitatively similar to those in the cluster, then we say that these are not significantly distinguishable from the cluster; and so they fall into the class of research libraries. Thus, we define criteria for research libraries and determine which institutions meet those criteria.

We begin by discussing the HEGIS data and the methodology for identifying an initial group of research libraries.

II. LIBRARY DATA AND THE METHODOLOGY FOR IDENTIFYING ACADEMIC RESEARCH LIBRARIES

We are seeking to describe the quantitative characteristics of academic research libraries in the United States. For this purpose we begin with the most comprehensive data file on U. S. academic libraries, the HEGIS survey. At the time this project was begun, the latest HEGIS library data available on computer tape were those from the Fall, 1979, survey (containing some data for FY 78-79).

The universe for this survey was 3,190 college and university libraries, of which 2,945 institutions responded. Two of the respondents lacked data on volumes held, staff, and expenditures. These two were deleted from our working file, on the grounds that their data were too sparse to be useful for this inquiry. Our final file of libraries therefore comprised 2,943 institutions.

To the library data we also added data from other HEGIS surveys: Fall Enrollments 1978 and 1979; Earned Degrees Conferred 1978-79 and 1979-80; Faculty Salaries 1978-79 and 1979-80; and Financial Statistics of Institutions of Higher Education, 1979. From all of these data we selected for analysis 48 basic variables on library collections, expenditures, staffing, and services; FTE and headcount enrollments of undergraduate and of graduate and professional students; associate's, bachelor's, master's, and doctor's degrees; headcount faculty; and educational and general expenditures by colleges and universities.

It should be noted that the HEGIS surveys exhibit some of the disabilities that afflict self-reported data. Missing values are a particular problem in statistical analysis. Confusion between missing values and zeros, either in reporting or in coding, can create ambiguities. For example, in the library survey over a third of the institutions report no data for microforms of books. Does this mean that they have no microforms of books, or merely that they are not reporting how many they have? When we find that even university libraries are coded as having no microforms of books, we can reasonably suspect the data.[3]

Another example: 72 libraries are coded as having answered no directional questions; but these same libraries did answer reference questions. If there were reference questions, then it is likely that there were also directional questions, especially since some of the libraries in this category are university libraries. So in at least some of these cases a zero for directional questions in fact indicates a missing value. For some variables, such as microforms, the patterns of ambiguous reporting or coding are extensive enough that the data should be taken with a grain or two of salt. Fortunately, for crucial variables only a few libraries exhibit missing or zero values. For example, only 16 lack values for volumes held; 37, values for volumes added, gross; 28, values for current periodical subscriptions. Where zero is coded for variables like volumes held or total staff, we have recoded the values as missing, on the grounds that it is unlikely that an academic library has no volumes or no staff.

We turn then to the problem of identifying an initial group of research libraries from our file of 2,943 libraries.

Although a knowledgeable librarian might not be able to say precisely what a research library is, he or she undoubtedly would be able to name some research libraries. Harvard, Yale, Berkeley, Stanford, Illinois, Cornell, and others would come immediately to mind. These would be the largest libraries in terms of collections, staffing, and expenditures. How could the smaller research libraries be identified? A priori it is not evident that all university libraries are research libraries or that all doctorate-granting institutions have research libraries. For example, in the state of Virginia the three largest academic libraries are the University of Virginia, Virginia Polytechnic Institute, and Virginia Commonwealth University. Would there be general agreement among librarians that all three of these are research libraries? If not, how would we decide which ones are the same kind of library, on a smaller scale, as Harvard, Yale, and Berkeley?

A pragmatic approach to identifying a sample of research libraries might be to select those that have received Title II-C grants. Those institutions have been judged, according to the Government's criteria, to be research libraries. But it is not clear how representative this sample might be -- whether it may be weighted by larger institutions, for example. A second approach would be to choose the (for 1978-79) 89 U. S. academic members of the Association of Research Libraries. Those libraries have been selected as research libraries according to carefully worked out quantitative criteria. But again a priori it is not evident how inclusive this sample would be. A third approach might be to use the Carnegie Council's classification of institutions of higher education.[4] The Council classifies colleges and universities into six categories (doctorate-granting institutions, comprehensive universities and colleges, liberal arts colleges, and so on). The category Doctorate-Granting Institutions is subdivided into Research Universities and Doctorate-Granting Universities. The Council lists 98 Research Universities in 40 states. Of the 98 libraries in these institutions, 76 are members of the Association of Research Libraries; 22 are not members. But even granted that the Council has identified a distinct group of Research Universities, it does not follow that every Research University has a research library.

Rather than begin with prior assumptions derived from the II-C grants or ARL membership or Carnegie classification, we start with the statistical method of cluster analysis. In this method selected variables are analyzed in order to group like cases together. For example, from data on the numbers of different kinds of teeth, cluster analysis can find various groupings of similar animals. An obvious question to put to cluster analysis, therefore, is what clusters it can find among our 2,943 libraries. Is there a cluster that includes cases known to be research libraries--Harvard, Yale, Berkeley, Stanford, etc.?

In order to use cluster analysis, we must decide which variables to include in the analysis. From our 48 variables we are interested, in the first place, in

the library variables. We do not know a priori whether or to what extent
university variables (such as enrollments, degrees, expenditures) may be related
to library characteristics. We therefore exclude the university variables from
the cluster analysis. Among library variables some are merely linear combinations
of others and contribute no additional information to an analysis. For example,
total FTE staff here is taken as equal to FTE professional staff plus FTE nonprofessional staff. If the latter two variables are in the analysis, then total
staff is not needed. Other library variables available in the HEGIS file have not
been of concern in library literature on quantitative characteristics. Some
examples are part-time women nonprofessionals or microforms of serials or numbers
of titles of government documents. For the purpose of classifying and describing
libraries librarians have been more interested in variables such as volumes held
or professional staff or circulation.

When we exclude these variables, we are left with 14 variables that measure
library characteristics.[5] Four measure collections, four expenditures, two staffing,
and four activities and services. These 14 variables are

Volumes held

Volumes added, gross

Total microforms

Current periodical subscriptions

Expenditures for library materials

Expenditures for binding

Total salaries and wages

Other operating expenditures

FTE professional staff

FTE nonprofessional staff

Interlibrary loans lent

Interlibrary loans borrowed

Circulation

Total reference, directional, and group transactions

These are the variables to be used in cluster analysis.

III. QUANTITATIVE CHARACTERISTICS OF ACADEMIC RESEARCH LIBRARIES

A. Cluster Analysis

The goal of cluster analysis is to classify objects into groups, or clusters, suggested by the data, rather than defined a priori.[6] The objects in one cluster are quantitatively similar to one another and dissimilar to objects in different clusters. Various types of clusters are possible. In disjoint clusters each object is placed in one and only one cluster. An example might be a two-cluster arrangement of a deck of cards, in which one cluster comprises all red cards and the other all black. A sophisticated procedure is hierarchical clustering, in which one cluster is contained within another. For example, the red cluster in a deck of cards can be divided into two clusters of hearts and diamonds, and similarly the black cluster can be divided into spades and clubs; and each of these four groups can be further divided (into face cards and others, say). Other clustering procedures (which are harder to interpret for large data sets) allow overlapping clusters, in which an object can belong to more than one cluster.

For this paper we applied a hierarchical procedure based on Ward's method, a widely-used clustering algorithm. Other methods, however, such as disjoint clustering based on Euclidean distances, produce similar results to the ones reported here.

Cluster analysis examines the 14 variables, listed above, for each library in the data file. At the highest level the analysis finds two clusters. One of these clusters is further divided into two groups, so that at this level there are three clusters. Again, one of the clusters is divided, making four clusters. And so on, down to the level where each library comprises a separate cluster. There is, in short, a hierarchy of groupings among the libraries. Looking at the highest level, we find that 127 libraries are in one cluster, and all other libraries are in the other cluster. This cluster of 127 libraries is the group of particular interest. The cluster contains 88 of the 89 ARL libraries in the HEGIS file. (The missing ARL library is Brigham Young University, which did not report data on expenditures and so was excluded from the cluster analysis.) Of 98 institutions classed as Research Universities by the Carnegie Council, the libraries of 85 are included in this cluster. There are only 30 libraries in the cluster that are not ARL members or are not the libraries of Carnegie Council Research Universities. These 30 libraries include 26 from doctorate-granting institutions, 3 from master's degree institutions, and 1 from a two-year college. Over two-thirds of the libraries in the cluster are ARL members, including the large research libraries like Harvard, Berkeley, Yale, Stanford, as well as the smaller research library members of the ARL. The remaining one-third of the cluster comprises almost entirely libraries of doctorate-granting universities. We might well suspect that these libraries are quantitatively similar to the large libraries in the ARL that are known to be research libraries. The conclusion seems inescapable that this cluster on the whole delineates a group of research libraries in the data.

It is interesting to follow the cluster analysis to further levels of the hierarchy. The "research library" cluster divides into two groups of 12 and 115 libraries. The group of 12 comprises the largest libraries, such as Harvard, Berkeley, Illinois, and others. Thus, at the level of three clusters there are 12 very large research libraries, 115 others in a research library-like group, and a third cluster containing all other libraries. At the fourth level a group of 387 libraries splits off from this third cluster. These 387 are predominantly smaller university libraries and large college libraries. In other words, the analysis finds a fourfold grouping of libraries at this level: the 12 largest research libraries, 115 other "research libraries," 387 university or large college libraries, and a remaining cluster of mostly two-year institutions and smaller colleges.

In summary, cluster analysis points to a basic group of 127 libraries that share research library characteristics. We could, in fact, simply stop here and call these the research libraries in the HEGIS file. But it is possible, as it were, to fine-tune the analysis. For example, the 127 libraries in the cluster include a two-year college library. Did that library fall into the cluster merely because it has large collections, staffing, and services like circulation spread over many branch locations? On the other hand, there may be other libraries outside the cluster that are closely related to the 127. Or again the cluster analysis does not tell us which of our 14 variables are more significant in distinguishing between the 127 libraries and the others. In short, cluster analysis is a kind of rough-and-ready first step in classifying libraries. For fine-tuning we turn first to the statistical procedure of discriminant analysis and then to principal component analysis.

B. Discriminant Analysis

Discriminant analysis is a powerful statistical tool for identifying the characteristics that can discriminate between two or more groups.[7] Discriminant analysis begins with separate groups--say, male and female library professionals. It then analyzes discriminating variables--salaries, salary increases, rank, etc.-- to identify the combinations of variables that best distinguish between the groups. One product of the analysis can be a formula that distinguishes males from females merely on the basis of their salaries, rank, and so on.

In the present instance we have two groups, or clusters, of libraries and data for 14 variables for each library. We want to know (1) which of these 14 variables are necessary for discriminating between the two clusters, and (2) which of the 14 are sufficient for discrimination. We use a method in discriminant analysis called stepwise selection. The analysis then finds that only 12 of our 14

variables are needed for maximum discrimination. The other two variables--Current
periodical subscriptions and Interlibrary loans lent--add nothing significant to
the discriminating power of the other variables. The 12 variables that the analysis
identifies as useful for discrimination are

> Volumes held
>
> Volumes added, gross
>
> Total microforms
>
> Expenditures for library materials
>
> Expenditures for binding
>
> Total salaries and wages
>
> Other operating expenditures
>
> FTE professional staff
>
> FTE nonprofessional staff
>
> Interlibrary loans borrowed
>
> Circulation
>
> Total reference, directional, and group transactions

What discriminant analysis is telling us is this: If we know how many volumes an
academic library had, how many volumes added, how many microforms, etc., then we
can determine fairly accurately whether that library falls in the "research
library" cluster or in the other cluster. We still need to determine, however,
(1) whether any of the libraries in our cluster of 127 are basically dissimilar
to the known research libraries, and (2) whether there are libraries outside the
cluster that in fact are similar to research libraries. To answer these questions,
we turn to principal component analysis.

C. Principal Component Analysis

   Principal component analysis is one of the set of statistical techniques
generically called factor analysis.[8] Component analysis begins with the twelve

variables for our cluster of 127 libraries. It asks, in effect, what hypothetical variable or component is most closely related to the twelve variables. This componen is derived in such a way that it has the highest possible correlations with the twelve variables. The analysis then calculates the correlations of the variables wit the component. We take the component to be a summary measure of library collections, expenditures, staffing, and activities and services.

When the component analysis is performed, here are the correlations of the twelve variables with the library size component:

Volumes held	.93
Volumes added, gross	.92
Total microforms	.50
Expenditures for library materials	.91
Expenditures for binding	.81
Total salaries and wages	.95
Other operating expenditures	.75
FTE professional staff	.88
FTE nonprofessional staff	.93
Interlibrary loans borrowed	.45
Circulation	.77
Total reference, directional, and group transactions	.24

From these figures we can see that the 127 libraries are most alike in volumes held, total salaries, and FTE nonprofessionals. They are less similar in microforms, interlibrary borrowing, and reference transactions.

From these correlations between the twelve variables and the library size component, what are called component score coefficients are derived. These coefficients are directly proportional to the correlations. Here are the component score coefficients for the data from the 127 libraries:

Volumes held	.12530
Volumes added, gross	.12410
Total microforms	.06770
Expenditures for library materials	.12255
Expenditures for binding	.10986
Total salaries and wages	.12851
Other operating expenditures	.10117
FTE professional staff	.11842
FTE nonprofessional staff	.12567
Interlibrary loans borrowed	.06112
Circulation	.10347
Total reference, directional, and group transactions	.03251

These coefficients are no more than weights for each of the twelve variables. When the weights are multiplied by the data from an individual library, the sum of the twelve products is a component score for that library.

It is worth emphasizing again that the weights, or coefficients, are directly proportional to the correlation of each variable with library size. Where a correlation is higher (say, for total salaries), more of the variation in library size is explained by that variable, which therefore is given a higher weight. The weights thus accurately mirror the ways in which the 127 libraries are alike or different; they reflect and measure what is common among the 127 libraries.

From these weights we can compute component scores for individual libraries. The data for each of the twelve variables are transformed to a standard normal form and multiplied by the corresponding weight. The formula for computing component scores is:

$$.12530 \text{ (log of vols. held} - 14.1235)/.6773$$

+ .12410 (log of vols. added - 10.8661)/.6372

+ .06770 (log of microforms - 11.7778)/4.8702

+ .12255 (log of expend. for lib. materials - 14.0521)/.5319

+ .10986 (log of expend. for binding - 11.3047)/.8031

+ .12851 (log of total salaries - 14.5587)/.5764

+ .10117 (log of other operating expend. - 12.7151)/.8067

+ .11842 (log of prof. staff - 3.9796)/.5680

+ .12567 (log of nonprof. staff - 4.5709)/.6455

+ .06112 (log of interlib. borrowing - 8.1983)/1.0976

+ .10347 (log of circulation - 13.1478)/.6672

+ .03251 (log of ref. transactions - 8.2017)/.8358

The score for an individual library indicates its rank or position in regard to the size and resources deployed of the 127 libraries. Taken together, the 127 scores range from 2.689 to -4.629. Their mean (and median) is approximately 0, and their standard deviation is 1. The scores have the useful property that they are approximated by a standard normal curve or distribution. In this kind of distribution most of the values fall between +2 and -2; we would expect no more than six or seven out of 127 to be greater than +2 or less than -2. And indeed there are three scores greater than +2 (Harvard, Berkeley, and Yale) and three less than -2 (Northern Virginia Community College, Tennessee State University, and Mills College). In a standard normal distribution, moreover, we would expect about 95% of the scores to be greater than or equal to -1.65. For our 127 libraries we would expect about 121 scores to be -1.65 or greater; and in fact 124 scores are -1.65 or greater. From this feature of the distribution we can make valuable inferences about libraries outside our sample of 127. We use the component score formula above to compute scores for other libraries. If there is a group of other libraries that are in fact like the cluster in respect to library size and resources deployed, then at least 95% of that group should score -1.65 or higher. Or in different terms the probability is no more than 5% that a library essentially like the sample would fail to score at least -1.65.

In summary, if we use the component score formula for our 127 libraries to calculate scores for all 2,943 libraries in the total data file, we can set a score cutoff point. For libraries with scores above that point, we say that those libraries cannot be significantly distinguished from Harvard, Yale, Berkeley, Stanford, and others in the cluster of 127. For scores below the cutoff point, we say that there is a significant quantitative distinction. How do we determine the cutoff point? There is no hard-and-fast rule in statistics for selecting the point. In social sciences a common procedure is to choose a point associated with a .05 probability level. (Interestingly, the U. S. Supreme Court has used a .05 significance level in discrimination cases.)[9] We hypothesize, for example, that library X shows the same quantitative characteristics as Harvard, Yale, Berkeley, and other known research libraries. If we find a probability of 5% or less, then we reject this hypothesis. As we have seen, a .05 significance level is associated with a component score of -1.65. Consequently, we can form a decision rule: If a given library scores -1.65 or higher, then accept that it shows the characteristics of Harvard, Yale, Berkeley, and other research libraries. If it scores less than -1.65, then reject the hypothesis that it shows the essential research library characteristics.

Of the 2,943 libraries in our data file, it turns out that 181 exhibit scores of -1.65 or greater. These libraries are listed in Table 1, in descending rank order by component score. The Table also includes two columns headed "ARL" and "Carnegie". An x in the ARL column indicates that the library was a member of the Association of Research Libraries in 1978-79. An x in the Carnegie column indicates that the library is in an institution classified by the Carnegie Council as a "Research University."[10]

The Appendix displays the scores for the 2,943 libraries in the data file, arranged by state and by component score.[11]

TABLE 1

Principal Component Scores of Libraries Scoring −1.65 or Higher, 1978-79

Rank	Library	Score	ARL	Carnegie
1.	Harvard University	2.689	X	X
2.	U of Cal-Berkeley	2.122	X	X
3.	Yale University	2.088	X	X
4.	U of Cal-Los Angeles	1.942	X	X
5.	U of Ill Urbana Campus	1.780	X	X
6.	U of Texas at Austin	1.766	X	X
7.	Stanford University	1.720	X	X
8.	U Michigan-Ann Arbor	1.653	X	X
9.	University of Washington	1.614	X	X
10.	U of Wisconsin Madison	1.613	X	X
11.	Columbia U Main Division	1.536	X	X
12.	U of Minn Mnpls Snt Paul	1.363	X	X
13.	Indiana U Bloomington	1.286	X	X
14.	University of Chicago	1.227	X	X
15.	Ohio State U Main Campus	1.122	X	X
16.	Cornell U Endowed Colleges	1.070	X	X
17.	University of Florida	1.038	X	X
18.	U of Virginia Main Campus	1.035	X	X
19.	U of Pennsylvania	1.013	X	X
20.	Princeton University	0.966	X	X
21.	U of Cal-Davis	0.906	X	X
22.	U of NC at Chapel Hill	0.872	X	X
23.	Northwestern University	0.856	X	X
24.	New York University	0.813	X	X
25.	Duke University	0.752	X	X
26.	U of Southern California	0.707	X	X
27.	University of Iowa	0.672	X	X
28.	Michigan State University	0.665	X	X
29.	University of Georgia	0.665	X	X
30.	University of Utah	0.664	X	X
31.	University of Arizona	0.632	X	X
32.	PA State U Main Campus	0.595	X	X
33.	U of Pittsbg Main Campus	0.583	X	X
34.	U of Md College Park Cam	0.567	X	X
35.	U of Kansas Main Campus	0.555	X	X
36.	Rutgers U New Brunswick	0.538	X	X
37.	U of Cal-San Diego	0.535	X	X
38.	Arizona State University	0.460	X	
39.	Sthn Illinois U Carbondl	0.441	X	X
40.	U of Cal-Santa Barbara	0.424	X	X
41.	Florida State University	0.394	X	X
42.	U of Hawaii at Manoa	0.388	X	X
43.	University of Kentucky	0.342	X	X
44.	U of Missouri-Columbia	0.333	X	X
45.	VA Poly Inst and State U	0.304	X	X
46.	SUNY at Buffalo Main Cam	0.297	X	X
47.	Temple University	0.270	X	X
48.	U of NM Main Campus	0.215	X	X
49.	Mass Inst of Technology	0.207	X	X
50.	Washington University	0.194	X	X
51.	Washington St University	0.167	X	X
52.	U of SC at Columbia	0.166	X	X
53.	Wayne State University	0.158	X	X
54.	Johns Hopkins University	0.150	X	X
55.	Purdue U Main Campus	0.144	X	X
56.	Vanderbilt University	0.105	X	X
57.	University of Rochester	0.088	X	X
58.	U of Cincinnati Main Cam	0.086	X	X
59.	Iowa State U Sci & Techn	0.083	X	X
60.	LA State U and A&M C	0.063	X	X
61.	U of Nebraska-Lincoln	0.053	X	X
62.	U of Colorado at Boulder	0.043	X	X
63.	Texas A&M U Main Campus	0.030	X	X
64.	U of Cal-Irvine	0.021	X	X
65.	Syracuse U Main Campus	−0.015	X	X
66.	U of South Florida	−0.027	X	X
67.	U of Mass Amherst Campus	−0.042	X	X
68.	University of Connecticut	−0.046	X	X
69.	Emory University	−0.054	X	X
70.	U of Houston Cen Campus	−0.123	X	X

TABLE 1 (Continued)

Rank	Library	Score	ARL	Carnegie
71.	U of Oregon Main Campus	-0.129	X	X
72	Georgetown University	-0.160	X	X
73.	Boston University	-0.163	X	X
74.	Texas Tech University	-0.205	X	X
75.	U of Tennessee Knoxville	-0.218	X	X
76.	Howard University	-0.220	X	X
77.	U of Cal-Riverside	-0.221	X	
78.	NC State U Raleigh	-0.240	X	X
79.	Brown University	-0.270	X	X
80.	University of Miami	-0.305	X	X
81.	Case Western Reserve U	-0.351	X	X
82.	Dartmouth College	-0.360	X	X
83.	SUNY at Stony Bk Main Cam	-0.367	X	X
84.	San Diego State U	-0.369		
85.	Ball State University	-0.397		
86.	U of Wisconsin Milwaukee	-0.415		
87.	SUNY at Albany	-0.429	X	
88.	University of Notre Dame	-0.438	X	
89.	Auburn U Main Campus	-0.468		X
90.	Colorado State University	-0.480	X	X
91.	Tulane U of Louisiana	-0.485	X	X
92.	Northern Ill University	-0.547		
93.	U of Oklahoma Norman Cam	-0.648	X	X
94.	Kent State U Main Campus	-0.690	X	
95.	North Texas St University	-0.724		
96.	U of Akron Main Campus	-0.750		
97.	George Wash University	-0.753		X
98.	University of Alabama	-0.773	X	
99.	U of PR Rio Piedras	-0.792		
100.	University of Delaware	-0.821		
101.	University of Louisville	-0.825		
102.	San Francisco State U	-0.842		
103.	San Jose State U	-0.846		
104.	Cal State U-Northridge	-0.854		
105.	Okla State U Main Campus	-0.863	X	X
106.	U of Ill Chicago Circle	-0.864		
107	Cal State U-Sacramento	-0.871		
108.	Illinois State University	-0.931		
109.	U Vt & State Agrl College	-0.961		X
110.	Boston College	-0.976		
111.	Oregon State University	-1.004		X
112.	GA Inst of Techn Main Cam	-1.034		X
113.	Memphis State University	-1.049		
114.	Southern Meth University	-1.067		
115.	U of New Hampshire	-1.070		
116.	Miami Univ Oxford Cam	-1.072		
117.	Western Mich University	-1.073		
118.	Ind-Purdue U Indianapolis	-1.074		
119.	U of Cal-Santa Cruz	-1.079		
120.	U of Ill Medl Ctr Chigo	-1.080		
121.	Georgia State University	-1.091		
122.	Fordham University	-1.111		
123.	U Alabama in Birmingham	-1.113		
124.	Kansas St U Agr & App Sci	-1.117		X
125.	Ohio U Main Campus	-1.152		
126.	NM State U Main Campus	-1.155		
127.	Wake Forest University	-1.157		
128.	Cal State U-Los Angeles	-1.158		
129.	Cal Poly St U-Sn Luis OB	-1.174		
130.	Rice University	-1.186	X	
131.	Bowling Grn St U Main Cam	-1.189		
132.	Marquette University	-1.196		
133.	Cal State U-Long Beach	-1.214		
134.	U of Nevada Reno	-1.230		
135.	Cleveland St University	-1.230		
136.	Hofstra University	-1.230		
137.	U of Arkansas Main Campus	-1.255		X
138.	University of Denver	-1.261		
139.	Wright St U Main Campus	-1.273		
140.	Tufts University	-1.277		X

TABLE 1 (Continued)

Rank	Library	Score	ARL	Carnegie
141.	West Virginia University	-1.287		
142.	U of Texas at El Paso	-1.298		X
143.	Portland State University	-1.307		
144.	Cal State U-Chico	-1.311		
145.	Clemson University	-1.316		
146.	U of NC at Greensboro	-1.318		
147.	University of Wyoming	-1.326		
148.	CUNY Queens College	-1.332		
149.	Northeastern University	-1.340		
150.	U of Missouri-Kansas City	-1.341		X
151.	Honnold Joint Library	-1.348		
152.	Sthn Illinois U Edwardsvl	-1.361		
153.	Loyola U of Chicago	-1.368		
154.	Central Mich University	-1.375		
155.	Eastern Ky University	-1.381		
156.	Mississippi St University	-1.384		X
157.	Western Ky University	-1.392		
158.	Cal State U-Fresno	-1.394		
159.	Cal State U-Fullerton	-1.405		
160.	Indiana State U Main Cam	-1.416		
161.	East Carolina University	-1.418		
162.	Yeshiva University	-1.425		X
163.	C of William and Mary	-1.436		
164.	University of Toledo	-1.443		
165.	Brandeis University	-1.448		X
166.	U of Rhode Island	-1.464		
167.	Northern Ariz University	-1.469		
168.	Catholic U of America	-1.472		X
169.	Baylor University	-1.499		
170.	Cornell U Statutory C	-1.505		
171.	Old Dominion University	-1.517		
172.	U of Northern Iowa	-1.522		
173.	American University	-1.559		
174.	Florida International U	-1.561		
175.	University of Montana	-1.570		
176.	U of Northern Colorado	-1.588		
177.	Wichita State University	-1.589		
178.	U of Southern Mississippi	-1.619		
179.	Saint John's University	-1.625		
180.	Adelphi University	-1.635		
181.	DePaul University	-1.640		

From our cluster of 127 libraries only three score below -1.65. The three, with their scores, are Northern Virginia Community College, -2.043; Tennessee State University, -2.107; and Mills College, -4.629. Brigham Young is the only ARL member not included in Table 1; because of missing data on expenditures its score cannot be calculated. There are six libraries of institutions in the Carnegie list of "Research Universities" that do not score -1.65 or higher. These, with their scores, are: St. Louis, -1.776; Utah State, -2.093; Carnegie-Mellon, -2.441; California Institute of Technology, -2.873; CUNY Graduate School, -3.928; Rockefeller, -4.035.

According to our decision rule, we accept that the 181 libraries of Table 1 are not significantly different from the group containing Harvard, Yale, Berkeley, and other research libraries. We therefore take these 181 to be the research libraries in our file of 2,943. The libraries that score less than -1.65 we judge to be significantly different from the 181.

The component scores of Table 1 are summary measures indicating a library's size in collections, expenditures, personnel, and services and activities. The scores are simply weighted sums of the data for twelve variables. Consequently, different combinations of data can produce the same score. For example, a library with a large number of volumes but relatively few professionals can exhibit the same score as a library with few volumes and many professionals. We can obtain a clearer picture of what is implied by our -1.65 dividing lines by looking at individual variables. In a normal distribution only 5% of the values would be expected to be less than 1.65 standard deviations below the mean. Returning to our sample of 127 libraries, from which the component score formula was derived, we find that the mean of the logarithm of professional staff is 3.9796, and the standard deviation is .5680. Then 1.65 standard deviations below the mean is $3.9796 - 1.65(.5680) = 3.0424$. The antilog of this number is 20.96, which can be rounded to 21. Thus, 21 serves as a dividing line for professionals. We would expect no more than about 5% of the libraries like Harvard, Yale, and other research libraries to have fewer professionals than 21.

The dividing lines for ten of the twelve variables used in principal component analysis are displayed in Table 2. (Two variables--Total microforms and Interlibrary loans borrowed--are omitted because the variability among the 181 libraries in respect to these variables is so great that useful dividing lines cannot be derived.) To these ten variables we add two linear combinations of variables: Total library expenditures and Total staff. Note that not all of the 181 research libraries pass each of these tests. For example, 6 of the 181 had fewer than 21 professionals. All 181 do pass the component score test because, as was observed above, a library deficient in professionals may balance that deficiency with a large number of volumes in the computation of its component score. Nevertheless, Table 2 does offer a useful guide to the characteristics of academic research libraries in 1978-79. In general, a research library had at least 445,000 volumes; 18,000 volumes added; $530,000 in expenditures for materials; and so on. The libraries that failed to meet a majority of these levels differed from research libraries.

TABLE 2

Approximate Dividing Lines for Academic Research Library Variables, 1978-79

Variable	Dividing Line
Volumes held	445,000
Volumes added, gross	18,000
Expenditures for library materials	$ 530,000
Expenditures for binding	$ 22,000
Total salaries and wages	$ 810,000
Other operating expenditures	$ 88,000
Total expenditures	$1,450,000
FTE professional staff	21
FTE nonprofessional staff	33
Total FTE staff	54
Circulation	170,000
Total reference, directional, and group transactions	900

IV. OTHER QUANTITATIVE CHARACTERISTICS OF ACADEMIC RESEARCH LIBRARIES:
     REGRESSION ANALYSIS

In the preceding section we have delineated a group of 181 libraries from our file of 2,943. We have seen how in 1978-79 research libraries on the whole owned at least 445,000 volumes, spent $1,450,000 or more, and had at least 54 FTE staff. In this section we discuss other quantitative relationships in the data of the 181 research libraries.

A useful statistical technique for describing the relations of one variable to others is multiple regression analysis. In principal component analysis we studied twelve variables, and asked what hypothetical variable, or component, is most closely related to the twelve and how strong the relationship is. In regression analysis we select a known variable, such as professional staff, and ask which other known variables are closely related to it, and again, how strong the relation is. For analysis we choose ten of the twelve variables in Table 2: Volumes held; Volumes added, gross; Expenditures for library materials; Expenditures for binding; Total salaries and wages; Other operating expenditures; Total expenditures; FTE professional staff; FTE nonprofessional staff; and Total staff. (The other two variables-- Circulation and Total reference, directional, and group transactions--are only weakly correlated with other variables, so that in their case the results of regression analysis are of doubtful utility.)

How do we select the variables that best "explain," or are most closely associated with volumes, volumes added, expenditures for materials, and the other variables? Regression techniques offer procedures for selecting subsets of explanatory variables. But one should not merely follow a procedure, such as step-wise regression, unthinkingly. For example, gross volumes added are most strongly related to net volumes added. But we will not gain much by learning that gross volumes added are associated with net volumes added. For this report we are seeking a small set of explanatory variables for each of our ten variables--if possible, no more than one or two explanatory variables in each set. For simplicity's sake, moreover, we would like to have the same set of explanatory variables for all or most of our ten variables. In other words, judgment needs to be exercised in the selection of explanatory variables.

As an aid in selection, we used a technique called all-subsets regression on the ten variables for various classes of libraries--the 181 research libraries, other doctorate-granting institutions, institutions with master's degrees or with bachelor's degrees as the highest offering, and two-year colleges. This analysis reveals that the "best" explanatory variables differ by type of library and by variable being explained. For example, for professional staff in the 181 research libraries the single explanatory variable that accounts for most variance is volumes; the best pair of explanatory variables consists of volumes and either faculty head-count 1979 or fulltime students 1978. In four-year colleges, on the other hand, the single variable most closely related to professional staff is current periodicals; and the best pair is current periodicals and fulltime students 1978. A pair of explanatory variables that recurs throughout the analysis, however, is volumes held and circulation. For research libraries this pair is the best, or is one of the two or three best, sets of explanatory variables. We offer a specific example of the use of these variables.

Consider professional staff in the 181 research libraries. The number of professionals is strongly related to volumes held and circulation. Regression analysis shows that this relationship is characterized by an R^2 of .80, meaning that 80% of the variance in numbers of professionals in research libraries can be "explained" by volumes held and circulation. The more volumes a research institution has, and the more books it circulates, the more professional staff it is likely to have. The analysis, moreover, presents a precise statement of the relationship by deriving an equation:

FTE professional staff = .00002208308 x Volumes held + .00001215037 x

Circulation + 14.996054.

This equation becomes more understandable when we note that .00002208308 x Volumes is approximately equivalent to 1 per each 45,000 volumes. Similarly, .00001215037 x Circulation can be converted to 1 per each 83,000 volumes circulated. Thus, the equation becomes

FTE professional staff = 1 per each 45,000 Volumes + 1 per each 83,000 Volumes circulated + 15.

The regression analysis also offers a way of judging how closely this equation predicts the actual number of professionals in given libraries. The difference between an actual number and a predicted number is a residual. The standard error of the residuals is approximately 16. We can expect in general that 95% of residuals would be greater than -1.65 standard errors. -1.65 times the standard error of 16 is approximately -26. Adding this to the equation above, we have

FTE professional staff = 1 per each 45,000 Vols. + 1 per each 83,000 Volumes circulated + 15 - 26 = 1 per each 45,000 Volumes + 1 per each 83,000 Volumes circulated - 11.

This equation presents the minimum number of professionals that one would expect in a research library. There is no more than a .05 probability that a research library would have fewer professionals than this equation predicts. From the principal component analysis we saw that a research library can be expected to have at least 21 professionals. From the regression analysis we now see that the number of professionals is also related to volumes and circulation. Any research library would be expected to have 21 professionals. A research library with 1,500,000 volumes and a circulation of 500,000 would be expected to have 1,500,000/45,000 + 500,000/83,000 - 11 = 28 professionals or more. While component analysis sets dividing lines for all research libraries, regression analysis sets dividing lines that vary according to volumes and circulation in individual institutions.

In the same ways in which a relation between professionals and volumes and circulation has been measured, we can measure the relations of our other variables to volumes and circulation. To explain the variable volumes, however, we cannot use volumes and circulation, since we would be relating a variable to itself. The single variable to which volumes are most closely related is doctorates awarded in 1978-79; and so we use that as the explanatory variable. Note that we are not concerned here with causes and effects. We are not saying that doctorates awarded are somehow a cause of library size in volumes, but only that there is a close statistical relationship between volumes and doctorates. The more doctorates an institution awards, the more volumes its library tends to own. If we know how many doctorates were granted in 1978-79, we can predict fairly accurately how many volumes a library had. But we cannot conclude that library size in some way depends upon degrees awarded.

The regression equations for our ten variables are displayed in Table 3. These models are intuitively attractive because they point up the ways in which added volumes, expenditures, and staffing are associated with library resources measured in volumes and library services measured in circulation. For example, in 1978-79 research libraries tended to spend $1.40 for each volume held and $1.50 for each circulation; the libraries had 1 staff member for each 14,500 volumes and 1 for each 24,500 circulations; they added 1 volume for each 50 volumes held and 1 for each 50 volumes circulated.

We can use these same models for other types of libraries. Among four-year college libraries, for example, the equation for FTE professional staff is 1 professional for each 61,500 volumes + 1 for each 24,800 circulations + 1 with an R^2 of .46. Research libraries have more professionals than college libraries per volumes held but approximately the same number of professionals per volumes circulated. Similarly with other variables and other types of libraries the regression equations differ from those for research libraries. By applying tests for heterogeneity of slopes in analysis of covariance, we find that these differences are significant. In other words, the regression equations of Table 3 are characteristic of research libraries but not of other types of libraries.

Thus, the regression equations offer a second way, in addition to the component scores, of characterizing research libraries.

TABLE 3

Regression Results for Selected Variables, 1978-79

Variable	Regression Equation	R^2	Standard Error of Residuals
Volumes held	Doctorates x 6,300 + 427,000	.63	778,000
Volumes added, gross	Vols/50 + Circ/50 + 12,400	.81	16,400
Expenditures for library materials	Vols x $.35 + Circ x $.40 + $509,000	.69	$391,000
Expenditures for binding	Vols x $.04 + Circ x $.04 + $14,000	.65	$ 43,000
Total salaries and wages	Vols x $.85 + Circ x $1.00 + $358,000	.89	$501,000
Other operating expenditures	Vols x $.20 + Circ x $.10 + $33,000	.76	$148,000
Total expenditures	Vols x $1.40 + Circ x $1.50 + $914,000	.88	$842,000
FTE professional staff	Vols/45,000 + Circ/83,000 + 15	.80	16
FTE nonprofessional staff	Vols/21,400 + Circ/35,000 + 15	.89	24
Total FTE staff	Vols/14,500 + Circ/24,500 + 30	.92	30

V. SUMMARY

In Part III of this report we derived approximate dividing lines that distinguish research libraries from other kinds of libraries. Table 2 shows that a typical research library in 1978-79 had at least 445,000 volumes, expenditures of $1,450,000, and a staff of 54. In Part IV we found that the variables in research library data are related in distinct ways. Table 3 shows, for example, that there was one professional for each 45,000 volumes plus one for each 83,000 circulations, plus 15. From the discussion in Part IV it can be seen that the minimum number of professionals that one would expect in a research library is

$$\text{Vols}/45{,}000 + \text{Circ}/83{,}000 + 15 - 1.65 \times 16 =$$

$$\text{Vols}/45{,}000 + \text{Circ}/83{,}000 - 11.$$

We can draw together these criteria by saying that in academic research libraries the number of professionals was (1) at least 21, and (2) at least equal to 1 for each 45,000 volumes plus 1 for each 83,000 circulations minus 11. These criteria and others are displayed in Table 4.

Also displayed in Table 4 are the numbers of libraries satisfying these criteria. In respect to professional staff, for example, 172 of the 181 research libraries have at least 21 professionals, and their professional staff is also equal to at least $\text{Vols}/45{,}000 + \text{Circ}/83{,}000 - 11$. 55 non-research libraries satisfy this criterion.

Clearly, any one criterion by itself does not sufficiently discriminate between research and non-research libraries. Sets of the criteria do, however, offer considerably better discrimination. Here are the numbers of libraries satisfying all ten criteria, nine of the ten, eight, and seven:

No. of Criteria Satisfied	Research Libraries	Non-Research Libraries
10	114	0
9	34	1
8	18	3
7	8	10

TABLE 4

Criteria for Academic Research Libraries, 1978-79

Variable	Criteria		No. of Libraries Satisfying Criteria	
	At Least:	And Equal To At Least:	Research Libraries	Non-Research Libraries
ɔlumes held	445,000	Doctorates x 6,500 - 856,000	164	45
ɔlumes added, gross	18,000	Vols/50 + Circ/50 -14,600	174	81
ⅹpenditures for library materials	$ 530,000	Vols x $.35 + Circ x $.40 - $140,000	168	30
ⅹpenditures for binding	$ 22,000	Vols x $.04 + Circ x $.04 - $57,000	170	77
ɔtal salaries and wages	$ 810,000	Vols x .$85 + Circ x $1.00 - $468,000	164	29
ther operating expenditures	$ 88,000	Vols x $.20 + Circ x $.10 - $212,000	161	109
ɔtal expenditures	$1,450,000	Vols x $1.40 + Circ x $1.50 - $475,000	175	27
ᴛE professional staff	21	Vols/45,000 + Circ/83,000 - 11	172	55
ᴛE nonprofessional staff	33	Vols/21,400 + Circ/35,000 - 25	166	57
ɔtal FTE staff	54	Vols/14,500 + Circ/24,500 - 20	170	45

92% of research libraries and only four non-research libraries pass at least eight of the ten tests. 96% of research libraries and 14 non-research libraries pass at least seven of the ten.[12] Suppose that these criteria were used to determine whether a given library is a research library. Then if we wanted a rigorous test, we would require the library to satisfy at least eight of the ten criteria. If we wanted a more inclusive test, we would require seven of the ten.

From this investigation, then, we are left with two ways of distinguishing research libraries from other types of libraries. The first way is to calculate principal component scores and require a score of -1.65 or higher. In this method the scores are weighted combinations of twelve library variables. For a given library with a score of -1.65 or greater the interrelations among the variables may or may not be typical of those in other research libraries. That is, in relation to volumes held and circulations the library may have, say, more volumes added and fewer professionals than a typical research library. But its component score will still class it with the research libraries. The second way of distinguishing research libraries is by the criteria of Table 4. If a library satisfies seven or eight of these criteria, it is classed with the research libraries. For a given library these criteria require that the values of individual variables be typical of research libraries. The library with a score of -1.65 or greater that has fewer professionals then the typical research library may fail to satisfy the Table 4 criterion for professional staff. Thus, the Table 4 criteria impose constraints not present in the component score method.

Both of the methods delineate approximately the same group of research libraries. The Table 4 criteria are perhaps preferable for applications because they are apt to make more intuitive sense to those to whom the component scores seem like mysterious mathematical mumbo-jumbo. The Table 4 criteria point out very straightforwardly that research libraries had, for example, 21 or more professionals, and that the number of professionals was related to library resources measured in volumes and library services measured in volumes circulated.

Do these methods potentially have practical uses? Undoubtedly the component
scores and Table 4 criteria offer objective ways of judging how similar a library
is to research libraries. It must be understood, however, that the component score
equation and the Table 4 criteria in this paper are based on 1978-79 data. One
would expect changes from year to year, especially in the minimum levels of Table 4.
Consequently, in order to use these methods in continuing applications, one would need
to recalculate the scores and the criteria as new HEGIS data become available. But
one would also need to decide to what extent organizations as multifarious as
research libraries should be judged by purely quantitative criteria, remembering,
however, that the search for non-quantitative criteria can lead into truly uncharted
lands.

APPENDIX:

COMPONENT SCORES OF

2,943 ACADEMIC LIBRARIES

(The methodology followed in computing these scores
is described on pages 11-15 of the preceding report.)

ALABAMA

(. = MISSING DATA)

STATE RANK	LIBRARY	SCORE	VOLUMES HELD	GROSS VOLUMES ADDED	CIRCULATION	TOTAL EXPENDITURES	TOTAL STAFF
1.	AUBURN U MAIN CAMPUS	-0.468	1,043,428	62,287	452,307	$2,547,029	95
2.	UNIVERSITY OF ALABAMA	-0.773	1,051,974	32,277	403,085	2,227,513	95
3.	U ALABAMA IN BIRMINGHAM	-1.113	619,947	45,012	279,923	2,066,472	78
4.	U OF SOUTH ALABAMA	-1.907	260,734	14,294	140,187	1,412,635	58
5.	SAMFORD UNIVERSITY	-2.826	252,570	14,680	136,962	841,014	32
6.	JACKSONVL ST UNIVERSITY	-2.875	364,844	20,859	86,075	962,858	26
7.	U ALABAMA IN HUNTSVILLE	-2.980	248,080	14,463	52,545	642,437	29
8.	ALABAMA STATE UNIVERSITY	-3.409	170,980	12,402	20,335	729,718	30
9.	TROY STATE U MAIN CAMPUS	-3.478	181,586	7,606	111,486	457,273	24
10.	TUSKEGEE INSTITUTE	-3.812	234,849	5,266	250,000	422,727	19
11.	ALABAMA A & M UNIVERSITY	-3.848	248,512	3,700	35,319	592,076	31
12.	U OF NORTH ALABAMA	-3.904	153,887	7,298	49,268	457,685	17
13.	AUBURN U AT MONTGOMERY	-4.395	97,442	8,013	34,749	335,220	13
14.	SPRING HILL COLLEGE	-5.013	152,500	3,500	83,452	152,005	8
15.	LIVINGSTON UNIVERSITY	-5.066	111,112	6,276	20,017	183,751	7
16.	BIRMINGHAM STHN CULLEGE	-5.240	128,495	3,850	21,230	171,235	9
17.	CHATTAHOOCHEE VALLEY CC	-5.384	37,459	6,799	24,422	287,485	7
18.	UNIVERSITY OF MONTEVALLO	-5.566	149,411	4,290	90,108	241,012	8
19.	GADSDEN STATE JR COLLEGE	-5.652	55,882	1,447	22,566	202,163	11
20.	OAKWOOD COLLEGE	-5.719	81,944	2,500	20,705	182,928	9
21.	JEFFERSON ST JR COLLEGE	-5.806	48,377	1,692	35,000	256,798	8
22.	GEO C WALLACE ST CC-DOTHN	-5.866	32,411	2,075	16,555	165,570	7
23.	SNEAD STATE JR COLLEGE	-5.977	35,057	1,967	13,091	129,997	6
24.	ENTERPRISE ST JR COLLEGE	-6.153	31,007	1,449	18,647	195,125	7
25.	MOBILE COLLEGE	-6.225	61,152	4,297	18,137	79,506	5
26.	MILES COLLEGE	-6.260	78,380	1,097	14,610	151,831	9
27.	S D BISHOP ST JR COLLEGE	-6.319	29,723	1,513	11,537	131,787	7
28.	JOHN C CALHOUN ST CC	-6.329	34,391	1,452	13,953	130,443	6
29.	HUNTINGDON COLLEGE	-6.349	96,956	1,944	16,642	100,423	5
30.	TALLADEGA COLLEGE	-6.384	68,321	1,001	22,794	90,311	4
31.	ALEXANDER CITY STATE JC	-6.401	32,240	928	5,498	138,993	9
32.	STILLMAN COLLEGE	-6.495	74,480	1,371	19,119	91,474	6
33.	ATHENS STATE COLLEGE	-6.615	62,778	1,328	14,357	85,691	5
34.	TROY ST U DOTHN-FT RUCKER	-6.649	20,424	2,503	6,159	104,456	6
35.	FAULKNER STATE JR COLLEGE	-6.742	32,900	1,168	16,122	112,855	4
36.	STHN UNION ST JR COLLEGE	-6.775	57,258	2,097	7,263	106,787	4
37.	GEO C WALLACE ST CC-SELMA	-6.777	21,836	1,619	10,531	115,894	5
38.	NTHEST ALA ST JR COLLEGE	-7.094	38,113	1,418	9,398	75,525	3
39.	LAWSON STATE CMTY COLLEGE	-7.196	39,550	550	510,313	85,749	5
40.	JUDSON COLLEGE	-7.216	52,878	1,227	11,598	50,369	5
41.	TROY STATE U MONTGOMERY	-7.289	9,852	1,565	22,202	59,821	3
42.	JEFFERSON DAVIS STATE JC	-7.388	29,755	1,528	15,329	58,789	3
43.	ALABAMA CHRISTIAN COLLEGE	-7.596	22,987	1,236	8,820	48,425	3
44.	LURLEEN B WALLACE ST JC	-7.604	22,085	1,889	13,178	91,509	7
45.	BREWER STATE JR COLLEGE	-7.725	23,682	1,292	8,175	94,639	4

ALABAMA

(. = MISSING DATA)

STATE RANK	LIBRARY	SCORE	VOLUMES HELD	GROSS VOLUMES ADDED	CIRCULATION	TOTAL EXPENDITURES	TOTAL STAFF
46.	STHESTN BIBLE COLLEGE	-7.952	25,589	892	11,514	$38,420	4
47.	GEO C WALLACE ST CC-HNCV	-7.965	11,520	1,700	8,544	67,215	3
48.	NTHWST ALA ST JR COLLEGE	-8.177	34,732	1,192	26,625	71,452	4
49.	MARION MILITARY INSTITUTE	-8.286	26,773	389	6,137	42,166	3
50.	PATRICK HENRY STATE JC	-8.320	27,011	1,016	6,396	46,403	3
51.	ALA LUTH ACAD AND COLLEGE	-8.725	11,689	400	2,000	35,141	2
52.	LOMAX-HANNON JC	-10.92	11,199	85	2,000	11,875	1
53.	SELMA UNIVERSITY	.	14,985	65	6,003	.	3
54.	WALKER COLLEGE	.	19,463	533	4,854	.	2

ALASKA

(. = MISSING DATA)

STATE RANK	LIBRARY	SCORE	VOLUMES HELD	GROSS VOLUMES ADDED	CIRCULATION	TOTAL EXPENDITURES	TOTAL STAFF
1.	U ALASKA FAIRBANKS CAMPUS	-2.442	436,547	13,242	64,480	$1,980,457	53
2.	U ALASKA ANCHORAGE JT LIB	-3.101	204,436	16,949	99,956	1,098,338	29
3.	U OF ALASKA JUNEAU JT LIB	-5.519	33,199	2,792	13,809	237,635	10
4.	STRATTON JOINT LIBRARY	-6.681	51,566	976	16,295	79,325	5
5.	U OF ALASKA KUSKOKWIM CC	-7.211	10,156	2,771	14,915	98,342	2
6.	U ALAS MATANUSKA-SUSITNA	-7.796	11,225	1,329	1,800	69,124	2
7.	U OF ALASKA KETCHIKAN CC	-8.439	26,081	2,050	2,354	63,576	2
8.	U OF ALASKA KENAI CC	-8.625	12,385	1,986	1,644	76,806	1
9.	U OF ALASKA KODIAK CC	-8.952	8,296	2,382	4,750	57,450	2
10.	ALASKA BIBLE COLLEGE	.	16,221	711	.	.	1

ARIZONA

(. = MISSING DATA)

STATE RANK	LIBRARY	SCORE	VOLUMES HELD	GROSS VOLUMES ADDED	CIRCULATION	TOTAL EXPENDITURES	TOTAL STAFF
1.	UNIVERSITY OF ARIZONA	0.632	1,411,264	100,355	701,161	$5,710,063	197
2.	ARIZONA STATE UNIVERSITY	0.460	1,537,019	92,941	1,201,252	4,398,578	166
3.	NORTHERN ARIZ UNIVERSITY	-1.469	483,137	29,543	584,044	1,353,391	42
4.	PIMA COMMUNITY COLLEGE	-3.290	97,000	12,825	66,449	657,974	33
5.	GLENDALE CMTY COLLEGE	-4.512	65,714	2,794	67,230	424,831	23
6.	CENTRAL ARIZONA COLLEGE	-4.580	71,582	6,964	16,617	272,044	11
7.	PHOENIX COLLEGE	-4.691	93,421	3,010	58,021	413,777	20
8.	MESA COMMUNITY COLLEGE	-4.721	49,274	2,083	82,652	380,203	23
9.	YAVAPAI COLLEGE	-4.852	39,837	4,956	26,882	223,550	13
10.	SCOTTSDALE CMTY COLLEGE	-5.681	31,612	1,836	30,137	225,687	10
11.	COCHISE COLLEGE	-5.681	47,858	2,053	17,964	166,923	10
12.	NORTHLAND PIONEER COLLEGE	-5.883	14,000	4,500	4,200	179,544	8
13.	GRAND CANYON COLLEGE	-6.105	116,948	40,043	28,225	84,246	5
14.	MOHAVE COMMUNITY COLLEGE	-6.278	19,139	3,550	15,556	146,420	6
15.	EASTERN ARIZONA COLLEGE	-6.339	39,056	5,025	28,320	116,888	4
16.	ARIZONA WESTERN COLLEGE	-6.467	35,044	754	23,789	121,057	7
17.	STHWSTN BAPT BIBLE C	-8.459	16,381	831	6,105	25,725	1
18.	COLLEGE OF GANADO	-8.758	15,022	1,350	3,304	34,282	3
19.	ARIZONA C OF THE BIBLE	-9.617	12,586	444	4,168	30,650	2
20.	PRESCOTT CENTER COLLEGE	-10.69	4,165	1,687	5,000	8,606	1
21.	AMER GRAD SCH OF MGMT	.	69,601	3,844	56,019	.	5
22.	MARICOPA TECH CC	.	40,000	3,000	23,375	.	6

ARKANSAS

(. = MISSING DATA)

STATE RANK	LIBRARY	SCORE	VOLUMES HELD	GROSS VOLUMES ADDED	CIRCULATION	TOTAL EXPENDITURES	TOTAL STAFF
1.	U OF ARKANSAS MAIN CAMPUS	-1.255	877,866	36,711	242,518	$1,828,642	71
2.	U OF ARK AT LITTLE ROCK	-2.131	302,789	22,497	91,307	1,230,929	37
3.	ARKANSAS STATE U MAIN CAM	-2.600	351,559	14,005	71,526	848,445	28
4.	U OF CENTRAL ARKANSAS	-3.061	277,078	17,468	88,156	614,201	21
5.	U OF ARK MEDL SCI CAMPUS	-3.268	116,127	4,530	37,969	698,296	43
6.	HARDING U MAIN CAM	-4.163	147,801	5,414	97,623	266,651	12
7.	HENDERSON ST UNIVERSITY	-4.574	154,860	5,169	40,615	377,041	21
8.	ARKANSAS TECH UNIVERSITY	-4.684	146,577	7,394	60,068	260,685	10
9.	STHN ARK U MAIN CAMPUS	-4.884	102,106	4,108	135,810	240,046	7
10.	U OF ARKANSAS PINE BLUFF	-5.042	120,369	5,729	43,001	431,408	25
11.	HENDRIX COLLEGE	-5.201	126,737	4,678	25,182	189,990	8
12.	U OF ARKANSAS-MONTICELLO	-5.235	75,045	5,591	17,468	208,265	7
13.	OUACHITA BAPT UNIVERSITY	-5.277	106,604	2,541	25,574	198,757	9
14.	HARDING GRAD SCH RELIGION	-6.073	58,438	2,542	20,765	86,206	4
15.	WESTARK COMMUNITY COLLEGE	-6.121	36,942	1,234	24,860	143,760	8
16.	JOHN BROWN UNIVERSITY	-6.335	69,263	2,705	22,639	106,128	3
17.	ARKANSAS COLLEGE	-6.561	64,242	2,012	6,445	102,343	2
18.	SOUTHERN BAPTIST COLLEGE	-6.844	47,498	2,142	7,144	54,296	4
19.	PHILLIPS CO CMTY COLLEGE	-6.860	29,219	1,270	11,068	100,771	4
20.	COLLEGE OF THE OZARKS	-7.015	68,399	1,820	6,043	56,350	3
21.	GARLAND CO CMTY COLLEGE	-7.533	13,639	1,505	6,289	106,152	6
22.	NORTH ARKANSAS CC	-7.908	9,947	2,297	20,000	80,840	3
23.	STHN ARK U STHWST TECH	-8.011	11,200	1,050	9,000	51,354	1
24.	STHN ARK U EL DORADO BR	-8.204	4,112	2,014	1,430	70,072	3
25.	EAST ARK CMTY COLLEGE	-8.409	7,170	668	2,005	95,461	4
26.	CENTRAL BAPTIST COLLEGE	-8.687	19,081	1,483	5,032	17,420	1
27.	CAPITAL CITY BUS COLLEGE	-9.558	5,926	612	1,048	22,186	1
28.	CROWLEY'S RIDGE COLLEGE	-11.13	11,950	40	350	9,816	1
29.	ARKANSAS STATE U BEEBE BR	.	35,511	2,672	13,248	.	3
30.	MISS CO CMTY COLLEGE	.	7,057	1,253	.	83,250	4
31.	PHILANDER SMITH COLLEGE	.	60,089	4,209	.	.	2

-39-

CALIFORNIA

(. = MISSING DATA)

STATE RANK	LIBRARY	SCORE	VOLUMES HELD	GROSS VOLUMES ADDED	CIRCULATION	TOTAL EXPENDITURES	TOTAL STAFF
1.	U OF CAL-BERKELEY	2.122	5,439,883	169,857	2,055,846	$13,131,279	435
2.	U OF CAL-LOS ANGELES	1.942	4,109,146	129,752	1,771,882	11,933,620	390
3.	STANFORD UNIVERSITY	1.720	4,577,827	89,596	1,047,620	11,450,141	442
4.	U OF CAL-DAVIS	0.906	1,525,544	74,421	1,454,279	6,811,443	250
5.	U OF SOUTHERN CALIFORNIA	0.707	1,949,756	92,379	736,937	5,613,865	216
6.	U OF CAL-SAN DIEGO	0.535	1,332,525	58,903	712,951	5,853,732	190
7.	U OF CAL-SANTA BARBARA	0.424	1,325,063	51,922	575,898	5,340,801	179
8.	U OF CAL-IRVINE	0.021	887,213	54,315	390,177	4,628,498	125
9.	U OF CAL-RIVERSIDE	-0.221	947,698	32,748	300,799	4,279,848	130
10.	SAN DIEGO STATE U	-0.369	755,775	32,099	587,062	3,103,408	107
11.	SAN FRANCISCO STATE U	-0.842	558,732	25,410	742,753	2,506,238	87
12.	SAN JOSE STATE U	-0.846	695,736	32,937	518,153	2,446,408	101
13.	CAL STATE U-NORTHRIDGE	-0.854	691,394	30,154	321,212	2,446,637	93
14.	CAL STATE U-SACRAMENTO	-0.871	635,252	30,899	451,793	2,262,854	76
15.	U OF CAL-SANTA CRUZ	-1.079	595,042	28,069	372,979	2,438,293	75
16.	CAL STATE U-LOS ANGELES	-1.158	750,788	22,404	628,864	2,284,338	78
17.	CAL POLY ST U-SN LUIS OB	-1.174	549,954	26,943	429,167	1,920,495	75
18.	CAL STATE U-LONG BEACH	-1.214	718,578	40,360	563,433	2,717,130	100
19.	CAL STATE U-CHICO	-1.311	551,794	24,682	446,029	1,737,404	63
20.	HONNOLD JOINT LIBRARY	-1.348	805,687	25,364	348,121	1,909,779	66
21.	CAL STATE U-FRESNO	-1.394	576,595	24,947	349,067	1,988,800	68
22.	CAL STATE U-FULLERTON	-1.405	487,910	19,955	296,678	2,132,351	75
23.	CAL STATE POLY U-POMONA	-1.744	342,095	19,020	219,289	1,677,362	56
24.	U OF CAL-SAN FRANCISCO	-1.830	457,021	13,998	150,838	1,482,765	66
25.	CAL STATE U-HAYWARD	-1.920	666,981	26,340	250,454	1,423,224	47
26.	LOMA LINDA UNIVERSITY	-2.120	356,309	13,571	177,272	1,045,315	49
27.	HUMBOLDT STATE U	-2.165	256,384	17,565	560,738	1,224,017	42
28.	UNIVERSITY OF SANTA CLARA	-2.207	359,982	14,907	223,996	1,181,682	38
29.	SONOMA STATE UNIVERSITY	-2.325	287,121	17,448	131,296	1,029,393	34
30.	U OF SAN FRANCISCO	-2.345	490,017	19,257	104,565	968,647	33
31.	LOYOLA MARYMOUNT U	-2.376	384,395	16,517	59,401	1,131,277	48
32.	CAL STATE U-DOMINGUEZ HLS	-2.449	230,440	17,697	164,500	1,195,700	39
33.	UNIVERSITY OF SAN DIEGO	-2.501	343,929	17,218	188,853	874,902	30
34.	CAL STATE C-SN BERNARDINO	-2.557	301,915	21,058	130,853	847,207	29
35.	UNIVERSITY OF THE PACIFIC	-2.836	330,406	11,843	97,819	754,452	31
36.	CAL INST OF TECHNOLOGY	-2.873	338,151	11,090	54,216	1,136,276	23
37.	CAL ST COLLEGE-BAKERSFLD	-3.161	196,332	16,054	71,269	685,211	21
38.	OCCIDENTAL COLLEGE	-3.281	329,023	10,222	81,162	581,463	23
39.	PEPPERDINE UNIVERSITY	-3.310	222,562	11,608	68,297	648,371	17
40.	CAL ST COLLEGE-STANISLAUS	-3.419	193,240	12,820	108,900	716,025	22
41.	CHABOT COLLEGE	-3.543	109,015	5,376	122,450	817,266	30
42.	GRAD THEOL UN JT LIBRARY	-3.716	531,472	7,375	75,672	466,923	11
43.	RAND GRAD INST POL STDIES	-3.729	83,794	2,470	42,089	660,385	32
44.	WHITTIER COLLEGE	-3.743	188,340	12,979	20,706	544,407	17
45.	U OF CAL HASTINGS C LAW	-3.849	197,393	16,421	89,115	518,708	13

CALIFORNIA

(. = MISSING DATA)

STATE RANK	LIBRARY	SCORE	VOLUMES HELD	GROSS VOLUMES ADDED	CIRCULATION	TOTAL EXPENDITURES	TOTAL STAFF
46.	GROSSMONT COLLEGE	-3.959	88,118	4,033	96,361	$749,776	31
47.	MOUNT SAN ANTONIO COLLEGE	-3.985	89,804	2,272	96,060	929,668	49
48.	DIABLO VALLEY COLLEGE	-4.071	73,353	3,829	148,498	690,374	24
49.	STHWSTN U SCHOOL OF LAW	-4.113	71,258	5,094	45,308	534,471	22
50.	BIOLA COLLEGE	-4.120	165,895	8,071	130,993	295,957	12
51.	PALOMAR COLLEGE	-4.135	125,146	8,861	57,267	613,929	36
52.	POINT LOMA COLLEGE	-4.178	161,564	4,723	55,150	554,158	13
53.	DE ANZA COLLEGE	-4.362	73,383	3,651	196,425	642,721	29
54.	ORANGE COAST COLLEGE	-4.406	92,306	4,073	78,811	520,809	21
55.	US INTERNATIONAL U	-4.449	230,126	4,431	427,217	253,995	14
56.	LONG BEACH CITY COLLEGE	-4.456	122,933	6,253	98,550	454,027	13
57.	CHAPMAN COLLEGE	-4.537	149,753	3,902	84,030	249,047	11
58.	GOLDEN WEST COLLEGE	-4.556	86,700	5,042	120,680	465,350	18
59.	SN FRISCO CC DISTRICT	-4.602	83,862	2,066	133,816	535,001	28
60.	MILLS COLLEGE	-4.629	185,653	4,753	52,676	274,185	10
61.	FOOTHILL COLLEGE	-4.646	101,878	3,888	159,480	477,495	19
62.	SADDLEBACK CMTY COLLEGE	-4.655	93,000	5,000	138,260	425,644	18
63.	SAN DIEGO MESA COLLEGE	-4.679	83,318	4,676	75,655	341,810	19
64.	EL CAMINO COLLEGE	-4.699	95,662	2,010	78,962	363,616	16
65.	PACIFIC UNION COLLEGE	-4.715	101,285	3,498	63,734	299,736	9
66.	SAN JOAQUIN DELTA COLLEGE	-4.726	68,283	3,149	103,653	373,604	16
67.	LOS ANG VALLEY COLLEGE	-4.776	115,215	4,372	86,224	269,859	14
68.	SOUTHWESTERN COLLEGE	-4.829	58,938	3,835	86,793	413,878	17
69.	SAN DIEGO CITY COLLEGE	-4.861	55,904	3,335	87,300	409,279	17
70.	SANTA ROSA JUNIOR COLLEGE	-4.882	83,028	3,700	69,957	288,779	11
71.	SN BERNARDINO VLY COLLEGE	-4.903	116,502	3,836	27,127	317,354	15
72.	OHLONE COLLEGE	-4.933	48,867	3,051	54,251	443,328	23
73.	FULLERTON COLLEGE	-4.948	91,833	1,831	138,660	511,792	23
74.	CITRUS COLLEGE	-4.987	76,162	1,804	75,739	283,212	16
75.	SAN JOSE CITY COLLEGE	-4.992	67,065	4,107	57,541	313,778	13
76.	CALIFORNIA INST OF ARTS	-4.996	68,649	2,823	26,499	271,879	12
77.	RIO HONDO COLLEGE	-5.013	74,929	3,670	35,652	370,068	18
78.	HARTNELL COLLEGE	-5.014	66,688	3,003	37,430	333,461	13
79.	CABRILLO COLLEGE	-5.019	50,121	2,355	142,796	393,353	10
80.	AMERICAN RIVER COLLEGE	-5.035	74,819	2,882	157,668	314,435	16
81.	FRESNO CITY COLLEGE	-5.043	49,004	2,156	95,149	353,146	21
82.	GLENDALE CMTY COLLEGE	-5.060	64,451	4,766	60,715	294,307	14
83.	COLLEGE OF MARIN	-5.092	74,681	2,511	56,335	299,634	13
84.	LANEY COLLEGE	-5.201	67,885	2,305	116,198	372,748	14
85.	WESTMONT COLLEGE	-5.257	121,227	4,758	30,549	209,800	8
86.	MOUNT SNT MARY'S COLLEGE	-5.268	129,947	2,445	39,428	195,008	13
87.	SANTA MONICA COLLEGE	-5.296	98,067	2,672	53,888	286,475	12
88.	SCH OF THEO AT CLAREMONT	-5.338	113,883	3,163	29,979	133,269	11
89.	SNT MARY'S COLLEGE OF CAL	-5.362	128,197	4,502	13,520	139,628	8
90.	CHAFFEY COLLEGE	-5.379	66,984	2,503	38,315	228,089	10

CALIFORNIA

(. = MISSING DATA)

STATE RANK	LIBRARY	SCORE	VOLUMES HELD	GROSS VOLUMES ADDED	CIRCULATION	TOTAL EXPENDITURES	TOTAL STAFF
91.	LOS ANG TR TECH COLLEGE	-5.406	88,500	3,200	31,560	$315,818	11
92.	MERCED COLLEGE	-5.471	36,315	2,809	44,979	253,956	14
93.	WEST LOS ANGELES COLLEGE	-5.483	49,196	1,451	40,000	342,225	17
94.	MODESTO JUNIOR COLLEGE	-5.507	61,000	1,700	52,910	267,735	15
95.	CAL LUTHERAN COLLEGE	-5.530	90,714	3,565	31,654	178,966	9
96.	SANTA ANA COLLEGE	-5.637	82,400	4,045	72,031	294,286	13
97.	CYPRESS COLLEGE	-5.639	55,895	1,207	35,150	232,964	10
98.	SHASTA COLLEGE	-5.654	61,114	802	62,140	281,723	15
99.	UNIVERSITY OF REDLANDS	-5.669	256,938	6,616	40,382	350,185	12
100.	CERRITOS COLLEGE	-5.688	67,495	3,152	199,937	542,158	23
101.	BAKERSFIELD COLLEGE	-5.709	61,445	3,226	64,968	346,880	23
102.	LOS ANG PIERCE COLLEGE	-5.773	98,676	3,063	191,148	390,706	17
103.	WOODBURY UNIVERSITY	-5.841	40,611	7,562	18,281	164,802	5
104.	SKYLINE COLLEGE	-5.843	44,698	2,245	42,637	204,543	6
105.	UNIVERSITY OF JUDAISM	-5.881	125,000	11,000	25,000	103,500	5
106.	COLLEGE OF ALAMEDA	-5.899	37,725	1,531	24,368	281,617	12
107.	CRAFTON HILLS COLLEGE	-5.914	66,686	5,762	12,360	144,461	5
108.	SIERRA COLLEGE	-5.921	56,474	2,324	39,104	213,044	12
109.	SANTA BARBARA CTY COLLEGE	-6.002	78,831	2,397	42,317	270,071	10
110.	COLLEGE OF SAN MATEO	-6.011	110,000	570	38,167	197,984	8
111.	WEST VALLEY COLLEGE	-6.014	50,000	2,700	114,668	540,638	27
112.	NORTHROP UNIVERSITY	-6.058	138,817	2,261	12,394	104,556	5
113.	AZUSA PACIFIC COLLEGE	-6.079	80,704	2,961	97,999	244,217	11
114.	CUESTA COLLEGE	-6.137	33,211	1,539	19,184	239,220	13
115.	RIVERSIDE CITY COLLEGE	-6.138	73,866	4,000	75,000	338,974	15
116.	MERRITT COLLEGE	-6.146	58,811	1,075	21,116	248,414	12
117.	MIRA COSTA COLLEGE	-6.164	26,590	2,062	21,487	199,733	7
118.	CUSUMNES RIVER COLLEGE	-6.181	61,288	1,964	30,368	288,741	15
119.	COLLEGE OF THE SEQUOIAS	-6.226	70,598	2,102	30,878	171,234	6
120.	EVERGREEN VALLEY COLLEGE	-6.362	28,878	2,871	33,644	392,911	17
121.	COLLEGE OF THE REDWOODS	-6.381	58,051	4,000	34,667	121,913	7
122.	WEST HILLS COLLEGE	-6.404	39,880	2,870	28,170	104,847	6
123.	BUTTE COLLEGE	-6.441	48,083	2,083	44,651	274,957	12
124.	REEDLEY COLLEGE	-6.450	27,881	580	22,876	158,920	11
125.	VICTOR VALLEY COLLEGE	-6.457	30,500	1,100	17,588	134,366	5
126.	ALLAN HANCOCK COLLEGE	-6.468	45,158	1,489	39,231	271,975	10
127.	ANTELOPE VALLEY COLLEGE	-6.479	39,951	1,258	11,385	150,439	7
128.	LOS MEDANOS COLLEGE	-6.483	10,711	520	29,006	329,737	13
129.	MOORPARK COLLEGE	-6.547	57,329	960	22,224	137,187	6
130.	DOMINICAN C OF SAN RAFAEL	-6.558	78,374	1,685	12,808	96,160	5
131.	GAVILAN COLLEGE	-6.566	40,900	2,400	12,335	112,490	4
132.	NAPA COLLEGE	-6.566	43,420	1,050	9,980	297,629	4
133.	INDIAN VALLEY COLLEGES	-6.566	31,596	1,593	18,114	135,998	8
134.	COLLEGE OF THE CANYONS	-6.566	35,561	2,200	17,262	200,831	9
135.	COLLEGE OF NOTRE DAME	-6.566	88,516	2,607	15,694	88,480	6

CALIFORNIA

(. = MISSING DATA)

STATE RANK	LIBRARY	SCORE	VOLUMES HELD	GROSS VOLUMES ADDED	CIRCULATION	TOTAL EXPENDITURES	TOTAL STAFF
136.	CERRO COSO CMTY COLLEGE	-6.578	15,990	838	8,473	$148,321	9
137.	JOHN F KENNEDY UNIVERSITY	-6.578	25,388	1,907	9,990	102,616	6
138.	BETHANY BIBLE COLLEGE	-6.581	45,718	1,682	12,931	87,708	5
139.	EAST LOS ANGELES COLLEGE	-6.654	76,402	1,402	34,048	336,920	14
140.	SAN FRANCISCO ART INST	-6.674	22,684	1,460	38,145	103,221	6
141.	ART CTR COLLEGE OF DESIGN	-6.686	19,830	1,805	24,541	83,106	6
142.	CHRISTIAN HERITAGE C	-6.705	35,591	9,440	22,444	77,499	6
143.	CONTRA COSTA COLLEGE	-6.708	58,038	1,837	38,277	270,196	9
144.	IMPERIAL VALLEY COLLEGE	-6.721	44,560	4,326	30,618	174,203	9
145.	LOS ANG SOUTHWEST COLLEGE	-6.748	62,435	2,900	13,636	245,544	12
146.	MONTEREY PEN COLLEGE	-6.757	64,730	4,454	34,051	130,258	8
147.	LOS ANG HARBOR COLLEGE	-6.799	74,622	5,960	70,277	221,341	10
148.	HOLY NAMES COLLEGE	-6.863	87,629	2,033	19,628	60,394	5
149.	CAL COLLEGE PODIATRIC MED	-6.870	13,641	1,417	9,733	92,500	4
150.	LOS ANGELES MISSION C	-6.905	25,992	2,682	6,363	244,475	10
151.	COLUMBIA COLLEGE	-6.977	28,204	2,813	17,718	116,921	5
152.	SOLANO COMMUNITY COLLEGE	-7.031	34,000	800	15,000	98,322	5
153.	CANADA COLLEGE	-7.039	46,626	986	10,825	213,619	9
154.	COLLEGE OF THE SISKIYOUS	-7.040	28,895	1,067	13,217	92,592	5
155.	NATIONAL UNIVERSITY	-7.102	9,577	2,691	11,394	183,421	9
156.	LOS ANG C OF CHIROPRACTIC	-7.109	12,081	1,272	11,682	66,030	3
157.	MENNONITE-PACIFIC JT LIB	-7.252	66,970	2,308	37,467	115,245	4
158.	MENLO COLLEGE	-7.270	43,920	1,171	10,926	63,768	4
159.	MENDOCINO COLLEGE	-7.289	14,755	1,463	8,772	92,760	4
160.	SOUTHERN CAL COLLEGE	-7.388	58,469	1,487	13,600	72,758	4
161.	PORTERVILLE COLLEGE	-7.407	20,298	863	13,468	72,172	4
162.	CHRIST COLLEGE IRVINE	-7.423	54,200	11,100	3,267	59,924	2
163.	CAL SCH PSYC BERKELEY	-7.453	15,000	1,009	10,819	52,648	2
164.	PACIFIC CHRISTIAN COLLEGE	-7.485	41,554	1,113	15,000	72,638	3
165.	LAKE TAHOE CMTY COLLEGE	-7.490	17,556	3,034	6,712	157,567	4
166.	PACIFIC OAKS COLLEGE	-7.549	23,800	1,036	11,516	44,365	3
167.	U OF WEST LOS ANGELES	-7.558	19,000	1,600	9,495	53,286	1
168.	TAFT COLLEGE	-7.571	25,447	1,126	2,095	68,116	6
169.	SAINT PATRICK'S SEMINARY	-7.604	56,032	616	4,203	31,107	2
170.	IMMACULATE HEART COLLEGE	-7.693	147,645	1,169	15,685	67,431	5
171.	MELODYLAND SCH THEOLOGY	-7.843	28,460	652	17,331	41,163	3
172.	MT SAN JACINTO COLLEGE	-7.872	31,402	1,672	11,101	94,741	5
173.	LASSEN COLLEGE	-7.901	13,219	625	6,700	128,270	5
174.	OXNARD COLLEGE	-7.962	21,000	400	2,769	120,275	5
175.	CAL SCH PROF PSYC SN DEGO	-7.984	8,083	968	7,500	43,581	2
176.	LINCOLN UNIVERSITY	-8.019	32,844	1,652	1,755	118,544	4
177.	SAN JUSE BIBLE COLLEGE	-8.042	29,149	857	22,131	34,604	2
178.	CAL SCH PROF PSYC FRESNO	-8.117	6,350	620	5,000	39,707	3
179.	BARSTOW COLLEGE	-8.175	30,683	1,363	9,145	103,058	4
180.	CENTER FOR EARLY ED	-8.205	11,102	1,716	9,990	27,308	1

CALIFORNIA

(. = MISSING DATA)

STATE RANK	LIBRARY	SCORE	VOLUMES HELD	GROSS VOLUMES ADDED	CIRCULATION	TOTAL EXPENDITURES	TOTAL STAFF
181.	COLLEGE OF THE DESERT	-8.252	46,367	1,066	11,772	$55,237	5
182.	PALO VERDE COLLEGE	-8.319	14,780	301	5,979	45,236	3
183.	SAN FRANCISCO CONSV MUSIC	-8.381	16,315	368	5,000	42,857	4
184.	SAINT JOHN'S COLLEGE	-8.526	50,501	1,500	8,000	20,314	1
185.	LOS ANGELES BAPT COLLEGE	-8.600	30,270	1,414	6,040	47,131	2
186.	MARYMOUNT PALOS VERDES C	-8.655	31,871	1,572	4,417	51,043	3
187.	SIMPSON COLLEGE	-8.849	48,806	888	15,005	35,966	3
188.	SAN DIEGO MIRAMAR COLLEGE	-8.918	3,040	592	6,087	64,457	3
189.	SAINT PATRICK'S COLLEGE	-8.949	60,000	1,700	1,756	34,750	2
190.	BROOKS INSTITUTE	-8.996	3,954	500	18,571	34,350	2
191.	FEATHER RIVER COLLEGE	-9.102	13,424	1,636	1,662	29,162	1
192.	NEW COLLEGE OF CALIFORNIA	-9.195	15,000	1,500	3,000	29,162	1
193.	PATTEN COLLEGE	-9.376	17,509	574	3,029	22,021	2
194.	COGSWELL COLLEGE	-9.450	9,400	1,100	3,700	32,927	1
195.	COLLEGE OSTED MED PACIFIC	-9.467	1,800	1,200	328	53,937	2
196.	ARMSTRONG COLLEGE	-9.526	17,072	642	3,382	23,230	1
197.	DON BOSCO TECHNICAL INST	-9.594	16,259	609	2,400	20,714	2
198.	THE WRIGHT INSTITUTE	-9.667	6,600	390	2,410	20,706	1
199.	HUMPHREYS COLLEGE	-9.773	14,907	395	805	19,772	2
200.	WEST COAST BIBLE COLLEGE	-10.18	22,798	495	5,000	17,908	1
201.	BROOKS COLLEGE	-10.84	1,500	0	2,000	16,300	2
202.	CALIFORNIA CHRISTIAN C	-11.66	8,975	447	950	2,346	0
203.	AMER ACAD DRAMATIC ARTS-W	.	707	242	.	.	1
204.	CAL BAPTIST COLLEGE	.	114,787	1,012	11,264	.	8
205.	CAL INST OF ASIAN STUDIES	.	19,000	1,000	5,000	.	1
206.	CAL SCH PROF PSYC LOS ANG	.	9,846	936	.	47,451	2
207.	CAL WESTERN SCHOOL OF LAW	.	68,154	1,938	9,231	287,196	.
208.	CALIFORNIA MARITIME ACAD	.	18,333	376	8,400	.	3
209.	COLEMAN COLLEGE	.	3,669	430	2,450	.	2
210.	DEEP SPRINGS COLLEGE	.	18,000	500	.	.	1
211.	FULLER THEOLOGICAL SEM	.	112,500	6,500	42,050	403,105	10
212.	GOLDEN GATE UNIVERSITY	.	100,093	5,137	23,984	.	.
213.	HOLY FAMILY COLLEGE	.	36,818	4,131	2,969	.	2
214.	LIFE BIBLE COLLEGE	.	13,751	2,401	.	66,389	5
215.	LOS ANGELES CITY COLLEGE	.	138,750	4,374	100,693	355,589	15
216.	MISSION COLLEGE	.	.	0	.	118,400	16
217.	MONTEREY INTRNATL STDIES	.	38,888	2,024	9,855	62,112	.
218.	OTIS ART INST PARSON SCH	.	.	509	4,042	.	2
219.	PASADENA CITY COLLEGE	.	113,680	3,531	.	440,326	17
220.	PASADENA COLLEGE CHIRO	.	5,281	900	.	17,908	1
221.	SACRAMENTO CITY COLLEGE	.	84,625	2,035	148,984	171,494	14
222.	SAN FERNANDO VALLEY C LAW	.	40,970	1,722	.	.	2
223.	STHN CAL C OF OPTOMETRY	.	.	0	10,104	.	3
224.	STHN CAL INSTITUTE ARCH	.	1,544	132	4,000	68,007	1
225.	UNIVERSITY OF LA VERNE	.	.	16,767	.	698,798	11

-44-

CALIFORNIA

(. = MISSING DATA)

STATE RANK	LIBRARY	SCORE	VOLUMES HELD	GROSS VOLUMES ADDED	CIRCULATION	TOTAL EXPENDITURES	TOTAL STAFF
226.	VENTURA COLLEGE	.	66,000	1,949	33,392	$282,132	.
227.	W COAST U ORANGE CO CTR	.	2,608	52	.	.	0
228.	WEST COAST U MAIN CAMPUS	.	6,548	377	3,221	.	0
229.	WORLD COLLEGE WEST	.	10,000	1,000	400	.	0
230.	WSTN ST U C LAW ORANGE CO	.	37,150	6,053	.	.	0
231.	WSTN ST U C LAW SAN DIEGO	.	27,221	2,768	43,500	.	0
232.	WSTN STATES COLLEGE ENGR	.	2,038	45	450	.	.
233.	YUBA COLLEGE	.	51,408	2,079	26,720	.	13

COLORADO

(. = MISSING DATA)

STATE RANK	LIBRARY	SCORE	VOLUMES HELD	GROSS VOLUMES ADDED	CIRCULATION	TOTAL EXPENDITURES	TOTAL STAFF
1.	U OF COLORADO AT BOULDER	0.043	1,811,881	50,250	739,260	$3,890,499	129
2.	COLORADO STATE UNIVERSITY	-0.480	863,434	31,679	490,710	2,650,885	112
3.	UNIVERSITY OF DENVER	-1.261	816,054	31,306	563,636	1,649,433	75
4.	U OF NORTHERN COLORADO	-1.588	389,562	12,215	513,456	1,455,620	77
5.	AURARIA JOINT LIBRARY	-1.997	340,140	29,550	143,655	1,547,117	74
6.	U OF COLO HLTH SCI CENTER	-3.232	156,479	7,138	42,985	712,331	33
7.	COLORADO COLLEGE	-3.708	290,750	6,843	55,083	405,906	19
8.	U OF COLO COLO SPRINGS	-3.789	122,213	11,553	42,737	422,632	13
9.	COLORADO SCHOOL OF MINES	-4.101	141,387	8,067	3,497	525,209	19
10.	U OF SOUTHERN COLORADO	-4.181	155,408	4,088	69,492	414,728	17
11.	WESTERN ST COLLEGE COLO	-4.495	127,493	4,443	53,221	297,478	10
12.	FORT LEWIS COLLEGE	-4.638	128,161	4,693	47,595	329,381	14
13.	ADAMS STATE COLLEGE	-4.945	188,766	3,787	80,286	203,795	9
14.	MESA COLLEGE	-5.048	92,994	4,037	31,251	216,189	9
15.	CC DENVER RED ROCKS CAM	-5.225	32,954	2,905	28,664	318,604	13
16.	PIKES PEAK CMTY COLLEGE	-5.252	37,773	2,046	26,756	330,141	14
17.	REGIS COLLEGE	-5.437	85,945	1,783	11,125	156,610	12
18.	ILIFF SCHOOL OF THEOLOGY	-5.673	104,824	1,950	15,366	155,032	6
19.	CC OF DENVER NORTH CAMPUS	-6.027	34,391	2,965	41,782	359,641	14
20.	ARAPAHOE CMTY COLLEGE	-6.111	33,078	1,485	28,336	159,660	7
21.	COLORADO WOMEN'S COLLEGE	-6.122	145,012	2,965	6,867	113,243	5
22.	LORETTO HEIGHTS COLLEGE	-6.242	103,000	1,709	18,458	113,109	5
23.	CONS BAPTIST THEOL SEM	-6.344	59,500	4,725	49,772	86,582	3
24.	TRINIDAD STATE JR COLLEGE	-6.450	58,641	2,730	12,361	83,564	5
25.	NORTHEASTERN JR COLLEGE	-6.639	41,274	2,664	5,882	75,798	10
26.	SAINT THOMAS SEMINARY	-6.683	90,300	4,550	7,308	77,775	3
27.	COLO MTN COLLEGE WEST CAM	-7.209	27,500	1,910	61,000	69,720	4
28.	AIMS COMMUNITY COLLEGE	-7.507	31,458	2,361	24,665	81,002	4
29.	COLO MTN COLLEGE EAST CAM	-7.890	17,731	1,554	12,212	67,891	4
30.	NAZARENE BIBLE COLLEGE	-7.918	25,303	2,723	33,676	54,168	3
31.	COLORADO NORTHWESTERN CC	-8.199	14,013	1,090	2,323	59,560	3
32.	LAMAR COMMUNITY COLLEGE	-8.979	21,281	275	5,087	30,254	2
33.	MORGAN COMMUNITY COLLEGE	-9.046	10,021	2,254	1,829	28,843	2
34.	ROCKMONT COLLEGE	-9.294	26,490	2,300	2,468	27,069	1
35.	INTERMOUNTAIN BIBLE C	-9.958	12,000	2,039	1,480	8,284	1
36.	COLO TECHNICAL COLLEGE	-11.15	3,463	200	281	5,773	1
37.	BAPT BIBLE C OF DENVER	.	24,872	700	5,500	.	1
38.	WESTERN BIBLE COLLEGE	.	19,050	725	3,325	.	1

-45-

CONNECTICUT

(. = MISSING DATA)

STATE RANK	LIBRARY	SCORE	VOLUMES HELD	GROSS VOLUMES ADDED	CIRCULATION	TOTAL EXPENDITURES	TOTAL STAFF
1.	YALE UNIVERSITY	2.088	7,072,345	189,195	1,162,377	$11,364,328	588
2.	UNIVERSITY OF CONNECTICUT	-0.046	1,594,990	64,170	293,773	3,739,540	143
3.	WESLEYAN UNIVERSITY	-2.088	788,260	18,537	182,099	1,058,896	42
4.	TRINITY COLLEGE	-3.070	512,580	11,984	93,751	609,772	26
5.	CENTRAL CONN ST COLLEGE	-3.184	280,010	11,619	55,969	698,173	27
6.	U OF CONN HEALTH CENTER	-3.226	112,480	7,175	28,278	813,029	30
7.	UNIVERSITY OF BRIDGEPORT	-3.272	311,794	4,979	62,960	599,970	30
8.	CONNECTICUT COLLEGE	-3.350	342,664	10,303	81,766	529,507	21
9.	UNIVERSITY OF HARTFORD	-3.396	269,755	10,024	98,435	541,500	25
10.	SOUTHERN CONN ST COLLEGE	-3.505	372,065	11,331	84,100	615,850	31
11.	FAIRFIELD UNIVERSITY	-3.663	155,743	7,081	71,606	422,708	21
12.	UNIVERSITY OF NEW HAVEN	-3.987	132,700	11,310	29,828	445,166	25
13.	QUINNIPIAC COLLEGE	-4.578	98,631	4,383	26,317	360,967	19
14.	WESTERN CONN ST COLLEGE	-4.751	139,510	4,479	40,321	357,416	15
15.	EASTERN CONN ST COLLEGE	-4.792	112,754	6,111	35,224	293,182	15
16.	SACRED HEART UNIVERSITY	-5.222	112,992	3,909	15,643	209,576	12
17.	SAINT JOSEPH COLLEGE	-6.049	96,066	3,576	14,138	82,063	7
18.	NORWALK COMMUNITY COLLEGE	-6.314	49,719	1,531	19,214	133,056	8
19.	HOUSATONIC REGIONAL CC	-6.359	29,212	1,030	5,000	165,268	6
20.	ALBERTUS MAGNUS COLLEGE	-6.537	83,889	2,025	23,450	55,611	5
21.	GREATER HARTFORD CC	-6.614	37,356	2,437	13,172	119,142	5
22.	SOUTH CEN CMTY COLLEGE	-6.804	21,910	2,300	35,522	153,710	7
23.	MIDDLESEX CMTY COLLEGE	-7.000	35,620	1,564	10,650	94,321	5
24.	MANCHESTER CMTY COLLEGE	-7.067	39,674	1,097	17,465	149,645	10
25.	MATTATUCK CMTY COLLEGE	-7.334	26,426	882	9,141	147,308	8
26.	QUINEBAUG VALLEY CC	-7.999	14,532	518	4,729	144,797	4
27.	TUNXIS COMMUNITY COLLEGE	-8.022	19,589	1,125	4,523	97,013	5
28.	ANNHURST COLLEGE	-8.187	45,391	3,200	12,906	20,696	3
29.	ASNUNTUCK CMTY COLLEGE	-8.216	20,468	939	7,684	62,157	3
30.	MOHEGAN COMMUNITY COLLEGE	-8.266	20,400	942	3,400	79,878	4
31.	POST COLLEGE	-8.394	21,612	1,900	1,650	61,777	2
32.	MITCHELL COLLEGE	-8.465	45,075	1,024	7,302	56,334	3
33.	HARTFORD GRADUATE CENTER	-8.586	21,094	554	2,381	59,900	3
34.	NORWALK ST TECH COLLEGE	-8.935	13,570	1,910	2,990	49,162	2
35.	SAINT THOMAS SEMINARY	-9.080	49,432	810	544	20,774	1
36.	HOLY APOSTLES COLLEGE	-9.136	31,035	2,168	2,438	13,025	4
37.	SAINT BASIL'S COLLEGE	-10.22	17,370	865	540	8,364	2
38.	THAMES VLY STATE TECH C	-10.62	7,150	25	1,140	29,168	2
39.	BRIDGEPORT ENGR INSTITUTE	.	10,000	500	15	.	3
40.	HARTFORD COLLEGE WOMEN	.	51,120	2,307	.	38,193	1
41.	HARTFORD ST TECH COLLEGE	.	8,000	50	1,870	.	2
42.	MT SACRED HEART COLLEGE	.	14,208	500	1,000	.	0
43.	NTHWSTN CONN CMTY COLLEGE	.	41,736	2,002	13,808	.	3
44.	SAINT ALPHONSUS COLLEGE	.	31,149	0	2,592	.	3
45.	WATERBURY ST TECH COLLEGE	.	8,500	250	1,000	.	2

DELAWARE

(. = MISSING DATA)

STATE RANK	LIBRARY	SCORE	VOLUMES HELD	GROSS VOLUMES ADDED	CIRCULATION	TOTAL EXPENDITURES	TOTAL STAFF
1.	UNIVERSITY OF DELAWARE	-0.821	1,174,002	46,889	395,183	$2,442,760	81
2.	DELAWARE STATE COLLEGE	-4.698	112,870	6,500	20,768	307,570	13
3.	WESLEY COLLEGE	-6.554	44,469	1,640	18,474	105,082	9
4.	BRANDYWINE C OF WIDENER U	-6.949	36,506	1,555	9,137	63,133	3
5.	DEL TECH & CC STANTON CAM	-7.443	15,818	1,755	17,688	124,883	6
6.	WILMINGTON COLLEGE	-7.632	53,561	1,209	2,301	50,792	3
7.	DEL TECH & CC STHN CAM	-7.783	25,414	1,045	11,219	103,323	6
8.	DEL TECH & CC WILMINGTON	-7.841	11,427	2,866	2,451	132,474	4
9.	DEL TECH & CC TERRY CAM	-8.043	13,280	2,542	7,182	96,050	5
10.	GOLDEY BEACOM COLLEGE	-8.252	9,239	504	10,977	50,884	3

DISTRICT OF COLUMBIA

(. = MISSING DATA)

STATE RANK	LIBRARY	SCORE	VOLUMES HELD	GROSS VOLUMES ADDED	CIRCULATION	TOTAL EXPENDITURES	TOTAL STAFF
1.	GEORGETOWN UNIVERSITY	-0.160	1,186,546	54,578	389,337	$3,531,056	134
2.	HOWARD UNIVERSITY	-0.220	1,058,514	46,021	200,545	4,614,485	158
3.	GEORGE WASH UNIVERSITY	-0.753	829,267	42,067	400,160	2,936,356	94
4.	CATHOLIC U OF AMERICA	-1.472	1,100,822	20,607	211,432	1,532,946	75
5.	AMERICAN UNIVERSITY	-1.559	466,837	26,675	248,000	1,486,953	62
6.	UNIVERSITY OF DC	-2.319	381,500	8,986	70,576	1,959,185	81
7.	GALLAUDET COLLEGE	-3.588	131,767	6,539	34,021	723,304	27
8.	TRINITY COLLEGE	-6.180	150,127	4,006	22,280	111,666	6
9.	MOUNT VERNON COLLEGE	-7.180	26,251	1,668	14,743	112,570	6
10.	WESLEY THEOLOGICAL SEM	-7.462	88,032	0	17,769	136,750	6
11.	DOMINICAN HOUSE STUDIES	-7.526	48,949	1,453	6,444	35,243	3
12.	STRAYER COLLEGE	-7.751	16,151	916	6,856	54,983	3
13.	CORCORAN SCHOOL OF ART	.	7,000	300	.	3,346	0
14.	SOUTHEASTERN UNIVERSITY	.	.	995	.	91,944	3

FLORIDA

(. = MISSING DATA)

STATE RANK	LIBRARY	SCORE	VOLUMES HELD	GROSS VOLUMES ADDED	CIRCULATION	TOTAL EXPENDITURES	TOTAL STAFF
1.	UNIVERSITY OF FLORIDA	1.038	2,079,344	139,413	550,050	$7,057,877	208
2.	FLORIDA STATE UNIVERSITY	0.394	1,353,613	75,655	525,580	5,563,703	141
3.	U OF SOUTH FLORIDA	-0.027	775,177	63,693	353,486	4,090,600	150
4.	UNIVERSITY OF MIAMI	-0.305	1,301,100	47,536	371,846	3,108,836	150
5.	FLORIDA INTERNATIONAL U	-1.561	324,103	5,121	183,105	2,780,071	71
6.	MIAMI-DADE CMTY COLLEGE	-1.767	309,561	31,280	229,815	1,674,149	75
7.	U OF CENTRAL FLORIDA	-1.811	299,561	33,280	126,408	1,821,550	57
8.	FLA ATLANTIC UNIVERSITY	-1.882	527,387	25,751	193,156	1,339,100	50
9.	U OF WEST FLORIDA	-2.035	333,454	19,013	159,011	1,355,015	37
10.	U OF NORTH FLORIDA	-2.084	213,015	17,592	229,318	1,357,877	36
11.	FLA JR COLLEGE JACKSONVL	-2.513	188,641	11,984	146,590	1,364,089	71
12.	FLA AGRICULTURAL & MECH U	-2.565	302,865	12,874	110,025	1,231,788	35
13.	BROWARD CMTY COLLEGE	-2.792	170,684	17,936	182,052	933,426	57
14.	SAINT PETERSBG JR COLLEGE	-3.212	179,378	11,017	120,514	753,238	38
15.	BREVARD CMTY COLLEGE	-3.476	114,471	8,169	87,965	646,628	30
16.	PENSACOLA JUNIOR COLLEGE	-3.745	103,992	8,136	67,116	602,457	32
17.	PALM BEACH JUNIOR COLLEGE	-3.838	111,655	4,931	71,942	504,022	29
18.	VALENCIA CMTY COLLEGE	-3.940	54,041	13,332	53,343	497,929	29
19.	STETSON UNIVERSITY	-4.180	199,999	6,717	48,432	291,110	17
20.	FLORIDA INST TECHNOLOGY	-4.197	125,880	6,192	44,967	302,048	17
21.	UNIVERSITY OF TAMPA	-4.345	165,976	7,820	17,488	291,715	15
22.	ROLLINS COLLEGE	-4.433	183,709	4,482	23,475	341,774	23
23.	SEMINOLE CMTY COLLEGE	-4.557	60,811	3,923	45,598	400,123	18
24.	JACKSONVILLE UNIVERSITY	-4.720	164,171	4,303	42,343	250,639	17
25.	FLORIDA SOUTHERN COLLEGE	-4.757	159,600	4,549	15,247	223,644	10
26.	POLK COMMUNITY COLLEGE	-4.839	69,190	5,972	32,149	295,963	18
27.	BARRY COLLEGE	-4.944	103,669	3,586	29,843	177,816	17
28.	GULF COAST CMTY COLLEGE	-4.957	44,508	2,850	17,160	273,066	12
29.	SANTA FE CMTY COLLEGE	-5.096	43,376	3,650	42,563	231,449	13
30.	ECKERD COLLEGE	-5.154	120,744	3,428	24,533	185,965	8
31.	EMBRY-RIDDLE AERON U	-5.164	35,000	2,900	12,568	292,635	13
32.	DAYTONA BCH CMTY COLLEGE	-5.423	54,200	2,244	33,342	516,662	27
33.	EDISON COMMUNITY COLLEGE	-5.557	58,291	3,943	96,280	328,638	17
34.	CENTRAL FLA CMTY COLLEGE	-5.562	48,263	2,574	28,409	218,532	10
35.	MANATEE JUNIOR COLLEGE	-5.658	47,251	2,107	52,547	219,594	13
36.	CHIPOLA JUNIOR COLLEGE	-5.677	46,233	2,151	74,169	172,854	8
37.	TALLAHASSEE CMTY COLLEGE	-5.692	54,748	2,212	16,925	250,610	13
38.	LAKE-SUMTER CMTY COLLEGE	-5.795	45,930	1,580	40,372	137,735	7
39.	SAINT LEO COLLEGE	-5.801	66,678	2,101	10,565	131,838	13
40.	OKALOOSA-WALTON JUNIOR C	-6.183	66,071	3,445	25,309	265,710	16
41.	INDIAN RIVER CMTY COLLEGE	-6.191	43,626	2,659	36,078	198,136	6
42.	EDWARD WATERS COLLEGE	-6.260	75,119	1,992	2,650	141,004	8
43.	LAKE CITY CMTY COLLEGE	-6.394	28,647	480	13,567	204,728	8
44.	BISCAYNE COLLEGE	-6.469	83,580	2,293	10,052	113,900	7
45.	HILLSBOROUGH CMTY COLLEGE	-6.542	29,440	2,027	52,469	283,329	11

FLORIDA

(. = MISSING DATA)

STATE RANK	LIBRARY	SCORE	VOLUMES HELD	GROSS VOLUMES ADDED	CIRCULATION	TOTAL EXPENDITURES	TOTAL STAFF
46.	PASCO-HERNANDO CC	-6.610	30,302	6,282	5,764	$247,336	9
47.	MIAMI CHRISTIAN COLLEGE	-6.639	24,669	1,898	8,450	77,187	5
48.	SAINT JOHNS RIVER CC	-6.654	49,563	2,072	7,026	107,130	7
49.	WARNER SOUTHERN COLLEGE	-6.846	51,332	5,442	11,600	71,188	3
50.	PALM BCH ATLANTIC COLLEGE	-6.939	40,905	1,889	14,698	81,189	4
51.	NORTH FLORIDA JR COLLEGE	-6.949	33,547	940	6,554	97,061	6
52.	FLAGLER COLLEGE	-7.174	49,537	4,533	13,758	122,323	6
53.	SOUTH FLORIDA JR COLLEGE	-7.331	29,727	1,441	6,772	78,803	4
54.	FLORIDA COLLEGE	-7.568	25,214	725	16,985	50,203	4
55.	FLORIDA MEMORIAL COLLEGE	-7.722	73,554	839	29,590	80,363	5
56.	FLORIDA KEYS CMTY COLLEGE	-7.790	25,162	1,082	7,710	97,623	6
57.	RINGLING SCHOOL OF ART	-8.462	9,914	0	21,000	67,930	4
58.	COLLEGE OF BOCA RATON	-8.505	27,780	1,600	1,328	23,524	2
59.	LUTHER RICE SEMINARY	-8.640	31,000	9,000	4,000	29,675	2
60.	TAMPA COLLEGE	-8.739	10,592	1,049	7,285	31,780	1
61.	WEBBER COLLEGE	-8.911	14,391	748	3,229	34,059	3
62.	JONES COLLEGE JACKSONVL	-9.473	10,720	458	5,000	22,609	2
63.	JONES COLLEGE ORLANDO	-9.953	6,980	601	2,566	18,748	1
64.	CLEARWATER CHRISTIAN C	-10.32	27,919	2,408	2,500	11,651	1
65.	UNIVERSITY OF SARASUTA	-10.41	37,638	0	400	22,432	1
66.	MORRIS C OF BUSINESS	-13.11	1,158	0	90	6,206	1
67.	BETHUNE COOKMAN COLLEGE	.	93,777	3,635	.	226,712	11
68.	NOVA UNIVERSITY	.	91,320	6,205	.	570,667	15
69.	SEM SAINT VINCENT DE PAUL	.	37,000	2,000	.	43,133	3
70.	SNT JOHN VIANNEY C SEM	.	47,000	12,500	.	.	2
71.	STHESTN C ASSEMBLIES GOD	.	42,065	2,394	26,388	.	3

GEORGIA

(. = MISSING DATA)

STATE RANK	LIBRARY	SCORE	VOLUMES HELD	GROSS VOLUMES ADDED	CIRCULATION	TOTAL EXPENDITURES	TOTAL STAFF
1.	UNIVERSITY OF GEORGIA	0.665	1,893,897	83,728	513,297	$5,012,116	216
2.	EMORY UNIVERSITY	-0.054	1,368,236	52,258	336,616	3,571,913	146
3.	GA INST OF TECHN MAIN CAM	-1.034	584,261	23,581	204,093	2,357,789	91
4.	GEORGIA STATE UNIVERSITY	-1.091	635,722	32,085	280,283	2,436,448	88
5.	VALDOSTA STATE COLLEGE	-2.954	205,434	13,817	112,943	672,593	28
6.	WEST GEORGIA COLLEGE	-3.154	216,577	10,612	162,792	547,896	30
7.	COLUMBUS COLLEGE	-3.345	138,681	12,911	73,702	560,964	24
8.	AUGUSTA COLLEGE	-3.443	234,961	20,593	73,062	433,946	15
9.	MEDICAL COLLEGE OF GA	-3.470	102,272	5,193	48,119	583,827	29
10.	MERCER U MAIN CAMPUS	-3.569	235,038	9,189	37,000	548,376	22
11.	GEORGIA COLLEGE	-3.955	140,409	3,519	110,055	383,638	16
12.	GEORGIA SOUTHERN COLLEGE	-4.024	264,893	16,522	123,500	786,803	37
13.	ATLANTA UNIVERSITY	-4.043	317,382	3,540	22,686	350,133	21
14.	FORT VALLEY STATE COLLEGE	-4.144	154,392	7,156	81,300	330,399	16
15.	GA SOUTHWESTERN COLLEGE	-4.292	117,942	3,836	25,157	325,171	14
16.	ARMSTRONG STATE COLLEGE	-4.474	111,644	2,302	54,412	278,218	15
17.	KENNESAW COLLEGE	-4.715	76,135	6,169	52,896	326,043	13
18.	BERRY COLLEGE	-4.726	110,026	6,219	33,872	240,794	9
19.	NORTH GEORGIA COLLEGE	-4.757	117,803	3,766	22,243	223,532	10
20.	SAVANNAH STATE COLLEGE	-4.804	130,136	6,490	30,595	261,086	16
21.	ALBANY JUNIOR COLLEGE	-4.832	62,161	3,983	71,410	208,355	11
22.	AGNES SCOTT COLLEGE	-4.904	158,506	4,923	36,023	216,077	9
23.	ALBANY STATE COLLEGE	-4.997	123,970	3,455	17,024	230,407	9
24.	GA INST TECHN-STHN TECH	-5.099	66,269	4,244	39,540	174,642	6
25.	MIDDLE GEORGIA COLLEGE	-5.104	74,074	2,473	120,808	169,300	10
26.	WESLEYAN COLLEGE	-5.218	107,608	4,242	30,565	211,527	5
27.	CLAYTON JUNIOR COLLEGE	-5.229	46,981	2,793	47,311	214,913	10
28.	GORDON JUNIOR COLLEGE	-5.509	39,178	4,037	12,988	208,255	8
29.	DALTON JUNIOR COLLEGE	-5.572	57,220	5,404	14,621	192,027	7
30.	ABRAHAM BALDWIN AGRL C	-5.582	53,728	2,134	21,671	150,632	8
31.	MERCER U IN ATLANTA	-5.584	47,708	3,622	18,361	155,690	7
32.	MACON JUNIOR COLLEGE	-5.595	54,261	2,151	26,414	158,000	8
33.	MORRIS BROWN COLLEGE	-5.635	60,325	3,896	51,512	140,915	7
34.	SHORTER COLLEGE	-5.825	78,060	2,950	47,332	98,228	4
35.	BRUNSWICK JUNIOR COLLEGE	-5.860	42,800	1,500	39,444	178,665	8
36.	FLOYD JUNIOR COLLEGE	-5.900	37,780	2,136	16,848	169,081	10
37.	GAINESVILLE JR COLLEGE	-6.144	42,825	1,707	19,179	106,262	6
38.	PAINE COLLEGE	-6.399	66,110	3,255	10,874	97,021	6
39.	OGLETHORPE UNIVERSITY	-6.482	61,551	1,953	10,704	93,219	5
40.	COLUMBIA THEOLOGICAL SEM	-6.483	77,342	2,000	19,326	77,652	4
41.	CLARK COLLEGE	-6.577	67,565	1,424	18,926	150,109	7
42.	SOUTH GEORGIA COLLEGE	-6.634	67,694	3,037	31,496	131,157	7
43.	TIFT COLLEGE	-6.656	59,095	2,193	9,601	70,941	3
44.	WAYCROSS JUNIOR COLLEGE	-6.681	15,218	2,014	5,410	106,593	4
45.	SPELMAN COLLEGE	-6.684	47,809	2,310	15,200	94,551	5

GEORGIA

(. = MISSING DATA)

STATE RANK	LIBRARY	SCORE	VOLUMES HELD	GROSS VOLUMES ADDED	CIRCULATION	TOTAL EXPENDITURES	TOTAL STAFF
46.	INTRDENOMINATL THEOL CTR	-6.764	80,098	1,960	22,500	$61,290	4
47.	TOCCOA FALLS COLLEGE	-6.803	46,117	4,393	39,734	54,212	2
48.	EMANUEL CO JUNIOR COLLEGE	-6.865	23,289	2,979	5,447	77,120	4
49.	PIEDMONT COLLEGE	-6.908	62,073	2,283	4,797	60,994	2
50.	BAINBRIDGE JUNIOR COLLEGE	-6.922	20,412	2,167	5,010	90,090	4
51.	BRENAU COLLEGE	-7.097	50,329	1,919	10,083	63,087	4
52.	REINHARDT COLLEGE	-7.241	28,813	1,630	9,235	67,053	5
53.	YOUNG HARRIS COLLEGE	-7.325	44,700	1,098	8,179	55,421	3
54.	ATLANTA JUNIOR COLLEGE	-7.455	17,447	1,893	1,399	175,052	7
55.	ATLANTA COLLEGE OF ART	-7.508	9,991	420	7,000	53,200	3
56.	BREWTON-PARKER COLLEGE	-7.528	22,218	1,167	8,526	36,947	3
57.	MERCER U STHN SCHOOL PHAR	-7.687	9,672	513	6,500	79,818	2
58.	EMMANUEL COLLEGE	-7.749	26,188	879	10,619	40,120	2
59.	COVENANT COLLEGE	-7.843	57,606	1,231	15,091	89,821	3
60.	ANDREW COLLEGE	-8.270	23,142	1,052	3,759	28,616	2
61.	TRUETT MCCONNELL COLLEGE	-8.374	25,823	641	3,500	43,556	2
62.	ATLANTA CHRISTIAN COLLEGE	-8.502	19,550	641	6,343	25,962	1
63.	GEORGIA MILITARY COLLEGE	-8.689	28,567	1,440	4,853	35,085	3
64.	LIFE CHIROPRACTIC COLLEGE	-10.5	13,518	0	266	40,894	4
65.	DRAUGHON'S JC BUSINESS	-11.13	2,980	258	1,466	12,982	1
66.	CRANDALL COLLEGE	.	1,080	84	1,300	.	1
67.	LA GRANGE COLLEGE	.	66,594	1,839	10,036	.	6
68.	THOMAS COUNTY CC	.	14,577	1,648	656	.	2

HAWAII

(. = MISSING DATA)

STATE RANK	LIBRARY	SCORE	VOLUMES HELD	GROSS VOLUMES ADDED	CIRCULATION	TOTAL EXPENDITURES	TOTAL STAFF
1.	U OF HAWAII AT MANOA	0.388	1,751,142	71,403	438,984	$4,869,418	161
2.	U OF HAWAII AT HILO	-3.612	133,081	19,048	37,105	555,396	17
3.	U OF HAWAII LEEWARD CC	-5.368	56,393	3,314	57,584	258,962	14
4.	U OF HAWAII HONOLULU CC	-6.110	38,987	2,703	22,047	302,646	15
5.	U OF HAWAII KAUAI CC	-6.323	26,758	2,287	18,590	205,460	7
6.	U OF HAWAII WINDWARD CC	-6.451	22,108	3,918	12,837	108,995	5
7.	CHAMINADE U OF HONOLULU	-6.619	50,000	2,132	19,551	117,723	6
8.	U OF HAWAII MAUI CC	-7.150	32,632	1,505	35,430	105,564	7
9.	U OF HAWAII KAPIOLANI CC	-7.483	29,813	1,638	8,739	120,545	6
10.	U OF HAWAII WEST OAHU C	-8.370	8,548	2,208	2,570	58,176	2
11.	HAWAII PACIFIC COLLEGE	-8.583	19,494	1,428	1,606	79,806	2
12.	HAWAII LOA COLLEGE	-8.689	35,938	1,431	4,862	69,227	3

IDAHO

(. = MISSING DATA)

STATE RANK	LIBRARY	SCORE	VOLUMES HELD	GROSS VOLUMES ADDED	CIRCULATION	TOTAL EXPENDITURES	TOTAL STAFF
1.	UNIVERSITY OF IDAHO	-1.956	555,582	30,933	198,676	$1,631,383	62
2.	BOISE STATE UNIVERSITY	-2.200	242,088	15,869	164,024	1,116,997	47
3.	IDAHO STATE UNIVERSITY	-2.546	289,080	16,314	108,365	1,279,056	36
4.	RICKS COLLEGE	-3.630	103,761	7,883	65,131	745,809	33
5.	NTHWST NAZARENE COLLEGE	-5.288	101,079	7,252	36,320	168,360	6
6.	LEWIS-CLARK ST COLLEGE	-5.454	77,852	3,495	33,678	183,653	7
7.	COLLEGE OF IDAHO	-5.648	119,733	2,764	19,062	138,820	7
8.	NORTH IDAHO COLLEGE	-6.471	29,650	1,368	9,192	109,917	6
9.	COLLEGE OF SOUTHERN IDAHO	.	89,824	1,604	7,802	146,716	.

ILLINOIS

(. = MISSING DATA)

STATE RANK	LIBRARY	SCORE	VOLUMES HELD	GROSS VOLUMES ADDED	CIRCULATION	TOTAL EXPENDITURES	TOTAL STAFF
1.	U OF ILL URBANA CAMPUS	1.780	5,759,666	161,279	1,758,309	$9,224,092	398
2.	UNIVERSITY OF CHICAGO	1.227	4,182,938	175,566	722,814	6,452,431	317
3.	NORTHWESTERN UNIVERSITY	0.856	2,505,509	67,233	700,000	6,884,971	223
4.	STHN ILLINOIS U CARBONDL	0.441	1,643,598	59,008	485,355	5,032,570	184
5.	NORTHERN ILL UNIVERSITY	-0.547	967,971	43,696	357,707	3,284,131	143
6.	U OF ILL CHICAGO CIRCLE	-0.864	680,675	27,103	296,297	2,874,164	113
7.	ILLINOIS STATE UNIVERSITY	-0.931	815,638	36,359	332,210	2,553,456	108
8.	U OF ILL MEDL CTR CHGO	-1.080	372,048	28,397	912,751	2,042,546	104
9.	STHN ILLINOIS U EDWARDSVL	-1.361	687,127	25,525	176,004	1,840,716	64
10.	LOYOLA U OF CHICAGO	-1.368	702,154	24,035	215,583	1,863,375	66
11.	DEPAUL UNIVERSITY	-1.640	343,570	16,387	146,850	1,609,585	86
12.	WESTERN ILL UNIVERSITY	-1.841	458,477	16,323	92,459	1,533,345	56
13.	EASTERN ILL UNIVERSITY	-1.888	406,600	22,814	197,748	1,212,749	62
14.	NTHESTN ILL UNIVERSITY	-2.237	318,547	18,017	125,731	1,214,395	53
15.	SANGAMON STATE UNIVERSITY	-2.445	232,214	19,297	136,698	1,195,312	46
16.	CHICAGO STATE UNIVERSITY	-2.557	228,957	10,074	108,985	1,063,692	55
17.	ILLINOIS INST TECHNOLOGY	-2.777	248,372	14,881	65,293	940,099	27
18.	COLLEGE OF DUPAGE	-3.034	93,050	7,831	87,982	1,322,609	48
19.	GOVERNORS ST UNIVERSITY	-3.312	170,452	11,054	72,971	791,095	41
20.	RUSH UNIVERSITY	-3.549	85,000	5,000	95,651	576,606	27
21.	BRADLEY UNIVERSITY	-3.651	305,167	8,131	45,558	557,067	23
22.	WM RAINEY HARPER COLLEGE	-3.727	95,766	4,520	56,027	662,439	35
23.	WHEATON COLLEGE	-3.881	145,863	12,681	141,084	363,205	17
24.	ELMHURST COLLEGE	-3.890	132,372	9,662	48,475	379,510	15
25.	SCH ART INSTITUTE CHICAGO	-4.033	12,068	4,496	55,949	524,000	25
26.	PARKLAND COLLEGE	-4.077	66,283	5,302	83,109	640,325	26
27.	AUGUSTANA COLLEGE	-4.149	205,344	7,532	42,064	329,142	13
28.	ILL WESLEYAN UNIVERSITY	-4.361	141,000	5,480	40,000	316,458	12
29.	CHGO C OSTEOPATHIC MED	-4.401	34,041	2,451	16,970	651,699	17
30.	JOHN MARSHALL LAW SCHOOL	-4.448	85,015	11,803	22,559	597,043	13
31.	ROSARY COLLEGE	-4.497	177,867	4,835	47,313	252,506	11
32.	KNOX COLLEGE	-4.527	191,606	6,504	54,796	285,385	10
33.	JESUIT-MCCORMICK JT LIB	-4.543	368,490	5,272	34,504	339,231	11
34.	LAKE FOREST COLLEGE	-4.563	171,662	7,284	34,785	300,350	10
35.	OLIVET NAZARENE COLLEGE	-4.605	115,869	4,536	71,863	196,864	12
36.	LINCOLN LAND CMTY COLLEGE	-4.612	66,285	2,889	48,792	398,462	18
37.	MORAINE VLY CMTY COLLEGE	-4.721	66,129	4,859	74,216	326,033	16
38.	LEWIS UNIVERSITY	-4.756	110,334	4,519	78,564	216,064	10
39.	MILLIKIN UNIVERSITY	-4.799	149,398	4,034	42,881	204,461	10
40.	NORTH PARK C & THEOL SEM	-4.827	146,040	2,718	31,410	241,602	13
41.	QUINCY COLLEGE	-4.861	194,790	4,053	42,000	171,012	7
42.	MUNDELEIN COLLEGE	-5.004	128,211	4,655	23,486	159,811	11
43.	JOLIET JUNIOR COLLEGE	-5.044	49,030	2,171	37,335	325,277	15
44.	GEORGE WILLIAMS COLLEGE	-5.109	87,649	5,468	30,660	165,279	9
45.	COLLEGE OF LAKE COUNTY	-5.109	76,040	4,034	102,949	486,308	24

ILLINOIS

(. = MISSING DATA)

STATE RANK	LIBRARY	SCORE	VOLUMES HELD	GROSS VOLUMES ADDED	CIRCULATION	TOTAL EXPENDITURES	TOTAL STAFF
46.	U HLTH SCI-CHGO MEDL SCH	-5.122	36,200	4,200	7,575	$267,712	14
47.	GARRETT-EVANGELCL THEOL	-5.132	166,584	3,133	20,820	181,620	8
48.	ILLINOIS CENTRAL COLLEGE	-5.143	63,463	2,649	64,386	459,212	19
49.	COLLEGE OF SAINT FRANCIS	-5.291	109,492	4,197	23,466	138,654	10
50.	ELGIN COMMUNITY COLLEGE	-5.317	43,988	3,608	20,804	240,443	12
51.	CITY C CHICAGO WRIGHT C	-5.326	70,317	1,951	27,635	305,488	16
52.	TRITON COLLEGE	-5.379	75,300	6,703	120,173	419,017	15
53.	CONCORDIA COLLEGE	-5.383	125,350	2,629	50,759	181,183	7
54.	CITY C CHGO TRUMAN C	-5.384	51,326	4,999	21,875	250,413	9
55.	SAINT XAVIER COLLEGE	-5.392	64,903	4,965	26,191	185,285	9
56.	BELLEVILLE AREA COLLEGE	-5.394	51,794	2,938	34,383	192,680	8
57.	WAUBONSEE CMTY COLLEGE	-5.396	47,169	2,152	41,168	228,869	11
58.	OAKTON COMMUNITY COLLEGE	-5.397	49,012	2,500	69,800	449,578	17
59.	THORNTON CMTY COLLEGE	-5.561	31,528	1,871	19,903	252,166	11
60.	ILLINOIS COLLEGE	-5.570	96,392	3,369	16,380	130,302	5
61.	ILLINOIS VLY CMTY COLLEGE	-5.583	62,385	1,196	12,500	210,767	10
62.	NATL COLLEGE ED MAIN CAM	-5.621	96,133	1,156	24,000	194,958	13
63.	MCHENRY COUNTY COLLEGE	-5.640	25,272	2,184	16,376	286,715	11
64.	MOODY BIBLE INSTITUTE	-5.699	102,579	4,440	70,201	96,973	4
65.	CITY C CHICAGO LOOP C	-5.816	46,688	1,644	27,000	334,731	13
66.	MONMOUTH COLLEGE	-5.868	120,538	3,183	16,419	113,537	4
67.	BLACK HAWK C QUAD-CITIES	-5.874	48,615	1,957	13,533	192,877	8
68.	AURORA COLLEGE	-5.886	86,777	2,517	18,179	116,054	7
69.	BETHANY-NTHN BAPT JT LIB	-5.926	130,695	2,200	13,679	127,229	7
70.	PRAIRIE STATE COLLEGE	-5.928	47,685	4,283	46,525	166,788	14
71.	MACMURRAY COLLEGE	-5.941	132,404	1,542	20,709	132,712	6
72.	TRINITY COLLEGE	-5.948	54,917	2,284	21,137	135,555	8
73.	LEWIS AND CLARK CC	-5.975	32,705	1,192	36,948	182,494	11
74.	MORTON COLLEGE	-5.979	36,977	1,646	31,868	141,895	9
75.	BARAT COLLEGE	-6.016	74,375	1,675	10,273	109,429	5
76.	ROCK VALLEY COLLEGE	-6.035	50,051	1,852	31,491	165,864	10
77.	NORTH CENTRAL COLLEGE	-6.042	96,748	2,824	8,139	111,875	5
78.	GREENVILLE COLLEGE	-6.071	95,025	1,923	25,409	125,375	6
79.	ILL ESTN CC WABASH VLY C	-6.190	17,500	2,750	25,167	121,722	5
80.	MCKENDREE COLLEGE	-6.234	55,637	2,736	8,777	113,245	4
81.	TRINITY EVANGELCL DIV SCH	-6.245	69,534	4,093	40,152	177,830	8
82.	BLACKBURN COLLEGE	-6.261	69,500	1,455	14,000	89,288	4
83.	KANKAKEE CMTY COLLEGE	-6.282	19,647	2,594	12,587	150,257	9
84.	NATL COLLEGE CHIROPRACTIC	-6.302	17,741	1,705	17,602	145,530	5
85.	REND LAKE COLLEGE	-6.407	27,024	2,451	10,226	103,583	7
86.	SAUK VALLEY COLLEGE	-6.421	41,206	2,231	35,888	119,917	7
87.	CITY C CHGO MALCOLM X C	-6.442	39,834	1,255	17,250	165,877	8
88.	CATHOLIC THEOL UNION	-6.455	79,059	3,110	10,493	73,769	4
89.	LINCOLN CHRISTIAN COLLEGE	-6.518	59,745	907	73,785	64,713	3
90.	CARL SANDBURG COLLEGE	-6.598	33,750	1,479	17,246	146,756	12

ILLINOIS

(. = MISSING DATA)

STATE RANK	LIBRARY	SCORE	VOLUMES HELD	GROSS VOLUMES ADDED	CIRCULATION	TOTAL EXPENDITURES	TOTAL STAFF
91.	LINCOLN COLLEGE	-6.676	37,016	1,584	19,427	$77,222	6
92.	JOHN A LOGAN COLLEGE	-6.694	27,000	1,050	62,000	162,528	8
93.	EUREKA COLLEGE	-6.807	75,940	1,305	9,431	69,841	4
94.	CHICAGO THEOLOGICAL SEM	-6.824	90,000	1,885	8,500	74,178	3
95.	SPOON RIVER COLLEGE	-6.831	23,115	3,630	25,025	144,769	6
96.	DANVILLE AREA CMTY C	-6.913	29,857	922	28,858	158,917	8
97.	COLUMBIA COLLEGE	-6.949	36,728	3,837	14,232	187,514	5
98.	JUDSON COLLEGE	-6.964	47,245	4,113	20,080	98,816	4
99.	HIGHLAND CMTY COLLEGE	-7.060	33,181	1,551	21,000	67,375	3
100.	SNT MARY OF THE LAKE SEM	-7.094	132,778	1,237	2,171	57,285	4
101.	ILL COLLEGE OF OPTOMETRY	-7.101	12,636	991	20,550	77,449	4
102.	SEABURY-WESTERN THEOL SEM	-7.197	75,432	1,727	5,611	62,304	2
103.	SOUTHEASTERN ILL COLLEGE	-7.260	25,000	1,450	10,291	67,769	5
104.	CITY C CHICAGO DALEY C	-7.272	38,057	918	28,240	237,803	11
105.	KASKASKIA COLLEGE	-7.278	42,788	830	6,465	146,051	6
106.	SHAWNEE COLLEGE	-7.392	34,486	823	9,801	63,513	2
107.	RICHLAND CMTY COLLEGE	-7.434	20,284	923	7,054	155,517	8
108.	KISHWAUKEE COLLEGE	-7.528	29,582	1,768	12,987	84,169	5
109.	LAKE LAND COLLEGE	-7.709	29,835	1,795	16,739	78,986	4
110.	NATL COLLEGE ED URBAN CAM	-7.768	23,905	301	4,474	64,158	4
111.	SPRINGFLD COLLEGE IN ILL	-7.847	30,545	738	2,956	40,805	3
112.	ILL ESTN LINCOLN TRAIL C	-7.869	19,700	1,300	5,000	50,975	3
113.	FELICIAN COLLEGE	-7.894	43,927	2,202	12,348	30,914	6
114.	ILL ESTN CC OLNEY CEN C	-7.943	27,370	404	6,012	68,966	5
115.	SPERTUS COLLEGE JUDAICA	-7.998	60,110	744	4,700	92,922	5
116.	MALLINCKRODT COLLEGE	-8.062	27,890	986	2,154	38,509	2
117.	STATE COMMUNITY COLLEGE	-8.144	27,505	831	4,358	78,094	4
118.	AMERICAN CONSV OF MUSIC	-3.287	5,630	2,036	2,425	38,916	2
119.	BLACK HAWK C EAST CAMPUS	-8.595	12,600	700	6,436	61,118	3
120.	ILL ESTN CC FRONTIER CC	-9.354	2,100	600	250	19,088	4
121.	KENDALL COLLEGE	-9.417	27,000	375	900	33,105	2
122.	DEVRY INST OF TECHNOLOGY	-9.605	7,399	1,063	7,239	20,922	1
123.	ALFRED ADLER INST CHICAGO	-10.36	4,500	700	1,045	8,547	1
124.	AERO-SPACE INSTITUTE	.	4,000	1,500	450	.	2
125.	CENTRAL YMCA CMTY COLLEGE	.	31,035	1,276	16,865	.	7
126.	CITY C CHGO OLIVE-HARVEY	.	47,669	1,712	18,676	.	10
127.	DELOURDES COLLEGE	.	19,255	1,015	1,195	.	2
128.	HEBREW THEOL COLLEGE	.	41,210	425	.	.	3
129.	ILL BENEDICTINE COLLEGE	.	112,499	4,394	14,812	.	10
130.	ILL COLLEGE PODIATRIC MED	.	9,075	1,283	15,034	.	4
131.	JOHN WOOD CMTY COLLEGE	.	2,792	700	12,608	.	.
132.	KELLER GRAD SCHOOL MGMT	.	600	50	.	.	0
133.	MEADVL-LOMBARD THEOL SCH	.	90,075	0	.	.	0
134.	MIDSTATE COLLEGE	.	6,847	907	6,829	.	2
135.	MORRISON INST OF TECHN	.	2,180	0	.	.	0

ILLINOIS

(. = MISSING DATA)

STATE RANK	LIBRARY	SCORE	VOLUMES HELD	GROSS VOLUMES ADDED	CIRCULATION	TOTAL EXPENDITURES	TOTAL STAFF
136.	NATIVE AMERICAN EDUC SERV	.	424	0	150	.	.
137.	PRINCIPIA COLLEGE	.	135,085	5,000	.	266,262	12
138.	TRINITY CHRISTIAN COLLEGE	.	43,000	1,500	.	55,979	2
139.	VANDERCOOK C OF MUSIC	.	18,000	700	2,000	.	1

INDIANA

(. = MISSING DATA)

STATE RANK	LIBRARY	SCORE	VOLUMES HELD	GROSS VOLUMES ADDED	CIRCULATION	TOTAL EXPENDITURES	TOTAL STAFF
1.	INDIANA U BLOOMINGTON	1.286	3,254,702	112,206	1,293,062	$7,467,545	303
2.	PURDUE U MAIN CAMPUS	0.144	1,388,152	30,377	725,987	4,250,478	209
3.	BALL STATE UNIVERSITY	-0.397	1,006,906	38,536	1,586,830	3,026,865	132
4.	UNIVERSITY OF NOTRE DAME	-0.438	1,383,114	41,180	340,537	2,608,393	119
5.	IND-PURDUE U INDIANAPOLIS	-1.074	559,869	26,497	260,442	1,982,207	83
6.	INDIANA STATE U MAIN CAM	-1.416	801,220	34,164	272,869	1,583,805	75
7.	VALPARAISO UNIVERSITY	-3.187	306,020	14,162	55,319	523,845	21
8.	IND-PURDUE U FORT WAYNE	-3.379	204,482	16,376	66,694	550,268	20
9.	UNIVERSITY OF EVANSVILLE	-3.677	195,578	8,506	50,235	481,826	21
10.	PURDUE U CALUMET CAMPUS	-3.955	125,183	11,391	34,237	395,104	17
11.	INDIANA U AT SOUTH BEND	-4.044	164,869	8,895	59,195	381,986	14
12.	DEPAUW UNIVERSITY	-4.079	220,092	4,008	59,999	319,439	21
13.	ANDERSON COLLEGE	-4.145	166,737	7,309	84,318	333,618	14
14.	EARLHAM COLLEGE	-4.239	260,746	13,821	54,227	271,840	10
15.	INDIANA ST U EVANSVL CAM	-4.375	134,033	9,508	21,173	285,721	15
16.	INDIANA CEN UNIVERSITY	-4.701	100,307	7,807	35,112	231,130	11
17.	INDIANA U SOUTHEAST	-4.703	86,499	5,307	37,732	242,483	12
18.	INDIANA U NORTHWEST	-4.726	140,614	8,279	24,007	254,233	8
19.	SAINT MARY'S COLLEGE	-5.012	148,774	4,500	25,064	227,353	12
20.	VINCENNES UNIVERSITY	-5.077	60,290	3,434	22,029	254,168	16
21.	MANCHESTER COLLEGE	-5.110	150,760	3,650	50,362	159,936	7
22.	SAINT JOSEPH'S COLLEGE	-5.183	146,177	3,180	23,284	157,064	7
23.	GRACE COLLEGE	-5.185	84,696	3,863	51,546	138,500	7
24.	INDIANA U AT KOKOMO	-5.315	79,495	2,377	27,439	193,418	7
25.	CONCORDIA THEOLOGICAL SEM	-5.634	96,262	5,162	19,601	140,976	7
26.	TAYLOR UNIVERSITY	-5.686	123,786	3,511	24,725	165,782	5
27.	CALUMET COLLEGE	-5.831	97,118	4,434	13,549	115,817	6
28.	TRI-STATE UNIVERSITY	-5.970	90,268	3,471	14,345	109,968	7
29.	MARION COLLEGE	-6.018	80,986	4,454	35,571	91,688	5
30.	SNT MEINRAD C JT LIBRARY	-6.126	120,999	3,640	19,810	86,916	6
31.	FRANKLIN COLLEGE INDIANA	-6.179	99,947	2,310	8,723	122,007	6
32.	GOSHEN COLLEGE	-6.209	100,664	2,433	18,759	109,343	5
33.	CHRISTIAN THEOLOGICAL SEM	-6.239	94,205	2,400	15,056	87,552	5
34.	PURDUE U NORTH CEN CAMPUS	-6.357	39,457	1,785	8,371	98,914	5
35.	ROSE-HULMAN INST OF TECHN	-6.571	50,895	1,228	11,189	84,353	6
36.	SAINT MARY-OF-THE-WOODS C	-6.603	131,825	2,234	13,286	83,648	5
37.	MENNONITE BIB SEM JT LIB	-6.625	77,817	2,198	11,262	66,784	5
38.	MARIAN COLLEGE	-6.682	102,142	2,985	11,841	42,384	4
39.	INDIANA UNIVERSITY EAST	-6.828	26,949	3,048	5,915	95,827	4
40.	OAKLAND CITY COLLEGE	-6.967	61,082	2,090	31,706	47,616	1
41.	SAINT FRANCIS COLLEGE	-6.979	67,729	1,356	6,390	62,949	5
42.	FORT WAYNE BIBLE COLLEGE	-7.100	49,463	1,438	34,234	58,530	5
43.	BETHEL COLLEGE	-7.200	50,757	1,764	7,554	51,855	2
44.	IND VOC TECH C-LAFAYETTE	-8.321	5,870	260	3,123	56,358	5
45.	INDIANA INST TECHNOLOGY	-8.375	45,926	176	3,578	32,072	1

INDIANA

(. = MISSING DATA)

STATE RANK	LIBRARY	SCORE	VOLUMES HELD	GROSS VOLUMES ADDED	CIRCULATION	TOTAL EXPENDITURES
46.	IND VOC TECH C-CEN IND	-8.535	7,049	789	16,578	$65,362
47.	IND VOC TECH C-STHCEN	-9.429	3,513	1,175	2,200	56,390
48.	IND VOC TECH C NORTHEAST	-9.779	4,984	146	1,600	28,213
49.	IND VOC TECH-WABASH VLY	-9.939	3,761	182	650	53,640
50.	HOLY CROSS JUNIOR COLLEGE	-10	8,474	317	946	7,790
51.	IND VOC TECH C-SOUTHWEST	-10.1	3,471	223	1,368	22,136
52.	LOCKYEAR COLLEGE	-10.17	7,464	120	800	26,372
53.	IND VOC TECH C-KOKOMO	-10.37	1,950	263	90	45,022
54.	IND VOC TECH C-COLUMBUS	-10.87	1,789	56	450	28,122
55.	ANCILLA DOMINI COLLEGE	.	27,290	865	23,645	.
56.	BUTLER UNIVERSITY	.	187,761	5,759	25,102	.
57.	HUNTINGTON COLLEGE	.	51,528	1,061	124	.
58.	IND NTHN GRAD SCH MGMT	.	7,650	100	.	.
59.	IND VOC TECH C-NTH CEN	.	7,283	168	7,145	.
60.	INDIANA C MORTUARY SCI	.	1,432	4	10	.
61.	INTERNATIONAL BUSINESS C	.	2,000	200	200	.
62.	WABASH COLLEGE	.	207,933	4,474	.	197,620

IOWA

(. = MISSING DATA)

STATE RANK	LIBRARY	SCORE	VOLUMES HELD	GROSS VOLUMES ADDED	CIRCULATION	TOTAL EXPENDITURES	TOTAL STAFF
1.	UNIVERSITY OF IOWA	0.672	2,216,970	89,522	966,121	$5,255,171	189
2.	IOWA STATE U SCI & TECHN	-0.083	1,296,074	47,252	792,989	3,869,258	163
3.	U OF NORTHERN IOWA	-1.522	502,831	29,329	210,041	1,546,006	59
4.	DRAKE UNIVERSITY	-2.433	460,637	19,093	94,363	1,034,716	38
5.	GRINNELL COLLEGE	-3.893	252,382	9,900	61,175	375,212	15
6.	LUTHER COLLEGE	-4.292	244,379	5,779	43,386	306,807	15
7.	COE COLLEGE	-4.424	176,295	6,015	36,758	250,968	11
8.	CENTRAL U OF IOWA	-5.075	120,000	5,000	87,000	188,830	6
9.	WARTBURG COLLEGE	-5.309	130,510	3,968	22,835	173,760	8
10.	MORNINGSIDE COLLEGE	-5.375	119,532	1,513	59,192	169,005	8
11.	LORAS COLLEGE	-5.401	196,593	3,543	33,958	165,655	6
12.	CORNELL COLLEGE	-5.427	116,582	3,429	15,411	167,690	8
13.	GRACELAND COLLEGE	-5.454	88,044	2,730	41,567	139,780	9
14.	SAINT AMBROSE COLLEGE	-5.463	101,600	2,066	22,231	160,000	8
15.	DORDT COLLEGE	-5.655	82,698	4,262	84,103	132,510	7
16.	NORTHWESTERN COLLEGE	-5.683	81,423	2,739	22,799	141,557	5
17.	GRAND VIEW COLLEGE	-5.704	65,350	4,568	28,050	111,835	5
18.	MOUNT MERCY COLLEGE	-5.707	62,947	1,800	31,331	120,451	8
19.	SOUTHEASTERN CMTY COLLEGE	-5.741	40,856	1,927	16,936	173,759	10
20.	PALMER C OF CHIROPRACTIC	-5.810	13,872	2,022	21,837	167,452	9
21.	KIRKWOOD CMTY COLLEGE	-5.822	47,244	4,326	26,812	141,172	11
22.	IOWA WESLEYAN COLLEGE	-5.894	93,305	2,310	14,266	113,254	7
23.	IOWA WESTERN CMTY COLLEGE	-5.896	54,252	2,426	17,881	183,659	7
24.	DES MOINES AREA CC	-5.912	71,399	3,868	36,214	266,370	14
25.	SIMPSON COLLEGE	-5.928	109,544	3,124	26,205	110,856	6
26.	IOWA CENTRAL CC	-5.990	60,687	1,199	20,234	166,797	9
27.	N IOWA AREA CMTY COLLEGE	-5.994	32,920	1,353	20,170	206,297	8
28.	MARYCREST COLLEGE	-6.000	94,638	2,660	33,575	77,004	7
29.	UNIVERSITY OF DUBUQUE	-6.084	139,489	5,388	3,707	146,670	4
30.	INDIAN HILLS CC	-6.309	31,208	5,214	13,182	128,899	5
31.	CLARKE COLLEGE	-6.448	102,112	2,500	16,745	57,263	4
32.	BRIAR CLIFF COLLEGE	-6.552	81,295	1,717	23,000	63,946	3
33.	WILLIAM PENN COLLEGE	-6.630	70,043	1,474	18,246	62,220	3
34.	NTHEST IA TECH INSTITUTE	-6.642	17,934	2,051	17,466	101,480	6
35.	WARTBURG THEOLOGICAL SEM	-6.861	72,170	3,949	8,444	64,265	4
36.	WESTMAR COLLEGE	-6.891	89,409	1,450	17,925	71,678	5
37.	IOWA LAKES CC NORTH CTR	-6.945	22,287	782	11,336	89,358	5
38.	DIVINE WORD COLLEGE	-6.957	83,903	1,557	10,112	49,850	5
39.	UPPER IOWA UNIVERSITY	-7.027	79,036	1,474	2,780	69,135	6
40.	MARSHALLTWN CMTY COLLEGE	-7.074	27,551	740	14,005	94,863	5
41.	ELLSWORTH CMTY COLLEGE	-7.206	23,994	1,317	32,983	105,637	6
42.	WESTERN IOWA TECH	-7.515	10,145	1,557	4,726	163,569	6
43.	SCOTT COMMUNITY COLLEGE	-7.543	22,337	1,645	18,995	102,567	6
44.	SOUTHWESTERN CMTY COLLEGE	-7.624	16,717	938	8,700	124,111	8
45.	WALDORF COLLEGE	-7.636	30,764	1,117	8,482	47,596	3

IOWA

(. = MISSING DATA)

STATE RANK	LIBRARY	SCORE	VOLUMES HELD	GROSS VOLUMES ADDED	CIRCULATION	TOTAL EXPENDITURES	TOTAL STAFF
46.	HAWKEYE INST TECHNOLOGY	-7.745	15,643	1,284	5,479	$108,158	4
47.	CLINTON COMMUNITY COLLEGE	-7.991	14,090	710	6,455	55,455	3
48.	MUSCATINE CMTY COLLEGE	-8.336	17,033	574	4,980	97,387	2
49.	SIOUX EMPIRE COLLEGE	-8.448	14,000	1,960	8,101	19,797	2
50.	IOWA LAKES CC SOUTH CTR	-8.608	10,899	533	9,480	66,690	3
51.	NTHWST IOWA TECH C	-8.997	30,212	939	2,500	27,532	2
52.	VENNARD COLLEGE	-9.234	41,676	706	13,729	30,927	2
53.	MOUNT SAINT CLARE COLLEGE	-9.680	19,403	1,450	2,778	13,473	2
54.	OPEN BIBLE COLLEGE	-10.13	15,210	670	2,120	11,028	1
55.	AQUINAS INST OF THEOLOGY	.	72,171	3,949	8,444	64,265	.
56.	BUENA VISTA COLLEGE	.	72,896	3,180	19,437	114,026	.
57.	COLLEGE OSTEO MED-SURGERY	.	22,055	463	.	76,550	4
58.	FAITH BAPT BIBLE COLLEGE	.	35,256	2,024	.	51,928	4
59.	MAHARISHI INTRNATL U	.	47,000	3,500	8,000	62,495	.

KANSAS

(. = MISSING DATA)

STATE RANK	LIBRARY	SCORE	VOLUMES HELD	GROSS VOLUMES ADDED	CIRCULATION	TOTAL EXPENDITURES	TOTAL STAFF
1.	U OF KANSAS MAIN CAMPUS	0.555	1,958,429	81,349	1,500,000	$4,329,266	164
2.	KANSAS ST U AGR & APP SCI	-1.117	858,845	26,853	283,367	2,205,087	73
3.	WICHITA STATE UNIVERSITY	-1.589	608,735	29,587	199,791	1,687,613	52
4.	EMPORIA STATE UNIVERSITY	-2.278	619,223	37,891	113,192	886,132	23
5.	WASHBURN U OF TOPEKA	-3.064	250,048	14,846	94,473	626,955	23
6.	U OF KANS MEDICAL CENTER	-3.139	122,557	6,263	193,809	647,834	36
7.	FORT HAYS ST UNIVERSITY	-3.397	300,512	6,805	32,907	578,522	17
8.	PITTSBURG ST UNIVERSITY	-3.484	203,528	5,872	56,428	644,545	17
9.	BENEDICTINE COLLEGE	-4.828	285,343	5,293	37,629	129,700	10
10.	BETHEL COLLEGE	-5.919	97,090	3,516	20,556	88,581	5
11.	FRIENDS UNIVERSITY	-5.947	81,603	2,825	14,356	105,147	5
12.	BETHANY COLLEGE	-5.968	77,513	4,809	10,240	110,983	4
13.	KANSAS CITY KANS CMTY JC	-5.998	50,853	2,200	40,364	128,817	8
14.	MARYMOUNT COLLEGE KANSAS	-6.144	75,122	1,937	20,308	94,609	5
15.	SOUTHWESTERN COLLEGE	-6.311	92,679	3,236	17,948	77,482	4
16.	MCPHERSON COLLEGE	-6.356	66,844	1,729	12,137	79,840	3
17.	BAKER UNIVERSITY	-6.368	96,187	2,547	13,968	104,663	6
18.	MID-AMERICA NAZARENE C	-6.396	62,630	2,003	17,960	93,872	5
19.	KANSAS NEWMAN COLLEGE	-6.445	68,317	2,684	17,458	86,781	4
20.	DODGE CTY CMTY JR COLLEGE	-6.448	32,296	1,412	15,431	121,844	7
21.	KANSAS WESLEYAN	-6.460	74,867	1,874	4,533	90,169	5
22.	STERLING COLLEGE	-6.467	77,572	1,724	15,861	76,202	4
23.	JOHNSN CO CMTY JR COLLEGE	-6.523	38,500	3,380	49,539	228,368	8
24.	COLBY COMMUNITY COLLEGE	-6.645	27,731	994	18,581	88,645	5
25.	HUTCHINSN CMTY JR COLLEGE	-6.715	37,522	1,902	15,320	100,619	7
26.	SAINT MARY COLLEGE	-6.938	110,188	2,084	12,428	29,904	6
27.	BUTLER CO CMTY JR COLLEGE	-6.973	30,622	1,708	13,084	72,742	4
28.	OTTAWA UNIVERSITY	-7.127	89,479	980	8,225	68,276	3
29.	COFFEYVL CMTY JR COLLEGE	-7.195	25,611	662	10,024	84,136	4
30.	SAINT MARY PLAINS COLLEGE	-7.251	57,472	1,646	13,257	47,280	5
31.	SEWARD CO CMTY JR COLLEGE	-7.383	20,238	1,134	13,118	57,754	2
32.	GARDEN CITY COMMUNITY JC	-7.444	30,612	1,069	4,871	62,744	3
33.	TABOR COLLEGE	-7.595	54,370	1,797	10,362	63,245	4
34.	COWLEY CO CMTY JR COLLEGE	-7.605	18,764	1,137	7,476	77,068	3
35.	ALLEN CO CMTY JR COLLEGE	-7.703	38,221	1,382	10,115	43,278	2
36.	BARTON CO CMTY JR COLLEGE	-7.881	24,361	420	71,877	85,809	7
37.	SAINT JOHN'S COLLEGE	-7.920	43,969	757	13,294	45,757	4
38.	HESSTON COLLEGE	-7.993	28,660	991	19,011	48,158	1
39.	HIGHLAND CMTY JR COLLEGE	-8.042	25,012	654	12,000	40,171	3
40.	NEOSHO CO CMTY JR COLLEGE	-8.099	20,718	1,185	17,401	58,408	3
41.	CLOUD CO CMTY JR COLLEGE	-8.230	18,489	814	9,120	61,621	5
42.	LABETTE CMTY COLLEGE	-8.252	19,739	1,312	4,136	53,937	2
43.	FT SCOTT CMTY JR COLLEGE	-8.279	19,751	943	11,665	57,355	3
44.	FRIENDS BIBLE COLLEGE	-8.303	18,376	1,262	5,100	34,589	1
45.	DONNELLY COLLEGE	-8.524	30,461	1,116	11,884	25,319	4

KANSAS

(. = MISSING DATA)

STATE RANK	LIBRARY	SCORE	VOLUMES HELD	GROSS VOLUMES ADDED	CIRCULATION	TOTAL EXPENDITURES	TOTAL STAFF
46.	KANSAS TECHNICAL INST	-8.698	15,531	1,023	2,649	$62,394	3
47.	CENTRAL COLLEGE	-9.009	18,045	670	11,200	27,034	1
48.	MANHATTAN CHRSTN COLLEGE	-9.329	22,173	813	3,000	21,335	2
49.	CENTRAL BAPTIST THEOL SEM	.	65,526	818	12,787	.	3
50.	HASKELL INDIAN JR COLLEGE	.	20,101	1,128	5,505	211,377	.
51.	INDEPENDENCE COMMUNITY JC	.	27,871	1,243	11,172	.	3
52.	PRATT CMTY JUNIOR COLLEGE	.	23,949	874	12,000	.	3

KENTUCKY

(. = MISSING DATA)

STATE RANK	LIBRARY	SCORE	VOLUMES HELD	GROSS VOLUMES ADDED	CIRCULATION	TOTAL EXPENDITURES	TOTAL STAFF
1.	UNIVERSITY OF KENTUCKY	0.342	1,244,935	56,333	542,205	$4,516,981	191
2.	UNIVERSITY OF LOUISVILLE	-0.825	831,537	32,669	225,602	2,576,023	116
3.	EASTERN KY UNIVERSITY	-1.381	465,928	37,656	290,943	1,511,515	85
4.	WESTERN KY UNIVERSITY	-1.392	468,644	41,161	181,354	1,638,783	88
5.	MURRAY STATE UNIVERSITY	-2.206	474,267	32,485	75,439	926,681	41
6.	NORTHERN KY UNIVERSITY	-2.242	251,386	19,877	116,143	1,330,081	38
7.	U OF KENTUCKY CC SYSTEM	-2.409	348,592	15,142	243,671	1,081,492	69
8.	MOREHEAD STATE UNIVERSITY	-2.578	375,077	16,443	325,294	836,118	48
9.	SOUTHERN BAPT THEOL SEM	-3.771	267,347	20,881	124,283	385,930	21
10.	KENTUCKY STATE UNIVERSITY	-3.934	135,248	9,115	46,604	362,090	20
11.	BEREA COLLEGE	-4.048	230,673	7,220	73,348	318,504	14
12.	CENTRE COLLEGE OF KY	-4.834	130,284	3,792	33,015	207,418	10
13.	ASBURY COLLEGE	-4.863	94,386	5,957	47,435	223,681	10
14.	ASBURY THEOLOGICAL SEM	-5.020	118,052	6,241	39,741	227,952	13
15.	CUMBERLAND COLLEGE	-5.393	87,569	3,038	35,000	153,235	12
16.	GEORGETOWN COLLEGE	-5.720	127,799	2,893	11,995	116,760	6
17.	SPALDING COLLEGE	-5.757	108,482	2,478	24,974	84,960	9
18.	BELLARMINE COLLEGE	-5.873	78,137	1,794	14,084	155,118	9
19.	UNION COLLEGE	-5.879	71,213	1,863	18,371	111,711	5
20.	LOUISVL PRESB THEOL SEM	-5.941	83,924	1,817	20,220	147,040	5
21.	KENTUCKY WESLEYAN COLLEGE	-6.053	88,754	3,081	7,648	106,111	7
22.	CAMPBELLSVILLE COLLEGE	-6.248	85,352	3,816	15,043	95,031	6
23.	THOMAS MORE COLLEGE	-6.498	79,896	1,488	8,227	70,039	8
24.	BRESCIA COLLEGE	-6.505	62,710	2,437	7,065	59,420	6
25.	LEXINGTON THEOL SEMINARY	-6.574	91,032	3,062	16,150	92,500	3
26.	SEMINARY OF SAINT PIUS X	-6.989	33,090	2,024	7,978	59,772	4
27.	TRANSYLVANIA UNIVERSITY	-7.028	93,286	1,408	7,573	114,814	8
28.	PIKEVILLE COLLEGE	-7.055	85,057	1,467	25,301	105,202	5
29.	ALICE LLOYD COLLEGE	-8.063	29,162	838	23,720	53,165	4
30.	LEES JUNIOR COLLEGE	-8.626	27,198	1,009	6,148	38,564	3
31.	LINDSEY WILSON COLLEGE	-8.843	18,859	525	3,141	26,324	2
32.	MIDWAY COLLEGE	-8.905	27,459	942	4,096	33,130	1
33.	KY CHRISTIAN COLLEGE	-9.068	23,577	909	5,126	11,322	1
34.	LOUISVILLE SCHOOL OF ART	-9.184	6,591	390	1,980	18,497	1
35.	SULLIVAN JC BUSINESS	-9.897	4,410	854	2,873	24,885	2
36.	DRAUGHUN'S COLLEGE	.	2,800	105	1,200	.	1
37.	KENTUCKY BUSINESS COLLEGE	.	3,600	0	1,500	.	1
38.	OWENSBORO BUSINESS C	.	2,700	200	.	22,050	1
39.	SAINT CATHARINE COLLEGE	.	16,576	704	2,202	.	2
40.	SUE BENNETT COLLEGE	.	35,520	1,122	4,212	.	2

LOUISIANA

(. = MISSING DATA)

STATE RANK	LIBRARY	SCORE	VOLUMES HELD	GROSS VOLUMES ADDED	CIRCULATION	TOTAL EXPENDITURES	TOTAL STAFF
1.	LA STATE U AND A&M C	0.063	1,767,635	56,253	352,203	$3,822,135	136
2.	TULANE U OF LOUISIANA	-0.485	1,346,910	36,889	214,398	2,628,808	125
3.	UNIVERSITY OF NEW ORLEANS	-2.122	369,985	20,060	97,775	1,284,954	58
4.	U OF STHWSTN LOUISIANA	-2.585	444,235	18,135	139,000	1,045,036	42
5.	LOYOLA U IN NEW ORLEANS	-2.628	380,078	13,830	87,647	793,751	40
6.	NORTHEAST LOUISIANA U	-2.818	296,187	13,600	87,315	942,555	35
7.	MCNEESE STATE UNIVERSITY	-2.989	197,812	11,991	107,057	612,656	33
8.	LOUISIANA TECH UNIVERSITY	-3.168	242,955	10,380	105,019	769,311	34
9.	SOUTHERN U A&M C MAIN CAM	-3.249	280,787	11,159	214,602	648,549	35
10.	NICHOLLS STATE UNIVERSITY	-3.324	184,708	6,392	98,472	598,128	25
11.	LA ST U MEDICAL CENTER	-3.406	122,048	6,219	138,936	587,810	23
12.	NTHWSTN ST U OF LA	-3.604	244,289	8,159	52,411	568,363	27
13.	STHESTN LA UNIVERSITY	-3.839	208,534	11,421	49,501	604,847	21
14.	GRAMBLING STATE U	-3.895	177,962	9,528	50,805	473,355	16
15.	LA STATE U SHREVEPORT	-3.923	111,104	7,657	34,227	418,891	18
16.	XAVIER UNIVERSITY OF LA	-4.426	98,194	4,622	26,949	359,682	19
17.	STHN U IN NEW ORLEANS	-4.627	150,946	9,161	47,458	279,300	15
18.	LA STATE U ALEXANDRIA	-4.727	100,146	5,602	13,467	298,588	11
19.	CENTENARY C OF LOUISIANA	-5.167	131,918	4,964	23,400	162,941	7
20.	NEW ORLS BAPT THEOL SEM	-5.231	145,965	3,719	42,027	133,563	13
21.	LA STATE U EUNICE	-5.349	75,386	4,528	7,072	169,797	8
22.	DILLARD UNIVERSITY	-5.611	120,076	2,144	11,475	191,907	9
23.	LOUISIANA COLLEGE	-5.758	96,158	3,822	18,156	132,033	7
24.	SAINT MARY'S DOMINICAN C	-6.440	71,661	2,040	8,395	73,205	7
25.	DELGADO COLLEGE	-6.442	32,278	714	23,281	310,657	16
26.	STHN U SHREVEPORT-BOSSIER	-6.561	26,600	1,035	7,714	129,590	6
27.	BOSSIER PARISH CC	-7.523	18,261	2,501	12,500	45,870	3
28.	SAINT JOSEPH SEM COLLEGE	-7.912	63,000	2,250	2,500	23,229	1
29.	SAINT BERNARD PARISH CC	-8.191	20,000	845	6,145	58,842	4
30.	NUTRE DAME SEM SCH THEO	.	73,054	2,111	8,406	.	2

MAINE

(. = MISSING DATA)

STATE RANK	LIBRARY	SCORE	VOLUMES HELD	GROSS VOLUMES ADDED	CIRCULATION	TOTAL EXPENDITURES	TOTAL STAFF
1.	U OF MAINE AT ORONO	-2.072	544,432	22,075	116,388	$1,421,015	63
2.	BATES COLLEGE	-3.138	237,171	14,067	79,667	516,548	23
3.	BOWDOIN COLLEGE	-3.166	410,670	12,617	95,872	635,654	22
4.	U OF SOUTHERN MAINE	-3.230	276,729	7,312	115,313	525,436	29
5.	COLBY COLLEGE	-4.648	358,072	10,637	78,034	675,810	24
6.	MAINE MARITIME ACADEMY	-5.382	46,100	2,927	19,750	185,317	8
7.	U OF MAINE AT FARMINGTON	-5.576	86,385	5,460	55,665	137,757	9
8.	NASSON COLLEGE	-5.632	122,058	3,005	52,090	103,007	6
9.	U OF ME AT PRESQUE ISLE	-6.248	68,356	2,746	25,226	109,756	4
10.	U OF MAINE AT MACHIAS	-6.391	59,284	2,515	23,394	91,148	4
11.	SAINT JOSEPH'S COLLEGE	-6.983	49,020	2,000	5,500	57,349	3
12.	UNITY COLLEGE	-7.116	35,798	5,662	14,261	75,148	3
13.	U OF MAINE AT AUGUSTA	-7.324	31,210	1,452	9,000	102,321	5
14.	BANGOR THEOLOGICAL SEM	-7.416	69,383	1,179	6,480	44,421	2
15.	UNIVERSITY OF NEW ENGLAND	-7.482	65,648	3,348	4,515	95,731	6
16.	U OF MAINE AT FORT KENT	-7.847	38,563	2,084	7,600	74,803	5
17.	HUSSON COLLEGE	-8.630	28,544	1,687	4,344	42,757	3
18.	COLLEGE OF THE ATLANTIC	-8.634	12,777	800	2,699	57,141	3
19.	NTHN ME VOC TECH INST	-8.912	10,854	1,247	3,244	42,100	1
20.	THOMAS COLLEGE	-8.916	16,304	636	2,966	35,335	2
21.	PORTLAND SCHOOL OF ART	-9.094	10,633	649	6,253	25,471	1
22.	BEAL COLLEGE	-10.15	13,650	246	950	12,510	1
23.	ANDOVER COLLEGE	-10.89	4,655	722	1,080	6,858	1
24.	EASTERN ME VOC-TECH INST	.	15,200	700	1,249		1
25.	SOUTHERN ME VOC TECH INST	.	15,574	1,037	.	12,088	2
26.	WESTBROOK COLLEGE	.	.	0	15,117	63,982	5

MARYLAND

(. = MISSING DATA)

STATE RANK	LIBRARY	SCORE	VOLUMES HELD	GROSS VOLUMES ADDED	CIRCULATION	TOTAL EXPENDITURES	TOTAL STAFF
1.	U OF MD COLLEGE PARK CAM	0.567	1,335,018	57,712	1,122,558	$5,802,996	209
2.	JOHNS HOPKINS UNIVERSITY	0.150	2,214,282	36,795	501,656	4,237,584	176
3.	U OF MD BALT PROF SCHOOLS	-1.883	367,392	16,680	98,817	1,464,713	63
4.	U OF MD BALTIMORE CO CAM	-2.237	293,618	13,689	161,168	1,150,168	47
5.	UNIVERSITY OF BALTIMORE	-3.024	295,311	10,623	45,771	791,638	32
6.	MORGAN STATE UNIVERSITY	-3.057	197,271	19,228	54,047	960,130	40
7.	SALISBURY STATE COLLEGE	-3.559	169,866	9,695	80,768	476,405	20
8.	FROSTBURG STATE COLLEGE	-3.746	167,170	3,817	56,882	494,195	29
9.	MONTGOMERY C ROCKVILLE	-3.860	93,898	4,500	62,500	615,373	26
10.	LOYOLA-NOTRE DAME JT LIB	-3.957	184,391	6,449	41,200	361,377	19
11.	CATONSVILLE CMTY COLLEGE	-3.975	102,575	3,282	67,260	645,923	34
12.	PRINCE GEORGES CC	-4.237	68,675	4,275	43,775	641,468	26
13.	BOWIE STATE COLLEGE	-4.348	151,421	1,818	24,549	435,393	20
14.	CMTY COLLEGE OF BALTIMORE	-4.357	87,712	6,661	64,424	436,641	23
15.	COPPIN STATE COLLEGE	-4.588	113,303	3,569	50,000	358,067	17
16.	ANNE ARUNDEL CMTY COLLEGE	-4.618	80,816	4,739	51,479	241,056	14
17.	SNT MARY'S COLLEGE OF MD	-4.686	77,515	4,582	16,739	292,261	12
18.	ESSEX COMMUNITY COLLEGE	-4.692	85,870	3,369	33,401	329,779	17
19.	GOUCHER COLLEGE	-4.709	203,413	4,899	29,588	230,201	13
20.	U OF MD-EASTERN SHORE	-4.855	108,630	1,171	39,000	257,783	16
21.	WESTERN MARYLAND COLLEGE	-4.936	119,337	3,541	28,757	235,589	8
22.	HOOD COLLEGE	-4.972	123,833	4,656	33,865	210,604	9
23.	CHARLES CO CMTY COLLEGE	-5.048	32,915	2,213	21,517	262,099	15
24.	WASHINGTON COLLEGE	-5.172	104,365	2,787	31,216	184,226	10
25.	MONTGOMERY C TAKOMA PARK	-5.352	52,591	3,430	20,125	257,782	10
26.	MOUNT SNT MARY'S COLLEGE	-5.445	125,680	3,827	15,940	191,000	10
27.	COLUMBIA UNION COLLEGE	-5.687	105,667	3,614	15,500	183,738	6
28.	HOWARD COMMUNITY COLLEGE	-5.847	27,018	789	32,279	210,700	15
29.	HAGERSTOWN JUNIOR COLLEGE	-6.134	43,980	1,920	18,544	160,170	9
30.	HARFORD COMMUNITY COLLEGE	-6.155	37,207	1,952	52,527	163,420	13
31.	ALLEGANY CMTY COLLEGE	-6.296	40,941	901	44,269	107,963	6
32.	PEABODY INST OF JHU	-6.350	65,488	2,199	15,274	74,042	4
33.	MD INST COLLEGE OF ART	-6.401	39,000	1,064	20,926	110,950	7
34.	DUNDALK CMTY COLLEGE	-6.557	17,461	1,805	75,562	219,343	8
35.	SAINT JOHN'S C MAIN CAM	-6.822	78,654	2,150	16,215	70,914	3
36.	SAINT MARY'S SEMINARY & U	-6.897	76,459	1,436	4,304	78,516	5
37.	SNT JOHN'S C SANTA FE NM	-6.987	44,293	1,734	12,789	89,162	4
38.	CHESAPEAKE COLLEGE	-7.144	27,436	1,036	7,781	79,622	4
39.	FREDERICK CMTY COLLEGE	-7.193	27,916	1,340	11,108	175,271	11
40.	WASHINGTON BIBLE COLLEGE	-7.265	28,452	2,898	35,905	70,527	2
41.	VILLA JULIE COLLEGE	-7.759	26,568	1,803	4,468	35,627	2
42.	GARRETT COMMUNITY COLLEGE	-7.816	20,780	2,763	3,427	112,915	6
43.	CECIL COMMUNITY COLLEGE	-8.070	17,771	1,000	5,858	86,414	4
44.	DE SALES HALL SCH THEO	-8.942	35,817	551	1,662	19,227	1
45.	CAPITOL INST TECHNOLOGY	-9.623	8,841	360	2,676	24,021	1

MARYLAND

(. = MISSING DATA)

STATE RANK	LIBRARY	SCORE	VOLUMES HELD	GROSS VOLUMES ADDED	CIRCULATION	TOTAL EXPENDITURES	TOTAL STAFF
46.	MARYLAND C ART AND DESIGN	-9.751	6,360	871	4,113	$14,723	2
47.	BALTIMORE HEBREW COLLEGE	.	30,275	2,621	30,640	.	5
48.	MONTGOMERY C GERMANTOWN	.	22,553	12,000	9,431	.	7
49.	NER ISRAEL RAB COLLEGE	.	16,992	176	1,700	.	1
50.	TOWSON STATE UNIVERSITY	.	327,841	15,708	.	1,102,622	43

MASSACHUSETTS

(. = MISSING DATA)

STATE RANK	LIBRARY	SCORE	VOLUMES HELD	GROSS VOLUMES ADDED	CIRCULATION	TOTAL EXPENDITURES	TOTAL STAFF
1.	HARVARD UNIVERSITY	2.689	9,913,992	241,400	1,784,951	$16,623,983	791
2.	MASS INST OF TECHNOLOGY	0.207	1,759,971	71,388	451,555	3,874,085	198
3.	U OF MASS AMHERST CAMPUS	-0.042	1,258,294	50,940	621,377	3,618,858	148
4.	BOSTON UNIVERSITY	-0.163	1,287,618	42,098	285,762	3,652,755	174
5.	BOSTON COLLEGE	-0.976	810,932	24,097	271,372	2,114,523	94
6.	TUFTS UNIVERSITY	-1.277	566,582	18,874	271,519	1,692,726	72
7.	NORTHEASTERN UNIVERSITY	-1.340	434,225	13,761	303,375	2,261,172	111
8.	BRANDEIS UNIVERSITY	-1.448	609,329	23,175	330,117	1,651,241	61
9.	SMITH COLLEGE	-1.694	866,244	23,108	273,661	1,315,463	63
10.	UNIVERSITY OF LOWELL	-2.017	279,197	16,301	80,493	1,462,985	40
11.	WELLESLEY COLLEGE	-2.506	541,798	12,498	108,290	868,471	41
12.	AMHERST COLLEGE	-2.547	545,099	14,758	112,127	794,113	35
13.	MOUNT HOLYOKE COLLEGE	-2.660	437,071	17,282	74,716	677,290	30
14.	STHESTN MASS UNIVERSITY	-2.859	225,175	11,117	40,394	1,577,331	35
15.	U OF MASS BOSTON CAMPUS	-2.926	318,295	18,556	49,801	1,075,448	42
16.	CLARK UNIVERSITY	-3.033	347,758	11,994	65,153	577,615	24
17.	WILLIAMS COLLEGE	-3.045	490,496	16,585	106,183	653,358	25
18.	BRIDGEWATER STATE COLLEGE	-3.260	176,642	5,250	67,240	654,496	34
19.	SUFFOLK UNIVERSITY	-3.275	197,936	15,675	26,600	889,736	25
20.	WESTERN NEW ENG COLLEGE	-3.292	167,087	16,547	61,875	666,420	21
21.	COLLEGE OF THE HOLY CROSS	-3.327	364,277	10,518	64,320	452,750	22
22.	WORCESTER POLY INSTITUTE	-3.441	175,522	12,476	47,300	475,406	18
23.	SALEM STATE COLLEGE	-3.691	180,006	6,388	130,000	455,933	18
24.	BOSTON STATE COLLEGE	-3.721	146,723	10,756	37,210	532,925	22
25.	SIMMONS COLLEGE	-3.823	157,810	8,802	71,466	450,133	20
26.	WHEATON COLLEGE	-3.845	205,891	7,583	62,397	487,725	21
27.	WORCESTER STATE COLLEGE	-4.091	146,461	3,560	40,803	472,942	27
28.	U MASS MEDL SCH-WORCESTER	-4.166	74,379	4,820	10,621	572,333	17
29.	BENTLEY COLLEGE	-4.258	95,088	5,733	26,365	452,541	19
30.	ADL MGMT ED INSTITUTE	-4.267	39,000	4,000	7,500	633,300	20
31.	FRAMINGHAM STATE COLLEGE	-4.355	130,025	5,940	80,451	329,791	17
32.	HAMPSHIRE COLLEGE	-4.415	59,705	1,916	58,425	407,787	26
33.	BABSON COLLEGE	-4.795	80,968	3,698	36,786	348,650	16
34.	NORTH ADAMS STATE COLLEGE	-4.871	113,856	6,599	37,414	266,620	9
35.	SPRINGFIELD COLLEGE	-4.936	135,380	2,691	46,088	209,285	15
36.	LESLEY COLLEGE	-5.010	72,189	5,089	53,169	244,457	11
37.	NEW ENGLAND SCHOOL OF LAW	-5.014	72,735	5,669	27,000	303,716	9
38.	STONEHILL COLLEGE	-5.135	109,852	5,295	15,012	232,022	11
39.	ASSUMPTION COLLEGE	-5.177	149,203	3,776	25,045	153,126	6
40.	GORDON-CONWELL THEOL SEM	-5.198	94,464	5,058	59,804	143,339	7
41.	BRISTOL COMMUNITY COLLEGE	-5.239	40,486	2,057	33,347	332,004	14
42.	EMERSON COLLEGE	-5.281	62,786	2,179	29,363	209,962	11
43.	MASS C PHAR-HLTH SCI	-5.379	55,404	2,584	6,830	203,289	12
44.	MERRIMACK COLLEGE	-5.419	117,414	3,315	31,352	183,250	8
45.	ANDOVER NEWTON THEOL SCH	-5.472	195,034	2,564	17,252	130,134	8

MASSACHUSETTS

(. = MISSING DATA)

STATE RANK	LIBRARY	SCORE	VOLUMES HELD	GROSS VOLUMES ADDED	CIRCULATION	TOTAL EXPENDITURES	TOTAL STAFF
46.	HOLYOKE COMMUNITY COLLEGE	-5.566	46,964	1,825	13,736	$209,940	10
47.	NEW ENG CONSV OF MUSIC	-5.577	40,000	2,635	61,423	163,295	8
48.	GORDON COLLEGE	-5.715	117,967	2,766	48,266	146,159	8
49.	MASS BAY CMTY COLLEGE	-5.775	40,891	1,694	27,280	214,947	11
50.	GREENFIELD CMTY COLLEGE	-5.886	38,885	1,117	16,872	183,867	11
51.	SPRINGFIELD TECHNICAL CC	-5.890	43,590	3,058	18,066	160,947	8
52.	ATLANTIC UNION COLLEGE	-5.956	96,528	2,979	20,565	109,208	4
53.	EPISCOPAL DIVINITY SCHOOL	-5.960	102,748	1,645	18,136	98,777	8
54.	REGIS COLLEGE	-6.042	119,399	4,252	18,450	94,552	7
55.	WHEELOCK COLLEGE	-6.114	61,319	2,605	41,428	135,414	7
56.	AMERICAN INTRNATL COLLEGE	-6.174	120,506	1,823	11,397	109,474	6
57.	CURRY COLLEGE	-6.206	78,957	1,684	10,000	132,125	6
58.	EMMANUEL COLLEGE	-6.306	119,619	2,918	14,580	125,044	6
59.	DEAN JUNIOR COLLEGE	-6.370	34,083	1,053	4,011	119,384	7
60.	MIDDLESEX CMTY COLLEGE	-6.580	33,015	5,000	12,343	146,967	5
61.	MASS COLLEGE OF ART	-6.657	64,325	810	30,000	147,509	5
62.	COLLEGE OUR LADY OF ELMS	-6.760	69,823	2,774	13,679	41,187	8
63.	ENDICOTT COLLEGE	-6.794	47,844	863	34,745	79,756	7
64.	MT WACHUSETT CMTY COLLEGE	-6.834	53,121	1,803	10,681	93,524	4
65.	HELLENIC C-HOLY CROSS SCH	-6.917	68,857	4,253	4,196	83,671	4
66.	QUINSIGAMOND CMTY COLLEGE	-6.919	53,284	2,213	13,673	83,894	5
67.	PINE MANOR COLLEGE	-7.035	31,190	1,861	3,393	84,154	6
68.	ANNA MARIA COLLEGE	-7.102	47,753	1,647	5,168	49,715	4
69.	HEBREW COLLEGE	-7.131	64,703	1,353	16,020	52,043	3
70.	MASSASOIT CMTY COLLEGE	-7.163	60,217	1,200	24,478	183,197	8
71.	SIMON'S ROCK EARLY C	-7.167	45,571	2,850	10,040	97,653	5
72.	NEW ENGLAND C OPTOMETRY	-7.218	9,034	784	3,120	76,815	4
73.	BUNKER HILL CMTY COLLEGE	-7.290	21,015	2,176	10,923	207,843	9
74.	WORCESTER JOINT LIBRARY	-7.333	31,506	755	2,656	60,487	2
75.	BERKSHIRE CMTY COLLEGE	-7.348	39,214	2,032	14,884	101,389	5
76.	ESSEX AGRL-TECH INST	-7.381	13,270	1,168	8,806	67,580	3
77.	BECKER JC-WORCESTER	-7.522	29,054	1,115	9,287	64,076	3
78.	BERKSHIRE CHRISTIAN C	-7.578	34,693	3,500	3,562	34,025	2
79.	BRADFORD COLLEGE	-7.579	54,724	1,557	4,266	67,875	1
80.	EASTERN NAZARENE COLLEGE	-7.605	83,020	2,886	10,324	99,246	5
81.	WENTWORTH INST OF TECH	-7.624	50,534	1,691	5,180	121,145	4
82.	CAPE COD CMTY COLLEGE	-7.625	48,936	0	18,969	201,330	9
83.	BERKLEE COLLEGE OF MUSIC	-7.768	25,917	1,190	72,980	78,075	3
84.	MASS MARITIME ACADEMY	-7.827	35,453	1,556	2,364	111,200	6
85.	LASELL JUNIOR COLLEGE	-7.944	48,600	1,380	15,748	64,444	4
86.	LABOURE JUNIOR COLLEGE	-8.005	8,592	337	24,300	50,766	3
87.	FORSYTH SCH DENTL HYGNSTS	-8.233	6,996	173	2,600	39,724	1
88.	BAY PATH JUNIOR COLLEGE	-8.417	28,355	775	5,344	48,422	3
89.	SNI HYACINTH COLLEGE-SEM	-8.549	53,100	2,300	1,500	12,079	2
90.	SWAIN SCHOOL OF DESIGN	-8.589	12,101	724	8,043	17,809	2

MASSACHUSETTS

(. = MISSING DATA)

STATE RANK	LIBRARY	SCORE	VOLUMES HELD	GROSS VOLUMES ADDED	CIRCULATION	TOTAL EXPENDITURES	TOTAL STAFF
91.	BECKER JC-LEICESTER	-8.691	25,474	1,046	4,874	$35,979	3
92.	ROXBURY COMMUNITY COLLEGE	-8.918	1,449	1,449	1,500	119,275	5
93.	NEWBURY JUNIOR COLLEGE	-8.943	7,065	690	1,500	73,553	2
94.	AQUINAS JC AT MILTON	-9.041	8,332	456	2,100	17,928	1
95.	SCH OF MUSEUM FINE ARTS	-9.181	6,706	737	14,000	29,682	1
96.	AQUINAS JC AT NEWTON	-9.562	11,070	900	430	11,310	2
97.	QUINCY JUNIOR COLLEGE	-10.06	7,200	0	1,974	89,549	3
98.	BAY STATE JC OF BUS	-10.3	4,005	108	6,000	17,142	1
99.	CHAMBERLAYNE JR COLLEGE	-10.64	25,200	156	584	14,847	1
100.	BLUE HILLS REG TECH INST	.	4,731	402	.	28,987	2
101.	FISHER JUNIOR COLLEGE	.	22,119	1,238	3,076	.	2
102.	FITCHBURG STATE COLLEGE	.	150,000	6,434	60,045	.	13
103.	FRANKLIN INST OF BOSTON	.	7,708	281	405	.	1
104.	KATHARINE GIBBS SCHOOL	.	1,795	20	400	.	0
105.	MOUNT IDA JUNIOR COLLEGE	.	25,885	1,235	.	47,145	3
106.	NEW ENG INST APP ARTS-SCI	.	3,422	212	1,311	.	1
107.	NTHN ESSEX CMTY COLLEGE	.	48,576	2,984	.	.	7
108.	RADCLIFFE COLLEGE	.	24,000	1,748	.	262,809	16
109.	SAINT JOHN'S SEMINARY	.	120,220	2,227	.	64,942	3
110.	SCH WORCESTER ART MUSEUM	.	31,761	768	.	33,796	2
111.	WESTFIELD STATE COLLEGE	.	122,327	4,947	57,491	.	11

-73-

MICHIGAN

(. = MISSING DATA)

STATE RANK	LIBRARY	SCORE	VOLUMES HELD	GROSS VOLUMES ADDED	CIRCULATION	TOTAL EXPENDITURES	TOTAL STAFF
1.	U MICHIGAN-ANN ARBOR	1.653	5,076,602	118,478	1,287,102	$9,443,339	463
2.	MICHIGAN STATE UNIVERSITY	0.665	1,905,583	70,053	1,144,706	5,156,848	202
3.	WAYNE STATE UNIVERSITY	0.158	1,804,932	49,371	375,163	4,574,157	171
4.	WESTERN MICH UNIVERSITY	-1.073	753,870	36,631	330,861	2,144,416	78
5.	CENTRAL MICH UNIVERSITY	-1.375	536,369	28,000	219,030	2,146,632	69
6.	EASTERN MICH UNIVERSITY	-1.790	465,279	16,956	230,682	1,520,692	62
7.	UNIVERSITY OF DETROIT	-2.015	449,958	13,612	251,946	1,052,301	53
8.	ANDREWS UNIVERSITY	-2.345	382,986	17,431	274,451	816,370	31
9.	OAKLAND UNIVERSITY	-2.436	290,345	10,930	124,226	1,162,815	44
10.	FERRIS STATE COLLEGE	-2.480	187,038	12,587	623,693	970,037	45
11.	MICHIGAN TECHNOLOGICAL U	-2.534	455,367	28,259	109,518	734,577	29
12.	NORTHERN MICH UNIVERSITY	-3.016	347,782	18,053	124,336	660,918	22
13.	CALVIN COLLEGE JOINT LIB	-3.461	308,251	8,970	115,000	442,697	13
14.	U OF MICHIGAN-DEARBORN	-3.607	211,130	10,065	56,085	549,552	20
15.	GRAND VALLEY ST COLLEGES	-3.609	207,811	10,439	61,947	483,981	18
16.	MACOMB CO CC-SOUTH CAMPUS	-3.751	94,312	3,746	139,929	774,058	29
17.	LANSING COMMUNITY COLLEGE	-3.779	74,277	6,643	198,146	907,920	36
18.	OAKLAND COMMUNITY COLLEGE	-3.810	146,673	3,228	74,125	609,053	28
19.	U OF MICHIGAN-FLINT	-3.891	94,892	12,530	39,850	531,503	18
20.	HOPE COLLEGE	-3.920	189,134	7,923	38,153	381,239	13
21.	ALBION COLLEGE	-4.163	218,341	5,576	31,482	303,876	13
22.	KALAMAZOO COLLEGE	-4.305	223,303	7,665	55,380	278,543	13
23.	HENRY FORD CMTY COLLEGE	-4.465	87,077	2,249	154,845	445,633	16
24.	ALMA COLLEGE	-4.561	137,429	5,009	28,337	294,662	13
25.	LAKE SUPERIOR ST COLLEGE	-4.849	92,987	3,560	17,206	275,895	11
26.	DELTA COLLEGE	-4.861	84,754	3,825	47,841	336,105	11
27.	KALAMAZOO VALLEY CC	-4.866	60,352	3,659	37,736	306,915	18
28.	MERCY COLLEGE OF DETROIT	-4.886	118,000	5,074	36,340	213,247	11
29.	SAGINAW VLY STATE COLLEGE	-5.065	87,524	5,549	22,297	326,979	10
30.	MACOMB CO CC-CENTER CAM	-5.070	57,390	4,131	46,199	376,893	15
31.	AQUINAS COLLEGE	-5.100	105,835	2,812	17,176	225,748	10
32.	MADONNA COLLEGE	-5.241	94,685	3,708	69,925	155,268	13
33.	WAYNE COUNTY CMTY COLLEGE	-5.266	42,192	21,200	36,918	499,342	22
34.	WASHTENAW CMTY COLLEGE	-5.268	48,219	2,831	20,393	319,120	16
35.	SCHOOLCRAFT COLLEGE	-5.272	69,765	2,523	42,693	284,413	10
36.	LAKE MICHIGAN COLLEGE	-5.383	70,000	4,000	129,944	151,658	5
37.	NORTHWESTERN MICH COLLEGE	-5.390	44,390	2,110	18,684	228,681	10
38.	GRAND RAPIDS BAPT C & SEM	-5.428	65,065	8,005	26,079	103,125	7
39.	KELLOGG COMMUNITY COLLEGE	-5.442	39,143	3,379	28,580	329,344	12
40.	CHAS S MOTT CMTY COLLEGE	-5.492	90,806	2,548	25,022	251,818	8
41.	ADRIAN COLLEGE	-5.498	112,210	3,359	14,133	186,124	8
42.	MUSKEGON CMTY COLLEGE	-5.517	52,980	4,699	45,042	164,528	8
43.	OLIVET COLLEGE	-5.529	74,293	5,125	13,205	128,465	8
44.	HILLSDALE COLLEGE	-5.545	85,686	5,763	28,013	198,098	6
45.	SPRING ARBOR COLLEGE	-5.636	64,423	3,549	34,776	136,450	6

MICHIGAN

(. = MISSING DATA)

STATE RANK	LIBRARY	SCORE	VOLUMES HELD	GROSS VOLUMES ADDED	CIRCULATION	TOTAL EXPENDITURES	TOTAL STAFF
46.	MARYGROVE COLLEGE	-5.658	171,147	1,943	44,048	$139,640	8
47.	DETROIT COLLEGE OF LAW	-5.709	52,523	3,147	3,450	267,700	8
48.	SIENA HEIGHTS COLLEGE	-5.772	76,469	3,189	15,039	119,432	7
49.	LAWRENCE INST TECHNOLOGY	-6.032	47,321	1,796	17,701	144,485	6
50.	JACKSON COMMUNITY COLLEGE	-6.033	39,197	3,447	56,919	133,976	4
51.	NAZARETH COLLEGE	-6.105	83,000	7,709	21,618	88,825	4
52.	SNT CLAIR CO CMTY COLLEGE	-6.194	41,871	2,044	62,313	214,294	9
53.	BAY DE NOC CMTY COLLEGE	-6.317	24,814	1,557	14,703	105,819	4
54.	GRAND RAPIDS JR COLLEGE	-6.411	48,866	2,138	41,723	216,000	10
55.	NORTHWOOD INSTITUTE	-6.539	45,059	1,633	21,723	91,072	8
56.	MONROE CO CMTY COLLEGE	-6.575	45,452	644	39,503	182,946	8
57.	WESTERN THEOLOGICAL SEM	-6.586	74,977	1,858	10,347	71,155	3
58.	SOUTHWESTERN MICH COLLEGE	-6.635	24,986	2,000	29,225	78,355	3
59.	CONCORDIA COLLEGE	-6.959	103,434	4,000	10,000	131,381	3
60.	MID MICHIGAN CMTY COLLEGE	-7.026	18,283	560	24,119	74,809	6
61.	SAINT MARY'S COLLEGE	-7.105	48,653	2,200	5,524	62,405	5
62.	ALPENA COMMUNITY COLLEGE	-7.108	29,053	1,082	17,976	97,994	4
63.	GOGEBIC COMMUNITY COLLEGE	-7.197	21,883	913	6,037	86,286	4
64.	DETROIT BIBLE COLLEGE	-7.382	39,264	1,157	4,818	65,485	3
65.	GLEN OAKS CMTY COLLEGE	-7.424	31,615	1,366	32,779	56,900	3
66.	KIRTLAND CMTY COLLEGE	-7.691	30,012	1,493	9,931	84,799	3
67.	KENDALL SCH OF DESIGN	-7.810	6,010	722	9,347	51,796	1
68.	GREAT LAKES BIBLE COLLEGE	-7.966	17,502	1,235	13,929	32,815	1
69.	MONTCALM CMTY COLLEGE	-7.971	21,261	645	5,401	61,218	3
70.	WALSH C ACCTY & BUS ADMIN	-8.148	12,500	756	10,893	44,166	2
71.	SACRED HEART SEMINARY C	-8.160	50,956	1,059	1,837	44,212	2
72.	CTR FOR CREATIVE STUDIES	-8.195	10,400	1,000	7,900	32,624	1
73.	WEST SHORE CMTY COLLEGE	-8.424	11,349	450	5,759	62,215	4
74.	NORTH CEN MICH COLLEGE	-8.441	21,239	348	3,528	44,790	2
75.	GRAND RAPIDS SCH BIBLE	-8.461	12,225	1,225	11,520	23,439	2
76.	MICH CHRISTIAN COLLEGE	-8.494	31,638	3,059	2,550	52,725	2
77.	DETROIT INST TECHNOLOGY	-8.518	61,424	398	5,160	61,854	4
78.	GENERAL MOTORS INSTITUTE	-8.557	40,519	2,501	24,100	102,190	0
79.	DETROIT C OF BUS ADMIN	-8.587	18,180	1,075	6,480	60,555	1
80.	JOHN WESLEY COLLEGE	-8.620	36,000	19	4,371	42,367	1
81.	DAVENPORT COLLEGE OF BUS	-9.478	12,676	602	3,240	45,702	1
82.	CLEARY COLLEGE	-9.631	10,708	310	600	19,548	1
83.	JORDAN COLLEGE	-9.633	13,000	3,000	2,500	10,656	1
84.	BAKER JUNIOR COLLEGE BUS	-10.04	3,000	375	3,390	29,766	3
85.	LEWIS C BUSINESS	-10.98	2,778	345	1,490	7,599	1
86.	CRANBROOK ACADEMY OF ART	.	20,179	378	3,950	.	1
87.	GRACE BIBLE COLLEGE	.	25,855	977	5,564	9,545	.
88.	HIGHLAND PK CMTY COLLEGE	.	.	0	3,773	85,206	5
89.	MERRILL-PALMER INSTITUTE	.	18,000	649	7,649	.	2
90.	MUSKEGON BUSINESS COLLEGE	.	3,597	636	1,405	.	1

MICHIGAN

(. = MISSING DATA)

STATE RANK	LIBRARY	SCORE	VOLUMES HELD	GROSS VOLUMES ADDED	CIRCULATION	TOTAL EXPENDITURES	TOTAL STAFF
91.	REFORMED BIBLE COLLEGE	.	34,465	1,675	9,449	.	2
92.	SHAW COLLEGE AT DETROIT	.	89,668	865	4,965	.	6
93.	SUOMI COLLEGE	.	22,348	511	11,092	.	2

MINNESOTA

(. = MISSING DATA)

STATE RANK	LIBRARY	SCORE	VOLUMES HELD	GROSS VOLUMES ADDED	CIRCULATION	TOTAL EXPENDITURES	TOTAL STAFF
1.	U OF MINN MNPLS SNT PAUL	1.363	3,738,168	92,338	1,363,321	$8,243,359	291
2.	SAINT CLOUD ST UNIVERSITY	-2.024	477,305	14,654	223,071	1,318,123	48
3.	U OF MINNESOTA DULUTH	-2.345	257,321	9,491	211,152	936,201	33
4.	MANKATO STATE UNIVERSITY	-2.399	369,281	14,739	216,080	1,323,714	45
5.	U MINN MAYO GRAD SCH MED	-2.712	219,692	4,963	562,495	756,504	29
6.	CARLETON COLLEGE	-3.287	260,021	11,000	141,105	581,777	17
7.	COLLEGE OF SAINT THOMAS	-3.459	196,110	5,212	56,154	512,195	23
8.	CONCORDIA C AT MOORHEAD	-3.516	204,121	6,627	119,586	423,611	17
9.	SAINT OLAF COLLEGE	-3.538	319,440	10,566	136,146	398,594	16
10.	MOORHEAD STATE UNIVERSITY	-3.716	248,750	13,027	138,832	500,990	21
11.	BEMIDJI STATE U	-3.750	204,511	5,762	110,145	504,266	19
12.	HAMLINE UNIVERSITY	-3.844	238,500	5,551	26,000	439,616	19
13.	SAINT JOHN'S UNIVERSITY	-3.890	283,358	6,254	55,004	398,247	16
14.	COLLEGE OF SNT CATHERINE	-3.910	206,382	6,005	69,528	346,267	19
15.	WINONA STATE UNIVERSITY	-3.925	170,209	5,855	75,102	467,019	19
16.	GUSTAVUS ADOLPHUS COLLEGE	-3.949	174,182	11,250	78,710	349,411	14
17.	MACALESTER COLLEGE	-4.254	271,332	4,846	70,289	267,959	14
18.	BETHEL COLLEGE	-4.387	125,000	6,653	66,299	247,220	11
19.	U OF MINNESOTA MORRIS	-4.539	111,957	5,153	31,635	286,503	10
20.	COLLEGE OF SAINT BENEDICT	-4.636	101,760	5,321	39,031	322,142	10
21.	AUGSBURG COLLEGE	-4.866	131,506	3,807	40,592	217,368	8
22.	STHWST STATE UNIVERSITY	-4.925	144,653	3,579	21,203	320,738	10
23.	NORMANDALE CMTY COLLEGE	-5.059	51,077	6,911	55,307	331,423	12
24.	COLLEGE OF SAINT TERESA	-5.272	130,583	3,282	32,125	123,350	8
25.	SAINT MARY'S COLLEGE	-5.326	137,388	3,848	30,186	157,700	8
26.	LUTHER NTHWSTN SEM JT LIB	-5.412	167,230	3,552	47,005	173,506	8
27.	COLLEGE SAINT SCHOLASTICA	-5.429	81,241	3,031	19,730	155,868	7
28.	N HENNEPIN CMTY COLLEGE	-5.689	27,003	1,234	40,240	256,240	9
29.	CONCORDIA C-SAINT PAUL	-5.691	82,741	2,968	18,205	134,645	6
30.	DR MARTIN LUTHER COLLEGE	-5.759	46,585	3,012	37,004	106,091	8
31.	MINNEAPOLIS C-ART DESIGN	-5.899	45,671	1,613	87,760	121,291	7
32.	BETHEL THEOL SEMINARY	-5.903	85,775	3,900	19,500	103,730	4
33.	INVER HILLS CMTY COLLEGE	-6.193	29,100	1,690	27,100	143,220	6
34.	LAKEWOOD CMTY COLLEGE	-6.517	26,791	1,159	40,614	164,876	6
35.	ROCHESTER CMTY COLLEGE	-6.594	46,590	2,167	20,325	124,757	7
36.	U MINN TECH COL CROOKSTON	-6.624	19,037	965	10,469	178,085	9
37.	SAINT PAUL BIBLE COLLEGE	-6.643	64,795	11,057	47,641	74,151	4
38.	U OF MINN TECH C-WASECA	-6.780	21,081	1,679	16,412	130,226	5
39.	GOLDEN VLY LUTH COLLEGE	-7.005	25,195	1,990	13,715	60,797	4
40.	SAINT PAUL SEMINARY	-7.008	62,450	850	4,893	50,340	4
41.	NORTHWESTERN COLLEGE	-7.090	48,208	1,191	13,384	81,638	4
42.	UNITED THEOLOGICAL SEM	-7.139	53,148	1,284	12,596	58,869	3
43.	HIBBING COMMUNITY COLLEGE	-7.326	23,525	696	6,741	69,983	4
44.	WORTHINGTON CMTY COLLEGE	-7.421	31,174	924	5,360	45,338	2
45.	ITASCA COMMUNITY COLLEGE	-7.479	19,384	609	5,744	69,201	2

MINNESOTA

(. = MISSING DATA)

STATE RANK	LIBRARY	SCORE	VOLUMES HELD	GROSS VOLUMES ADDED	CIRCULATION	TOTAL EXPENDITURES	TOTAL STAFF
46.	NTHWSTN C CHIROPRACTIC	-7.520	6,100	702	5,842	$62,190	4
47.	FERGUS FALLS CMTY COLLEGE	-7.543	25,663	850	7,041	69,470	3
48.	ANOKA-RAMSEY CMTY COLLEGE	-7.602	29,089	1,145	14,818	118,476	5
49.	AUSTIN COMMUNITY COLLEGE	-7.622	21,428	803	24,179	87,253	3
50.	SAINT MARY'S JR COLLEGE	-7.785	24,529	1,212	8,000	43,548	3
51.	BRAINERD CMTY COLLEGE	-7.967	15,340	450	7,208	58,264	1
52.	MESABI COMMUNITY COLLEGE	-8.371	28,136	577	4,720	48,940	1
53.	VERMILION CMTY COLLEGE	-8.391	16,000	1,056	4,896	53,242	1
54.	RAINY RIVER CMTY COLLEGE	-8.456	15,354	785	2,260	44,309	2
55.	NORTH CEN BIBLE COLLEGE	-8.641	25,252	1,161	10,663	28,271	2
56.	WILLMAR CMTY COLLEGE	-8.659	18,395	844	13,248	53,045	2
57.	NORTHLAND CMTY COLLEGE	-9.010	12,250	500	3,565	43,361	2
58.	CROSIER SEMINARY	-9.232	20,000	1,000	3,907	18,862	3
59.	MAYO MEDICAL SCHOOL	-9.831	2,574	402	6,364	39,352	2
60.	BETHANY LUTHERAN COLLEGE	.	.	1,000	2,113	38,140	2
61.	METROPOLITAN CMTY COLLEGE	.	.	0	12,906	111,767	6
62.	MINNESOTA BIBLE COLLEGE	.	17,022	907	3,869	.	2
63.	WM MITCHELL COLLEGE LAW	.	71,463	5,327	.	333,043	11

MISSISSIPPI

(. = MISSING DATA)

-78-

STATE RANK	LIBRARY	SCORE	VOLUMES HELD	GROSS VOLUMES ADDED	CIRCULATION	TOTAL EXPENDITURES	TOTAL STAFF
1.	MISSISSIPPI ST UNIVERSITY	-1.384	622,769	27,380	127,194	$1,825,415	55
2.	U OF SOUTHERN MISSISSIPPI	-1.619	427,652	21,278	205,909	1,513,466	58
3.	U OF MISSISSIPPI MAIN CAM	-2.107	602,203	21,111	192,438	1,433,327	61
4.	JACKSON STATE UNIVERSITY	-2.636	315,184	16,683	238,752	855,464	34
5.	DELTA STATE UNIVERSITY	-3.553	210,157	10,707	55,385	532,859	20
6.	U OF MISSISSIPPI MEDL CTR	-3.673	107,019	4,236	67,613	472,318	22
7.	HINDS JUNIOR COLLEGE	-3.715	71,231	6,878	111,280	534,864	22
8.	MISS UNIVERSITY FOR WOMEN	-3.790	220,893	8,098	48,854	372,188	19
9.	MISSISSIPPI COLLEGE	-3.845	223,739	12,618	64,842	364,706	17
10.	ALCORN STATE UNIVERSITY	-3.952	125,434	6,323	18,030	414,327	19
11.	MILLSAPS COLLEGE	-5.240	95,987	2,856	31,151	164,171	9
12.	JONES CO JUNIOR COLLEGE	-5.488	49,569	1,800	19,152	259,276	8
13.	MERIDIAN JUNIOR COLLEGE	-5.527	37,068	2,751	42,457	179,882	11
14.	WILLIAM CAREY COLLEGE	-5.602	77,076	3,861	10,214	166,972	8
15.	RUST COLLEGE	-5.751	64,658	5,957	36,649	146,689	5
16.	COPIAH-LINCOLN JR COLLEGE	-5.822	39,162	2,191	26,575	103,094	7
17.	REFORMED THEOLOGICAL SEM	-5.926	46,616	3,076	12,370	127,056	7
18.	ITAWAMBA JUNIOR COLLEGE	-5.929	36,416	2,487	10,100	167,416	8
19.	MISS VLY ST UNIVERSITY	-5.932	98,363	2,729	33,523	410,862	24
20.	MISS DELTA JUNIOR COLLEGE	-6.285	25,377	820	21,544	135,401	7
21.	MISS GULF CST JEFF DAVIS	-6.461	33,028	1,885	25,957	154,021	7
22.	MISS GULF CST JC JACKSON	-6.561	25,202	1,595	13,531	171,232	9
23.	BELHAVEN COLLEGE	-6.637	56,184	2,655	9,844	79,828	5
24.	NORTHWEST MISS JR COLLEGE	-6.643	28,873	1,715	24,222	113,121	6
25.	UTICA JUNIOR COLLEGE	-6.743	25,678	1,047	3,440	105,612	7
26.	SOUTHWEST MISS JR COLLEGE	-6.997	25,071	1,127	15,148	81,754	4
27.	HOLMES JUNIOR COLLEGE	-7.173	35,534	1,350	12,216	49,514	2
28.	EAST MISS JUNIOR COLLEGE	-7.273	20,498	978	7,982	52,808	3
29.	EAST CENTRAL JR COLLEGE	-7.679	26,471	1,177	4,363	69,359	3
30.	MARY HOLMES COLLEGE	-7.947	23,058	1,442	5,794	70,770	5
31.	BLUE MOUNTAIN COLLEGE	-8.066	44,722	996	9,519	50,594	2
32.	WOOD JUNIOR COLLEGE	-8.080	25,229	517	7,397	32,983	2
33.	MISS GULF CST JC PERKNSTN	-8.491	21,017	0	7,061	141,840	7
34.	WESLEY COLLEGE	-8.516	17,093	2,707	2,079	31,388	2
35.	PRENTISS NURM-INDUS INST	-9.471	6,307	832	1,500	24,360	2
36.	CLARKE COLLEGE	.	17,980	838	5,968	.	1
37.	CUAHOMA JUNIOR COLLEGE	.	26,143	1,161	5,124	.	9
38.	MINISTERIAL INST AND C	.	7,000	0	3,620	.	3
39.	MISS INDUSTRIAL COLLEGE	.	38,549	629	1,703	.	3
40.	NORTHEAST MISS JR COLLEGE	.	32,262	2,254	14,407	.	4
41.	PHILLIPS COLLEGE	.	1,149	352	4,208	.	1
42.	SOUTHEASTERN BAPT COLLEGE	.	9,475	575	.	.	0
43.	TOUGALOO COLLEGE	.	.	0	57,716	10,937	0
44.	WHITWORTH BIBLE COLLEGE	.	8,337	267	.	83,692	0

MISSOURI

(. = MISSING DATA)

STATE RANK	LIBRARY	SCORE	VOLUMES HELD	GROSS VOLUMES ADDED	CIRCULATION	TOTAL EXPENDITURES	TOTAL STAFF
1.	U OF MISSOURI-COLUMBIA	0.333	2,109,107	60,214	489,355	$4,240,841	167
2.	WASHINGTON UNIVERSITY	0.194	1,754,680	50,416	647,889	3,958,973	172
3.	U OF MISSOURI-KANSAS CITY	-1.341	634,796	24,624	191,966	1,580,667	75
4.	SAINT LOUIS U MAIN CAMPUS	-1.776	780,226	18,806	105,010	1,263,571	64
5.	U OF MISSOURI-SAINT LOUIS	-2.035	346,964	18,828	131,730	1,182,473	42
6.	CENTRAL MO ST UNIVERSITY	-2.126	312,704	13,516	163,068	1,068,908	52
7.	STHWST MO ST UNIVERSITY	-2.326	324,662	18,151	145,083	1,009,778	38
8.	STHEST MO ST UNIVERSITY	-2.631	249,882	10,218	164,064	967,291	42
9.	NTHEST MO ST UNIVERSITY	-2.986	236,141	15,876	147,581	716,825	27
10.	U OF MISSOURI-ROLLA	-3.610	284,892	13,153	34,859	563,286	25
11.	NTHWST MO ST UNIVERSITY	-3.664	206,254	7,057	94,663	427,388	20
12.	MISSOURI STHN ST COLLEGE	-3.937	129,204	6,775	67,783	574,828	14
13.	EDEN-WEBSTER JT LIBRARIES	-4.243	156,173	5,036	42,720	330,664	14
14.	MISSOURI WSTN ST COLLEGE	-4.286	104,154	7,806	53,228	340,641	11
15.	CONCORDIA SEMINARY	-4.721	145,963	3,678	70,535	247,210	11
16.	LINCOLN UNIVERSITY	-4.777	131,001	2,946	45,402	259,478	12
17.	STEPHENS COLLEGE	-4.833	117,819	3,718	41,882	272,522	16
18.	WILLIAM JEWELL COLLEGE	-4.981	131,657	3,676	52,645	177,502	9
19.	SNT LU CC-FLORISSANT VLY	-5.263	60,927	3,755	58,585	544,434	28
20.	SAINT LOUIS CC-MERAMEC	-5.349	58,679	3,454	50,826	485,278	24
21.	KANSAS CITY C OSTEO MED	-5.420	32,424	4,570	33,000	176,600	6
22.	SCHOOL OF THE OZARKS	-5.629	81,000	2,424	41,307	170,150	5
23.	SNT LU CC-FOREST PARK	-5.633	49,683	2,404	42,351	456,475	23
24.	CENTRAL BIBLE COLLEGE	-5.676	85,533	8,562	56,084	135,140	4
25.	MARYVILLE C-SAINT LOUIS	-5.715	93,000	3,000	37,408	151,727	10
26.	DRURY COLLEGE	-5.762	110,870	2,537	15,392	148,181	6
27.	EVANGEL COLLEGE	-5.880	87,950	2,957	14,616	109,177	6
28.	SOUTHWEST BAPTIST COLLEGE	-5.882	74,253	2,278	31,269	91,026	6
29.	ROCKHURST COLLEGE	-5.893	101,887	3,231	13,823	129,372	6
30.	WESTMINSTER COLLEGE	-5.931	53,026	1,864	12,315	103,783	6
31.	KIRKSVL COLLEGE OSTEO MED	-5.985	50,113	2,585	4,625	142,036	4
32.	THE LINDENWOOD COLLEGES	-6.049	87,457	3,942	17,325	101,475	6
33.	ASSEMBLIES GOD GRAD SCH	-6.065	29,029	3,178	17,538	115,098	7
34.	WILLIAM WOODS COLLEGE	-6.104	53,523	2,680	26,843	103,629	5
35.	STATE FAIR CMTY COLLEGE	-6.249	24,268	1,799	21,308	105,932	6
36.	JEFFERSON COLLEGE	-6.543	39,775	1,369	17,875	110,569	6
37.	AVILA COLLEGE	-6.570	66,007	1,369	21,037	56,018	5
38.	CHRIST SEMINARY-SEMINEX	-6.584	28,111	2,791	8,269	121,416	5
39.	CENTRAL METHODIST COLLEGE	-6.589	136,634	1,675	8,353	71,177	4
40.	COLUMBIA COLLEGE	-6.619	37,842	2,761	17,818	114,648	5
41.	LONGVIEW CMTY COLLEGE	-6.707	23,061	929	16,326	110,011	6
42.	CULVER-STOCKTON COLLEGE	-6.768	100,656	2,173	20,669	55,833	4
43.	SNT LOUIS COLLEGE OF PHAR	-6.809	31,750	1,252	19,914	83,126	4
44.	COVENANT THEOLOGICAL SEM	-6.878	35,790	1,614	16,864	63,226	5
45.	SNT PAUL SCH OF THEOLOGY	-6.898	60,381	1,708	8,275	77,492	4

MISSOURI

(. = MISSING DATA)

STATE RANK	LIBRARY	SCORE	VOLUMES HELD	GROSS VOLUMES ADDED	CIRCULATION	TOTAL EXPENDITURES	TOTAL STAFF
46.	SAINT MARY'S C O'FALLON	-7.012	43,665	1,298	45,733	$50,154	5
47.	MINERAL AREA COLLEGE	-7.034	23,075	1,569	10,324	75,334	4
48.	KANSAS CITY ART INSTITUTE	-7.044	28,403	1,200	11,580	56,772	4
49.	THREE RIVERS CMTY COLLEGE	-7.055	20,340	2,640	10,500	62,238	2
50.	HARRIS-STOWE STATE C	-7.136	55,604	1,404	11,450	74,724	3
51.	KENRICK SEMINARY	-7.219	62,232	968	5,757	54,423	3
52.	TARKIO COLLEGE	-7.246	65,612	1,280	5,612	40,483	2
53.	MISSOURI VALLEY COLLEGE	-7.275	84,754	1,051	14,575	44,690	3
54.	SAINT LOUIS U-PARKS C	-7.389	33,794	816	5,699	56,715	2
55.	NAZARENE THEOLOGICAL SEM	-7.545	53,923	2,638	28,000	75,092	3
56.	CROWDER COLLEGE	-7.622	26,454	1,135	9,919	60,623	3
57.	MISSOURI BAPTIST COLLEGE	-7.686	33,747	2,149	5,301	48,108	3
58.	HANNIBAL-LAGRANGE COLLEGE	-7.924	25,000	1,140	11,938	28,746	2
59.	CONCEPTION SEM COLLEGE	-7.927	87,015	2,591	5,108	21,303	4
60.	EAST CENTRAL MO DIST JC	-8.085	18,886	1,030	6,193	66,053	4
61.	SAINT PAUL'S COLLEGE	-8.275	32,516	845	4,942	34,564	2
62.	CARDINAL GLENNON COLLEGE	-8.312	62,835	1,222	5,747	28,935	1
63.	MAPLE WOODS CMTY COLLEGE	-8.316	18,228	362	18,850	82,934	4
64.	LOGAN C OF CHIROPRACTIC	-8.573	13,795	735	4,628	61,166	4
65.	SNT LOUIS CONSV OF MUSIC	-8.675	7,511	1,086	3,665	32,419	2
66.	MOBERLY JUNIOR COLLEGE	-8.740	14,392	344	3,747	44,094	3
67.	TRENTON JUNIOR COLLEGE	-8.805	12,271	711	4,906	33,555	2
68.	CLEVELAND CHIROPRACTIC C	-9.012	3,880	212	997	36,861	1
69.	CARDINAL NEWMAN COLLEGE	-9.202	5,987	2,267	3,400	38,889	2
70.	CEN CHRSTN C OF THE BIBLE	-9.322	16,945	792	4,894	15,782	1
71.	WENTWORTH MILITARY ACAD	-9.668	16,085	100	3,532	9,606	1
72.	KEMPER MILITARY SCH AND C	-10.18	20,662	694	1,145	11,387	1
73.	BAPTIST BIBLE COLLEGE	.	29,727	2,282	26,419	.	3
74.	CALVARY BIBLE COLLEGE	.	32,938	1,119	19,198	31,115	.
75.	FONTBONNE COLLEGE	.	85,873	1,384	.	94,038	.
76.	MISSOURI INST TECHNOLOGY	.	1,217	49	563	.	2
77.	PENN VALLEY CMTY COLLEGE	.	58,956	443	10,829	.	5
78.	PIONEER COMMUNITY COLLEGE	.	727	82	50	.	1
79.	SAINT MARY'S SEM-COLLEGE	.	56,919	1,467	.	20,096	2
80.	SNT LOUIS CHRISTIAN C	.	21,253	577	.	32,898	2

MONTANA

(. = MISSING DATA)

STATE RANK	LIBRARY	SCORE	VOLUMES HELD	GROSS VOLUMES ADDED	CIRCULATION	TOTAL EXPENDITURES	TOTAL STAFF
1.	UNIVERSITY OF MONTANA	-1.570	711,673	20,726	238,666	$1,570,057	50
2.	MONTANA STATE UNIVERSITY	-2.665	395,180	15,670	162,356	1,047,538	52
3.	EASTERN MONTANA COLLEGE	-4.940	126,919	5,143	27,516	264,840	11
4.	CARROLL COLLEGE	-5.755	75,068	4,278	35,549	132,685	5
5.	MONTANA C MINRL SCI-TECHN	-5.836	72,770	2,044	16,939	132,308	6
6.	NORTHERN MONTANA COLLEGE	-6.096	81,171	2,230	18,000	128,905	6
7.	ROCKY MOUNTAIN COLLEGE	-6.725	58,300	1,884	6,361	71,261	3
8.	COLLEGE OF GREAT FALLS	-7.297	54,015	1,893	24,645	102,067	6
9.	WESTERN MONTANA COLLEGE	-7.482	49,344	866	7,519	116,435	2
10.	MILES COMMUNITY COLLEGE	-8.364	11,233	748	9,000	58,635	2
11.	DAWSON COMMUNITY COLLEGE	-8.460	17,666	315	3,684	39,767	2
12.	FLATHEAD VLY CMTY COLLEGE	-8.636	9,680	716	4,740	60,429	1
13.	MONTANA INST OF THE BIBLE	-10.69	17,186	649	6	22,367	2

NEBRASKA

(. = MISSING DATA)

STATE RANK	LIBRARY	SCORE	VOLUMES HELD	GROSS VOLUMES ADDED	CIRCULATION	TOTAL EXPENDITURES	TOTAL STAFF
1.	U OF NEBRASKA-LINCOLN	0.053	1,441,515	60,379	376,989	$3,745,429	156
2.	U OF NEBRASKA AT OMAHA	-1.712	363,179	23,017	152,139	1,422,595	61
3.	CREIGHTON UNIVERSITY	-2.122	394,224	17,917	222,861	1,121,248	50
4.	U NEBRASKA MEDICAL CTR	-2.767	173,702	8,163	87,683	975,613	37
5.	KEARNEY STATE COLLEGE	-3.479	130,982	3,100	83,521	611,345	25
6.	WAYNE STATE COLLEGE	-4.148	149,548	6,163	41,157	343,031	16
7.	CHADRON STATE COLLEGE	-4.385	138,122	6,494	35,000	296,381	12
8.	PERU STATE COLLEGE	-4.898	81,907	5,820	119,963	200,936	7
9.	CONCORDIA TCHRS COLLEGE	-5.017	120,453	3,734	55,450	199,672	8
10.	NEBR WESLEYAN UNIVERSITY	-5.382	180,931	5,773	19,281	165,013	7
11.	METROPOLITAN TECHNICAL CC	-5.766	24,062	5,934	24,446	382,490	17
12.	CEN TECH CMTY C AREA	-5.848	43,375	1,555	9,876	255,513	12
13.	DOANE COLLEGE	-6.034	62,181	1,723	26,391	77,388	6
14.	HASTINGS COLLEGE	-6.058	95,786	2,776	21,200	92,469	5
15.	MIDLAND LUTHERAN COLLEGE	-6.288	75,588	1,992	21,237	108,580	5
16.	UNION COLLEGE	-6.289	115,670	2,481	21,620	137,036	4
17.	BELLEVUE COLLEGE	-6.433	43,150	4,042	18,360	97,586	3
18.	DANA COLLEGE	-6.732	84,753	2,178	17,269	63,874	3
19.	YORK COLLEGE	-7.098	25,497	630	12,260	62,598	4
20.	COLLEGE OF SAINT MARY	-7.193	61,784	1,745	11,763	54,180	2
21.	NEBRASKA WESTERN COLLEGE	-7.234	20,986	569	24,795	80,884	4
22.	NORTHEAST TECHNICAL CC	-7.288	22,966	1,125	13,044	76,972	3
23.	MCCOOK COMMUNITY COLLEGE	-7.736	20,050	2,500	16,848	64,363	5
24.	SOUTHEAST CC LINCOLN CAM	-7.798	14,513	1,276	13,914	91,847	4
25.	GRACE C OF THE BIBLE	-7.856	46,878	790	22,459	38,359	3
26.	SOUTHEAST CC MILFORD CAM	-7.868	5,608	593	4,572	86,161	4
27.	STHEST CC FAIRBY-BEATRICE	-7.892	10,623	510	3,441	48,262	3
28.	MID PLAINS CC	-8.242	16,127	826	4,560	43,341	2
29.	NEBR CHRISTIAN COLLEGE	.	20,025	601	4,800	9,848	.
30.	PLATTE VLY BIBLE COLLEGE	.	12,000	250	2,000	2,860	.

NEVADA

(. = MISSING DATA)

STATE RANK	LIBRARY	SCORE	VOLUMES HELD	GROSS VOLUMES ADDED	CIRCULATION	TOTAL EXPENDITURES	TOTAL STAFF
1.	U OF NEVADA RENO	-1.230	622,050	30,033	175,788	$2,231,020	71
2.	U OF NEVADA LAS VEGAS	-2.297	358,922	19,914	133,073	1,298,877	41
3.	WESTERN NEV CMTY COLLEGE	-5.080	27,503	4,790	13,334	263,638	11
4.	CLARK CO CMTY COLLEGE	-5.298	23,169	17,455	40,323	264,870	14
5.	NORTHERN NEV CMTY COLLEGE	-7.445	23,846	485	4,817	89,450	3
6.	SIERRA NEVADA COLLEGE	.	11,308	2,190	5,500	.	1

NEW HAMPSHIRE

(. = MISSING DATA)

STATE RANK	LIBRARY	SCORE	VOLUMES HELD	GROSS VOLUMES ADDED	CIRCULATION	TOTAL EXPENDITURES	TOTAL STAFF
1.	DARTMOUTH COLLEGE	-0.360	1,347,278	55,087	389,744	$2,871,931	133
2.	U OF NEW HAMPSHIRE	-1.070	780,242	29,364	352,227	1,911,497	87
3.	U NH PLYMOUTH ST COLLEGE	-3.868	171,499	10,089	77,677	447,766	22
4.	SAINT ANSELM'S COLLEGE	-4.112	130,254	8,022	25,380	329,641	17
5.	U OF NH KEENE ST COLLEGE	-4.260	149,596	8,252	59,562	266,607	12
6.	NEW ENGLAND COLLEGE	-4.797	81,739	3,452	25,525	208,667	13
7.	NEW HAMPSHIRE COLLEGE	-5.855	53,838	3,188	17,840	245,703	10
8.	FRANKLIN PIERCE LAW CTR	-5.892	57,872	3,297	7,300	177,627	6
9.	RIVIER COLLEGE	-6.343	90,523	1,994	14,442	47,847	6
10.	NH TECHNICAL INSTITUTE	-7.502	20,244	1,028	11,027	49,121	3
11.	DANIEL WEBSTER COLLEGE	-8.669	17,549	1,483	3,693	36,304	3
12.	NOTRE DAME COLLEGE	-9.148	40,625	0	9,700	30,684	5
13.	NH VOC-TECH C PORTSMOUTH	-9.512	7,839	883	2,503	24,077	1
14.	NH VOC-TECH C BERLIN	-9.513	6,142	168	10,900	23,071	1
15.	NH VOC-TECH C NASHUA	-9.518	5,967	457	2,090	25,072	1
16.	NH VOC-TECH C CLAREMONT	-9.601	7,155	566	4,000	20,732	1
17.	NH VOC-TECH C LACONIA	-9.659	6,648	667	2,936	24,022	1
18.	NH VOC-TECH C MANCHESTER	-9.740	7,414	526	1,164	21,086	1
19.	WHITE PINES COLLEGE	-9.761	17,705	698	1,895	15,524	2
20.	CASTLE JUNIOR COLLEGE	-11.39	4,447	0	6,186	12,343	1
21.	FRANKLIN PIERCE COLLEGE	.	.	0	20,312	88,362	3
22.	MCINTOSH COLLEGE	.	5,027	71	1,144	.	1

NEW JERSEY

(. = MISSING DATA)

STATE RANK	LIBRARY	SCORE	VOLUMES HELD	GROSS VOLUMES ADDED	CIRCULATION	TOTAL EXPENDITURES	TOTAL STAFF
1.	PRINCETON UNIVERSITY	0.966	3,172,238	82,632	726,407	$6,638,578	325
2.	RUTGERS U NEW BRUNSWICK	0.538	1,455,999	67,745	737,419	5,931,915	218
3.	MONTCLAIR STATE COLLEGE	-2.046	311,306	20,951	304,817	1,212,351	59
4.	WILLIAM PATERSON COLLEGE	-2.342	270,726	19,110	76,905	1,164,650	55
5.	TRENTON STATE COLLEGE	-2.359	380,654	24,981	129,063	1,087,493	48
6.	SETON HALL UNIVERSITY	-2.505	319,687	14,325	169,794	955,734	44
7.	RUTGERS U NEWARK CAMPUS	-2.506	433,025	8,984	114,138	1,238,181	51
8.	GLASSBORO STATE COLLEGE	-2.923	260,227	20,621	97,322	660,728	39
9.	RUTGERS U CAMDEN CAMPUS	-3.009	277,176	10,270	105,360	972,206	35
10.	DREW UNIVERSITY	-3.142	389,777	9,239	61,894	632,920	30
11.	KEAN C OF NEW JERSEY	-3.181	288,053	10,088	129,466	757,929	39
12.	RIDER COLLEGE	-3.247	312,310	11,727	126,724	538,153	.24
13.	FARLGH DCKSN TEANECK CAM	-3.403	233,456	5,260	119,923	738,160	45
14.	C MED & DENT OF NJ NEWARK	-3.456	100,000	6,775	58,028	732,940	29
15.	JERSEY CITY STATE COLLEGE	-3.457	224,795	9,773	126,802	661,148	29
16.	BROOKDALE CMTY COLLEGE	-3.506	64,780	6,746	95,385	1,102,920	67
17.	RAMAPO C OF NEW JERSEY	-3.614	137,632	8,542	77,881	615,156	33
18.	BERGEN COMMUNITY COLLEGE	-3.723	84,310	3,140	121,898	908,311	44
19.	STOCKTON STATE COLLEGE	-3.825	105,390	8,500	152,377	964,057	48
20.	COUNTY COLLEGE OF MORRIS	-3.913	82,389	5,010	142,727	570,283	33
21.	NJ INSTITUTE TECHNOLOGY	-3.956	125,450	6,146	47,253	497,368	17
22.	MONMOUTH COLLEGE	-3.999	208,898	7,752	35,266	430,369	22
23.	SAINT PETERS COLLEGE	-4.011	237,343	6,890	30,033	441,236	22
24.	FARLGH DCKSN U RUTHERFD	-4.156	161,177	2,527	64,922	489,209	30
25.	PRINCETON THEOLOGICAL SEM	-4.289	343,653	5,372	40,325	328,330	13
26.	FARLGH DCKSN MADISON CAM	-4.462	146,310	4,412	24,626	385,229	17
27.	BURLINGTON COUNTY COLLEGE	-4.463	56,437	4,649	281,131	202,223	19
28.	CAMDEN COUNTY COLLEGE	-4.704	69,981	6,202	46,453	324,148	15
29.	OCEAN COUNTY COLLEGE	-4.714	66,544	4,023	75,097	357,623	17
30.	STEVENS INST TECHNOLOGY	-4.720	95,792	3,950	12,982	296,055	11
31.	MERCER CO CMTY COLLEGE	-4.896	62,185	3,379	42,073	317,884	16
32.	MIDDLESEX COUNTY COLLEGE	-4.959	71,140	2,454	48,847	368,743	22
33.	SOMERSET COUNTY COLLEGE	-5.050	63,598	2,482	15,678	271,561	16
34.	UNION COLLEGE	-5.107	82,081	4,649	48,500	288,490	13
35.	COLLEGE OF SNT ELIZABETH	-5.163	145,839	5,179	32,821	124,038	9
36.	ESSEX COUNTY COLLEGE	-5.470	72,213	4,890	36,133	518,616	22
37.	UPSALA COLLEGE	-5.485	147,192	3,431	14,877	194,266	5
38.	BLOOMFIELD COLLEGE	-5.511	115,013	2,236	24,411	159,803	11
39.	GEORGIAN COURT COLLEGE	-5.666	70,221	2,949	35,423	118,538	9
40.	FELICIAN COLLEGE	-5.989	66,925	5,700	70,660	116,254	5
41.	ATLANTIC CMTY COLLEGE	-6.156	78,449	3,750	17,028	168,794	9
42.	GLOUCESTER COUNTY COLLEGE	-6.505	48,927	1,871	20,072	188,155	10
43.	PASSAIC CO CMTY COLLEGE	-6.517	24,482	3,878	9,953	201,677	12
44.	WESTMINSTER CHOIR COLLEGE	-6.594	31,500	670	33,649	127,350	9
45.	CUMBERLAND COUNTY COLLEGE	-6.707	47,686	1,750	18,286	116,967	6

NEW JERSEY

(. = MISSING DATA)

STATE RANK	LIBRARY	SCORE	VOLUMES HELD	GROSS VOLUMES ADDED	CIRCULATION	TOTAL EXPENDITURES	TOTAL STAFF
46.	CALDWELL COLLEGE	-6.807	96,675	2,575	12,604	$72,382	5
47.	CENTENARY COLLEGE	-7.814	43,421	2,017	72	66,714	4
48.	SALEM COMMUNITY COLLEGE	-7.853	18,468	2,365	8,200	73,517	5
49.	THE BERKELEY SCHOOL	-8.733	28,473	579	2,398	53,687	2
50.	RAB COLLEGE OF AMERICA	-9.578	6,000	50	10,000	10,470	2
51.	ASSUMPTION C FOR SISTERS	.	19,848	404	5,448	.	3
52.	DON BOSCO COLLEGE	.	50,869	500	3,646	.	2
53.	FARLGH DCKSN U EDW WMS C	.	10,030	173	5,280	.	1
54.	IMMACULATE CONCEPTION SEM	.	69,282	1,487	.	92,200	2
55.	KATHARINE GIBBS SCHOOL	.	3,189	11	.	3,875	0
56.	NEW BRUNSWICK THEOL SEM	.	133,577	1,061	5,492	.	4
57.	SNT MICHAELS PASIONST MON	.	19,000	275	.	.	1
58.	UNION CO TECHNICAL INST	.	18,770	2,079	5,175	.	3

NEW MEXICO

(. = MISSING DATA)

STATE RANK	LIBRARY	SCORE	VOLUMES HELD	GROSS VOLUMES ADDED	CIRCULATION	TOTAL EXPENDITURES	TOTAL STAFF
1.	U OF NM MAIN CAMPUS	0.215	1,143,247	72,972	506,329	$4,246,936	204
2.	NM STATE U MAIN CAMPUS	-1.155	611,922	54,493	228,276	1,689,013	75
3.	EASTERN NM U MAIN CAMPUS	-3.113	222,016	8,555	70,696	713,715	23
4.	NEW MEXICO HIGHLANDS U	-4.070	166,720	9,059	23,586	447,645	15
5.	NEW MEXICO JUNIOR COLLEGE	-5.001	80,407	4,642	125,348	199,992	10
6.	WESTERN NM UNIVERSITY	-5.126	117,723	3,917	39,524	181,350	11
7.	UNIVERSITY OF ALBUQUERQUE	-6.023	54,194	1,976	14,815	153,171	15
8.	NEW MEXICO MILITARY INST	-6.491	61,337	1,164	9,492	104,860	7
9.	COLLEGE OF SANTA FE	-6.496	85,000	3,900	20,921	41,557	4
10.	NM STATE U ALAMOGORDO	-6.521	27,468	1,672	19,690	78,937	6
11.	NM INST OF MINING & TECHN	-6.602	51,665	2,943	16,302	199,516	7
12.	EASTERN NM U ROSWELL CAM	-7.092	22,915	1,311	15,035	54,191	3
13.	NM STATE U SAN JUAN	-7.182	23,499	1,840	9,361	83,736	6
14.	COLLEGE OF THE SOUTHWEST	-7.641	34,816	2,663	2	92,767	5
15.	U OF NM GALLUP BRANCH	-7.700	14,745	1,124	3,883	47,763	3
16.	NM STATE U GRANTS BRANCH	-8.191	19,304	2,304	4,500	34,677	3
17.	NM STATE U CARLSBAD	-8.369	17,345	1,274	3,370	33,190	2

NEW YORK

(. = MISSING DATA)

STATE RANK	LIBRARY	SCORE	VOLUMES HELD	GROSS VOLUMES ADDED	CIRCULATION	TOTAL EXPENDITURES	TOTAL STAFF
1.	COLUMBIA U MAIN DIVISION	1.536	4,893,138	104,610	1,167,536	$8,538,285	406
2.	CORNEL U ENDOWED COLLEGES	1.070	3,544,853	93,298	845,254	6,641,195	300
3.	NEW YORK UNIVERSITY	0.813	2,700,201	104,658	656,194	6,013,034	241
4.	SUNY AT BUFFALO MAIN CAM	0.297	1,697,624	70,918	464,519	4,124,568	193
5.	UNIVERSITY OF ROCHESTER	0.088	1,835,704	54,873	657,124	3,481,608	141
6.	SYRACUSE U MAIN CAMPUS	-0.015	1,822,027	74,134	215,274	3,379,967	190
7.	SUNY AT STONY BK MAIN CAM	-0.367	1,018,864	42,779	219,924	2,985,451	146
8.	SUNY AT ALBANY	-0.429	878,569	46,652	242,612	3,149,057	132
9.	FORDHAM UNIVERSITY	-1.111	1,249,303	40,857	147,166	1,924,540	82
10.	HOFSTRA UNIVERSITY	-1.230	795,014	25,764	345,037	1,710,305	86
11.	CUNY QUEENS COLLEGE	-1.332	511,384	19,830	334,676	1,858,591	83
12.	YESHIVA UNIVERSITY	-1.425	770,826	29,400	159,759	1,749,810	75
13.	CORNELL U STATUTORY C	-1.505	730,537	18,665	474,480	1,755,908	74
14.	SAINT JOHN'S UNIVERSITY	-1.625	881,949	35,672	94,137	1,558,040	82
15.	ADELPHI UNIVERSITY	-1.635	350,761	20,023	172,345	1,585,828	75
16.	CUNY CITY COLLEGE	-1.664	937,302	14,315	139,808	1,733,727	69
17.	CUNY BROOKLYN COLLEGE	-1.800	580,500	16,329	129,453	1,767,734	84
18.	LONG IS U C W POST CENTER	-1.818	387,562	20,010	253,929	1,543,637	74
19.	SUNY COLLEGE AT BROCKPORT	-1.993	356,529	23,365	361,538	1,863,385	47
20.	SUNY COLLEGE AT BUFFALO	-2.156	408,415	19,059	271,948	1,149,101	60
21.	SUNY COLLEGE AT OSWEGO	-2.193	296,130	18,240	198,619	959,494	49
22.	VASSAR COLLEGE	-2.324	518,604	18,830	120,936	991,818	43
23.	CUNY HUNTER COLLEGE	-2.428	438,705	10,364	233,351	1,394,594	54
24.	SUNY COLLEGE AT ONEONTA	-2.462	366,097	20,807	204,685	875,030	45
25.	COLUMBIA U TCHRS COLLEGE	-2.627	393,978	9,423	200,787	901,864	68
26.	SUNY COLLEGE AT GENESEO	-2.655	325,544	11,017	157,379	735,747	38
27.	ROCHESTER INST TECHNOLOGY	-2.769	181,807	7,709	382,000	951,561	34
28.	SUNY COLLEGE AT FREDONIA	-2.771	313,613	9,687	154,682	666,566	33
29.	RENSSELAER POLY INSTITUTE	-2.792	284,600	8,430	39,960	866,410	39
30.	SUNY COLLEGE AT POTSDAM	-2.802	297,131	12,554	151,635	653,355	33
31.	UNION COLLEGE	-2.808	383,430	14,088	62,622	658,184	29
32.	SUNY COLLEGE AT NEW PALTZ	-2.873	295,558	12,901	138,932	754,313	38
33.	SUNY COLLEGE AT CORTLAND	-2.892	245,860	11,964	164,903	685,093	38
34.	CUNY LEHMAN COLLEGE	-2.893	364,075	13,241	266,595	786,192	36
35.	SUNY HEALTH SCI CTR BFLO	-2.913	187,319	9,135	89,767	794,047	33
36.	CUNY BERNARD BARUCH C	-2.992	252,299	10,779	123,259	799,717	42
37.	SUNY DOWNSTATE MEDL CTR	-3.012	237,715	6,571	73,117	729,961	35
38.	SUFFOLK CO CMTY COLLEGE	-3.073	143,337	11,021	93,189	864,938	50
39.	COLGATE UNIVERSITY	-3.121	325,383	8,896	72,883	638,957	24
40.	SUNY COLLEGE PLATTSBURGH	-3.125	227,160	3,680	116,250	756,582	37
41.	LONG IS U BROOKLYN CENTER	-3.198	219,089	9,725	317,933	554,705	26
42.	HAMILTON COLLEGE	-3.221	349,336	9,266	34,345	578,786	27
43.	SUNY COLLEGE AT PURCHASE	-3.263	147,942	9,485	72,138	576,265	23
44.	SKIDMORE COLLEGE	-3.294	218,635	9,413	135,553	461,740	21
45.	SUNY HLTH SCI CTR STNY BK	-3.302	159,254	10,667	39,988	682,380	20

NEW YORK

(. = MISSING DATA)

STATE RANK	LIBRARY	SCORE	VOLUMES HELD	GROSS VOLUMES ADDED	CIRCULATION	TOTAL EXPENDITURES	TOTAL STAFF
46.	SAINT LAWRENCE UNIVERSITY	-3.383	281,347	8,869	46,028	$452,444	20
47.	ITHACA COLLEGE	-3.393	259,731	5,954	124,739	619,244	32
48.	CORNELL U MEDICAL CENTER	-3.394	101,944	6,068	226,179	709,444	27
49.	SUNY UPSTATE MEDICAL CTR	-3.575	125,486	4,924	43,544	589,120	22
50.	POLYTECHNIC INST NEW YORK	-3.606	258,091	6,579	23,934	505,973	20
51.	PACE UNIVERSITY NEW YORK	-3.613	261,100	15,871	80,400	502,761	28
52.	HUDSON VLY CMTY COLLEGE	-3.631	92,121	5,752	63,729	580,160	33
53.	SINAI SCH OF MED CUNY	-3.644	32,817	2,519	89,739	789,993	33
54.	SAINT BONAVENTURE U	-3.655	245,762	8,814	41,240	354,909	21
55.	NIAGARA UNIVERSITY	-3.679	164,592	8,336	41,108	458,511	21
56.	SUNY COLLEGE OLD WESTBURY	-3.694	105,921	9,791	43,288	525,800	26
57.	MANHATTAN COLLEGE	-3.695	221,523	7,743	33,652	551,408	31
58.	NASSAU COMMUNITY COLLEGE	-3.714	137,921	5,021	98,964	839,038	41
59.	MERCY COLLEGE	-3.746	241,117	106,198	50,564	681,108	25
60.	NY INST TECHN MAIN CAMPUS	-3.802	84,850	6,600	31,565	591,036	27
61.	PACE U C OF WHITE PLAINS	-3.821	152,385	7,660	15,205	513,011	18
62.	ALBANY MEDICAL COLLEGE	-3.904	82,955	4,171	44,666	439,141	26
63.	CUNY GRAD SCH & U CENTER	-3.928	141,603	7,255	62,789	588,010	21
64.	ALFRED UNIVERSITY	-3.942	162,845	6,693	78,746	319,750	19
65.	ROCKEFELLER UNIVERSITY	-4.035	187,595	6,205	15,966	592,893	21
66.	SUNY AGRL TECH C FARMNGDL	-4.056	86,876	5,520	127,167	480,566	27
67.	CUNY JOHN JAY C CRIM JUST	-4.075	119,165	6,383	21,545	433,607	22
68.	ERIE COMMUNITY COLLEGE	-4.114	109,626	7,985	60,723	507,523	17
69.	PRATT INSTITUTE	-4.137	221,820	4,545	106,106	452,644	23
70.	RUSSELL SAGE C MAIN CAM	-4.167	182,949	8,595	45,123	368,195	21
71.	CUNY C OF STATEN ISLAND	-4.171	167,790	4,643	59,071	659,165	31
72.	CUNY QUEENSBOROUGH CC	-4.179	118,867	3,227	72,346	560,660	25
73.	CLARKSON COLLEGE OF TECHN	-4.193	87,586	4,451	32,775	443,153	17
74.	SIENA COLLEGE	-4.199	168,200	6,187	44,951	299,236	13
75.	NAZARETH C OF ROCHESTER	-4.208	179,240	6,947	41,140	306,415	17
76.	MANHATTANVILLE COLLEGE	-4.259	292,828	5,328	22,703	333,244	13
77.	ELMIRA COLLEGE	-4.286	134,345	4,855	26,555	304,409	16
78.	WAGNER COLLEGE	-4.306	251,169	4,655	51,949	287,729	15
79.	ONONDAGA CMTY COLLEGE	-4.349	78,553	4,546	43,476	463,013	24
80.	CANISIUS COLLEGE	-4.388	208,354	8,534	37,081	316,215	15
81.	SARAH LAWRENCE COLLEGE	-4.396	155,714	6,639	70,411	271,832	18
82.	HARTWICK COLLEGE	-4.399	156,488	6,008	38,693	280,772	10
83.	BARNARD COLLEGE	-4.399	146,829	3,490	124,017	714,563	17
84.	SUNY C OF TECH UTICA-ROME	-4.411	91,480	9,818	23,671	377,875	13
85.	PACE J PLSNTVL-BRCLF CAM	-4.450	193,897	5,389	41,801	307,585	16
86.	NEW SCH FOR SOC RESEARCH	-4.482	109,236	3,255	29,234	467,695	13
87.	UTICA C OF SYRACUSE U	-4.506	116,574	4,216	27,777	263,995	16
88.	SUNY C ENVRNML SCI-FORS	-4.520	75,090	2,450	36,640	314,100	15
89.	SUNY AGRL TECH C COBLESKL	-4.561	62,920	3,351	102,138	274,700	18
90.	COLLEGE OF SAINT ROSE	-4.630	125,490	5,483	59,908	177,409	10

NEW YORK

(. = MISSING DATA)

STATE RANK	LIBRARY	SCORE	VOLUMES HELD	GROSS VOLUMES ADDED	CIRCULATION	TOTAL EXPENDITURES	TOTAL STAFF
91.	COLLEGE OF NEW ROCHELLE	-4.655	137,172	5,214	38,334	$257,053	13
92.	DOWLING COLLEGE	-4.658	88,051	5,516	18,737	259,828	13
93.	D'YOUVILLE COLLEGE	-4.689	90,693	4,016	24,462	229,643	13
94.	LE MOYNE COLLEGE	-4.697	144,167	4,908	39,560	221,840	11
95.	SAINT JOHN FISHER COLLEGE	-4.697	120,410	5,480	54,771	297,400	8
96.	MOHAWK VLY CMTY COLLEGE	-4.722	65,036	3,344	17,830	304,106	16
97.	NEW YORK LAW SCHOOL	-4.780	119,731	13,108	22,549	390,037	8
98.	COLLEGE OF MT SNT VINCENT	-4.804	113,965	3,614	57,401	203,454	16
99.	CORNING COMMUNITY COLLEGE	-4.858	66,226	2,368	15,151	285,469	20
100.	CUNY BRONX CMTY COLLEGE	-4.883	76,869	2,443	116,493	537,283	25
101.	FASHION INST TECHNOLOGY	-4.895	54,615	3,694	86,284	551,365	28
102.	HOUGHTON COLLEGE	-4.987	164,663	5,441	28,406	183,960	9
103.	DUTCHESS CMTY COLLEGE	-5.000	76,545	5,270	26,862	250,828	12
104.	LONG IS U SOUTHAMPTON CTR	-5.018	104,000	3,500	23,000	192,733	10
105.	NEW YORK MEDICAL COLLEGE	-5.021	100,000	910	28,505	337,818	7
106.	SUNY AGRL & TECH C ALFRED	-5.039	54,750	2,551	53,860	206,536	13
107.	MONROE COMMUNITY COLLEGE	-5.090	73,967	2,617	45,344	298,772	13
108.	CUNY MEDGAR EVERS COLLEGE	-5.091	76,168	2,451	23,672	287,891	17
109.	ULSTER CO CMTY COLLEGE	-5.150	68,938	4,793	27,091	217,459	12
110.	BROOME COMMUNITY COLLEGE	-5.150	52,066	2,960	74,400	244,753	16
111.	ORANGE CO CMTY COLLEGE	-5.172	69,214	3,269	27,032	228,315	14
112.	NY ST C CERAMICS ALFRED U	-5.179	57,923	3,159	2,979	270,880	12
113.	COOPER UNION	-5.187	73,142	1,863	36,087	221,265	8
114.	WELLS COLLEGE	-5.208	195,122	3,239	14,981	167,231	8
115.	CUNY NEW YORK CITY CC	-5.245	118,960	2,992	31,978	411,013	22
116.	CUNY KINGSBOROUGH CC	-5.253	91,877	2,463	40,832	261,012	11
117.	BARD COLLEGE	-5.305	145,999	3,205	20,200	150,343	7
118.	SCHENECTADY COUNTY CC	-5.307	39,077	3,694	22,875	238,084	12
119.	RUSSELL SAGE JC OF ALBANY	-5.344	74,407	3,888	31,728	213,185	8
120.	BANK STREET COLLEGE OF ED	-5.374	92,580	2,864	50,132	187,525	8
121.	HERKIMER CO CMTY COLLEGE	-5.406	52,524	3,199	13,940	200,559	10
122.	DAEMEN COLLEGE	-5.415	99,564	3,672	19,355	127,102	8
123.	MOUNT SAINT MARY COLLEGE	-5.417	74,005	2,457	84,754	160,443	9
124.	MARYMOUNT COLLEGE	-5.466	107,603	2,695	33,467	129,498	10
125.	SAINT FRANCIS COLLEGE	-5.466	122,119	3,436	12,119	191,731	8
126.	KEUKA COLLEGE	-5.536	92,382	1,941	37,330	150,948	8
127.	EISENHOWER COLLEGE	-5.549	79,535	4,496	23,760	158,996	7
128.	COLG ROCH-BEXLEY-CROZER	-5.549	196,759	3,220	21,386	121,086	7
129.	JAMESTOWN CMTY COLLEGE	-5.555	46,882	1,820	22,459	201,639	11
130.	SUNY AGRL TECH C MORRISVL	-5.556	74,588	3,271	40,649	178,621	13
131.	SUNY MARITIME COLLEGE	-5.564	65,469	2,134	10,570	246,390	13
132.	CMTY COLLEGE FINGER LAKES	-5.621	40,635	1,717	25,558	152,321	11
133.	WESTCHESTER CMTY COLLEGE	-5.638	87,165	2,715	37,491	468,164	24
134.	MARIST COLLEGE	-5.694	80,690	1,795	16,000	164,335	10
135.	MARYMOUNT MANHATTAN C	-5.718	58,898	5,346	26,960	172,924	6

-91-

NEW YORK

(. = MISSING DATA)

STATE RANK	LIBRARY	SCORE	VOLUMES HELD	GROSS VOLUMES ADDED	CIRCULATION	TOTAL EXPENDITURES	TOTAL STAFF
136.	TOMPKINS-CORTLAND CC	-5.752	28,751	1,842	20,083	$191,193	11
137.	SULLIVAN CO CMTY COLLEGE	-5.757	42,947	2,497	68,281	158,698	9
138.	CUNY YORK COLLEGE	-5.856	119,438	2,912	32,051	257,578	14
139.	KING'S COLLEGE	-5.871	73,500	2,248	30,260	124,305	6
140.	NYACK COLLEGE	-5.940	63,932	2,259	20,590	111,338	6
141.	GENERAL THEOLOGICAL SEM	-5.951	192,253	2,734	8,999	134,247	7
142.	CLINTON COMMUNITY COLLEGE	-5.983	33,511	2,846	14,684	185,011	5
143.	ROBERTS WESLEYAN COLLEGE	-6.017	78,196	2,750	20,256	119,744	6
144.	SAINT THOMAS AQUINAS C	-6.051	78,480	3,418	12,281	130,946	8
145.	SNT JOSEPH'S C MAIN CAM	-6.158	107,711	3,249	44,942	65,175	6
146.	CUNY LA GUARDIA CC	-6.166	45,489	1,895	26,781	352,812	21
147.	LONG IS C HOSP SCH NURS	-6.168	15,070	1,370	5,720	143,514	5
148.	CUNY BORO OF MANHATTAN CC	-6.173	50,732	2,075	23,798	344,902	18
149.	NIAGARA CO CMTY COLLEGE	-6.197	36,512	1,143	18,788	317,592	19
150.	SUNY AGRL & TECH C CANTON	-6.258	34,309	1,333	16,569	134,858	7
151.	JEFFERSON CMTY COLLEGE	-6.266	56,248	1,142	16,268	112,964	8
152.	NY INST TECHN NY CTY CAM	-6.267	38,000	1,900	7,759	141,578	6
153.	DOMINICAN C OF BLAUVELT	-6.287	76,259	2,498	10,613	122,101	5
154.	FULTON-MONTGOMERY CC	-6.308	53,787	3,195	14,962	110,547	7
155.	SUNY STATE C OF OPTOMETRY	-6.320	17,827	1,616	17,272	112,024	5
156.	PARSONS SCHOOL OF DESIGN	-6.381	32,400	1,524	35,386	112,756	7
157.	MANHATTAN SCHOOL OF MUSIC	-6.442	90,073	3,151	21,480	91,973	6
158.	HILBERT COLLEGE	-6.445	43,083	1,370	64,276	81,083	4
159.	CONCORDIA COLLEGE	-6.465	40,846	1,810	27,085	85,179	4
160.	PAUL SMITH'S C ARTS & SCI	-6.608	33,120	1,322	23,841	79,417	6
161.	CHRIST THE KING SEMINARY	-6.630	70,542	5,753	7,383	65,072	4
162.	CULINARY INST OF AMERICA	-6.783	15,904	2,265	35,789	73,203	4
163.	CUNY HOSTOS CMTY COLLEGE	-6.814	26,847	2,475	6,671	227,278	9
164.	SNT JOSEPHS SEM & COLLEGE	-6.858	92,642	1,566	3,736	82,900	3
165.	SNT JOSEPHS C SUFFOLK CAM	-7.039	45,424	1,623	17,657	86,402	5
166.	LADYCLIFF COLLEGE	-7.061	76,960	1,587	18,309	73,573	7
167.	GENESEE COMMUNITY COLLEGE	-7.075	46,569	1,449	16,181	141,689	6
168.	MOUNT SAINT ALPHONSUS SEM	-7.113	72,410	2,260	3,804	52,130	3
169.	MARYKNOLL SCH OF THEOLOGY	-7.118	82,650	3,450	100	69,069	5
170.	TROCAIRE COLLEGE	-7.139	37,996	750	6,280	120,131	6
171.	ELIZABETH SETON COLLEGE	-7.141	40,611	1,737	7,330	42,330	5
172.	COLUMBIA-GREENE CC	-7.225	30,562	3,007	17,580	141,110	5
173.	WADHAMS HALL SEM-COLLEGE	-7.309	79,677	2,563	8,182	36,899	3
174.	ADIRONDACK CMTY COLLEGE	-7.363	44,442	800	7,302	114,317	8
175.	SEM IMMAC CONCEPTION	-7.379	43,692	1,815	9,100	33,042	2
176.	N COUNTRY CMTY COLLEGE	-7.523	30,600	1,852	4,204	95,731	5
177.	MARIA COLLEGE OF ALBANY	-7.526	42,725	1,400	35,000	22,257	3
178.	WEBB INST OF NAVAL ARCH	-7.608	32,136	1,734	3,348	50,351	2
179.	NY COLLEGE PODIATRIC MED	-7.677	5,847	557	12,153	47,682	3
180.	CTHOL C IMMAC CONCEPTION	-7.698	76,784	2,648	6,800	94,390	5

NEW YORK

(. = MISSING DATA)

STATE RANK	LIBRARY	SCORE	VOLUMES HELD	GROSS VOLUMES ADDED	CIRCULATION	TOTAL EXPENDITURES	TOTAL STAFF
181.	MEDAILLE COLLEGE	-7.776	89,175	2,100	5,575	$55,005	4
182.	MANNES COLLEGE OF MUSIC	-8.008	22,315	1,040	23,931	39,675	3
183.	MARIA REGINA COLLEGE	-8.148	37,986	861	22,078	18,806	4
184.	MOLLOY COLLEGE	-8.224	78,600	2,500	200	64,258	8
185.	N Y CHIROPRACTIC COLLEGE	-8.373	5,000	320	4,000	22,992	1
186.	CAZENOVIA COLLEGE	-8.384	35,158	682	16,711	54,217	4
187.	FIVE TOWNS COLLEGE	-8.439	8,300	2,100	3,500	23,622	2
188.	SNT VLADMR ORTH THEOL SEM	-8.465	37,000	1,000	1,092	37,508	2
189.	HARRIMAN COLLEGE	-8.985	32,900	1,104	5,108	30,620	2
190.	COLLEGE FOR HUMAN SERVICE	-9.184	19,543	3,500	2,150	30,205	2
191.	MATER DEI COLLEGE	-9.294	46,879	978	4,686	15,908	3
192.	BRAMSON ORT TRAINING CTR	-9.627	3,000	500	2,143	34,133	1
193.	MONROE BUSINESS INSTITUTE	-10.06	2,577	958	889	19,271	1
194.	TAYLOR BUSINESS INSTITUTE	-10.12	2,134	277	2,500	22,730	1
195.	NY SCH OF INTERIOR DESIGN	-10.54	1,979	160	2,233	13,829	1
196.	ALBANY BUSINESS COLLEGE	-11.19	4,073	90	492	9,348	1
197.	OLEAN BUSINESS INSTITUTE	-11.29	1,638	65	200	8,750	1
198.	THE WOOD SCHOOL	-12.28	500	81	136	5,359	0
199.	ROCHESTER BUS INSTITUTE	-12.93	2,279	10	500	1,565	0
200.	BERK-CLAREMONT HICKSVL	-14.11	243	67	30	2,125	0
201.	ACADEMY OF AERONAUTICS	.	24,581	1,904	6,023	.	4
202.	ALBANY COLLEGE PHARMACY	.	6,636	211	408	.	1
203.	ALBANY LAW SCHOOL	.	83,386	20,634	.	424,762	18
204.	BERK-CLAREMONT NY CITY	.	375	50	.	.	2
205.	BROOKLYN LAW SCHOOL	.	145,979	8,750	.	358,144	20
206.	BRYANT-STRATTON BUS INST	.	805	176	1,336	5,384	.
207.	BRYANT-STRATTON BUS INST	.	805	176	1,336	5,384	.
208.	CAYUGA CO CMTY COLLEGE	.	62,747	1,900	21,619	.	6
209.	COLLEGE OF INSURANCE	.	76,339	1,967	7,885	.	6
210.	INTERBORO INSTITUTE	.	3,542	500	.	.	1
211.	IONA COLLEGE	.	170,928	6,567	45,109	.	15
212.	KATHARINE GIBBS SCHOOL	.	1,500	50	480	.	0
213.	LAB INST OF MERCHANDISING	.	3,000	100	.	.	1
214.	NEW YORK THEOL SEMINARY	.	16,893	843	.	34,094	2
215.	POWELSON BUSINESS INST	.	1,182	100	960	.	0
216.	RABBI ISAAC ELCHANAN SEM	.	6,402	10	.	.	1
217.	ROCKLAND CMTY COLLEGE	.	126,966	5,213	.	423,872	19
218.	SAINT BERNARD'S SEMINARY	.	64,415	4,378	4,800	.	4
219.	SCHOOL OF VISUAL ARTS	.	20,000	1,500	32,500	.	6
220.	STENOTYPE INSTITUTE	.	200	10	.	.	0
221.	SUNY AGRL & TECH C DELHI	.	44,737	1,595	26,749	.	9
222.	SUNY AT BINGHAMTON	.	820,000	45,975	225,672	.	106
223.	SUNY EMPIRE STATE COLLEGE	.	4,387	70	40	31,040	.
224.	TECH CAREER INSTITUTES	.	2,051	49	6,380	.	0
225.	THE JUILLIARD SCHOOL	.	14,644	776	44,948	.	6

NEW YORK

(. = MISSING DATA)

STATE RANK	LIBRARY	SCORE	VOLUMES HELD	GROSS VOLUMES ADDED	CIRCULATION	TOTAL EXPENDITURES	TOTAL STAFF
226.	TOBE-COBURN SCH FASH CARS	.	2,266	51	.	$9,769	1
227.	TOURO COLLEGE	.	120,000	25,000	13,500	.	6
228.	UTICA SCHOOL OF COMMERCE	.	1,479	344	.	7,086	1
229.	VILLA MARIA COLLEGE BFLO	.	46,035	1,319	.	38,291	6

NORTH CAROLINA

(. = MISSING DATA)

STATE RANK	LIBRARY	SCORE	VOLUMES HELD	GROSS VOLUMES ADDED	CIRCULATION	TOTAL EXPENDITURES	TOTAL STAFF
1.	U OF NC AT CHAPEL HILL	0.872	2,315,237	110,528	1,010,718	$5,909,461	246
2.	DUKE UNIVERSITY	0.752	3,022,916	74,536	512,691	5,417,884	251
3.	NC STATE U RALEIGH	-0.240	890,024	76,124	396,783	3,398,289	125
4.	WAKE FOREST UNIVERSITY	-1.157	678,242	35,515	196,412	1,957,534	78
5.	U OF NC AT GREENSBORO	-1.318	551,700	30,006	287,147	1,771,126	79
6.	EAST CAROLINA UNIVERSITY	-1.418	577,578	29,059	268,971	2,538,839	104
7.	APPALACHIAN ST UNIVERSITY	-1.700	397,051	25,403	148,754	1,580,989	49
8.	U OF NC AT CHARLOTTE	-1.780	284,710	22,913	168,242	1,847,800	61
9.	WSTN CAROLINA UNIVERSITY	-2.234	295,152	20,697	93,016	1,229,241	35
10.	NC CENTRAL UNIVERSITY	-2.468	434,650	21,660	42,150	1,163,692	42
11.	NC AGRL & TECH STATE U	-2.592	288,694	12,160	65,264	1,002,098	39
12.	U OF NC AT WILMINGTON	-2.924	178,597	15,089	79,260	703,277	24
13.	DAVIDSON COLLEGE	-3.417	250,641	9,475	106,437	449,978	17
14.	PEMBROKE STATE UNIVERSITY	-3.937	151,554	12,224	24,603	432,127	15
15.	CAMPBELL UNIVERSITY	-4.289	153,889	5,833	100,613	259,279	18
16.	U OF NC AT ASHEVILLE	-4.371	107,871	5,027	37,425	301,565	13
17.	FAYETTEVL ST UNIVERSITY	-4.402	112,858	8,723	36,274	387,308	16
18.	WINSTON-SALEM STATE U	-4.434	144,238	7,009	52,026	323,424	17
19.	ELIZABETH CITY STATE U	-4.521	88,164	2,704	30,007	296,968	16
20.	CEN PIEDMONT CMTY COLLEGE	-4.591	67,192	3,059	78,390	363,979	17
21.	GARDNER-WEBB COLLEGE	-4.637	105,415	8,227	35,392	232,927	10
22.	STHESTN BAPTIST THEOL SEM	-4.785	115,769	3,380	66,294	222,760	11
23.	MEREDITH COLLEGE	-5.023	88,527	4,025	59,084	232,135	8
24.	GUILFORD COLLEGE	-5.026	143,572	5,682	34,640	196,125	10
25.	GUILFORD TECHNICAL INST	-5.079	36,694	3,241	32,163	330,585	18
26.	ELON COLLEGE	-5.146	122,105	3,593	41,493	162,276	8
27.	NC SCHOOL OF THE ARTS	-5.227	76,209	5,392	61,456	230,264	10
28.	LENOIR-RHYNE COLLEGE	-5.266	99,541	4,900	21,829	200,255	11
29.	CATAWBA COLLEGE	-5.280	121,754	4,703	26,695	144,927	8
30.	SAINT AUGUSTINES COLLEGE	-5.282	99,658	4,300	64,742	192,428	9
31.	MARS HILL COLLEGE	-5.353	62,872	3,553	19,963	152,545	13
32.	JOHNSN C SMITH UNIVERSITY	-5.392	92,903	3,427	61,095	175,977	12
33.	SOUTHEASTERN CMTY COLLEGE	-5.475	39,679	2,481	16,156	220,499	14
34.	PFEIFFER COLLEGE	-5.545	92,954	3,310	23,394	136,000	8
35.	SNT ANDREWS PRESB COLLEGE	-5.583	91,893	2,238	15,382	135,472	7
36.	PITT CMTY COLLEGE	-5.731	28,097	3,077	18,790	188,905	9
37.	WINGATE COLLEGE	-5.756	76,444	2,693	44,948	132,240	5
38.	HIGH POINT COLLEGE	-5.777	102,624	3,950	24,308	124,603	5
39.	SALEM COLLEGE	-5.832	106,031	2,146	15,070	135,220	5
40.	WAYNE COMMUNITY COLLEGE	-5.949	33,550	1,070	14,809	258,833	10
41.	WILKES COMMUNITY COLLEGE	-6.017	39,337	3,814	18,388	201,179	13
42.	QUEENS COLLEGE	-6.023	98,864	3,024	10,207	111,277	6
43.	CAPE FEAR TECHNICAL INST	-6.030	18,731	1,899	15,000	179,696	11
44.	DAVIDSON CO CMTY COLLEGE	-6.069	34,875	1,387	33,010	157,223	6
45.	CHOWAN COLLEGE	-6.162	62,500	3,175	19,324	122,682	5

NORTH CAROLINA

(. = MISSING DATA)

STATE RANK	LIBRARY	SCORE	VOLUMES HELD	GROSS VOLUMES ADDED	CIRCULATION	TOTAL EXPENDITURES	TOTAL STAFF
46.	BELMONT ABBEY COLLEGE	-6.177	79,717	4,620	7,104	$78,848	7
47.	NC WESLEYAN COLLEGE	-6.198	55,882	2,564	7,258	87,056	4
48.	LENOIR CMTY COLLEGE	-6.207	41,067	2,452	20,214	161,330	9
49.	BENNETT COLLEGE	-6.248	78,930	1,086	10,037	155,040	8
50.	CEN CAROLINA TECH C	-6.274	18,970	1,080	7,190	225,955	13
51.	WILSON CO TECHNICAL INST	-6.299	24,804	1,437	8,924	149,995	9
52.	SANDHILLS CMTY COLLEGE	-6.332	42,223	3,307	18,623	107,250	6
53.	RUCKINGHAM CMTY COLLEGE	-6.347	28,823	1,300	36,835	120,166	6
54.	WARREN WILSON COLLEGE	-6.361	72,132	2,798	20,012	106,468	5
55.	FAYETTEVILLE TECH INST	-6.432	29,642	3,069	22,325	245,524	15
56.	METHODIST COLLEGE	-6.465	65,280	1,442	15,883	92,348	6
57.	CATAWBA VALLEY TECH C	-6.528	25,824	1,914	28,371	125,310	7
58.	LIVINGSTONE COLLEGE	-6.548	69,285	2,613	5,553	91,393	7
59.	FURSYTH TECHNICAL INST	-6.707	26,583	1,417	22,655	138,300	6
60.	ROANOKE-CHOWAN TECH INST	-6.714	22,435	1,387	15,775	130,317	6
61.	HAYWOOD TECHNICAL INST	-6.718	20,490	1,299	8,332	122,839	6
62.	CLEVELAND CO TECH INST	-6.727	20,921	1,362	13,968	125,483	5
63.	GREENSBORO COLLEGE	-6.744	73,681	2,316	13,457	69,262	4
64.	ROBESON TECHNICAL INST	-6.776	29,224	2,954	7,777	81,119	5
65.	SURRY COMMUNITY COLLEGE	-6.776	27,803	1,740	12,563	96,826	6
66.	MITCHELL CMTY COLLEGE	-6.787	28,705	1,478	12,404	86,798	6
67.	RANDOLPH TECHNICAL C	-6.846	19,256	1,001	8,684	76,965	4
68.	GASTON COLLEGE	-6.858	41,904	1,187	10,316	114,106	5
69.	SAINT MARY'S COLLEGE	-6.872	30,243	1,591	12,170	77,726	4
70.	DURHAM TECHNICAL INST	-6.914	19,084	2,235	8,077	128,879	6
71.	TRI-COUNTY COMMUNITY C	-6.916	15,387	2,612	10,954	84,670	3
72.	EDGECOMBE TECH INST	-6.969	16,072	523	7,547	141,428	10
73.	MONTREAT-ANDERSON COLLEGE	-6.994	44,353	1,611	9,260	79,377	5
74.	LOUISBURG COLLEGE	-7.081	46,825	1,241	13,299	57,523	5
75.	WESTERN PIEDMONT CC	-7.134	31,194	1,180	17,523	165,389	9
76.	CALDWELL CC AND TECH INST	-7.146	21,816	1,432	13,689	112,153	8
77.	TECH C OF ALAMANCE	-7.153	22,000	825	9,242	86,649	4
78.	PIEDMONT TECHNICAL INST	-7.154	15,078	1,748	15,448	126,274	8
79.	BREVARD COLLEGE	-7.192	37,820	359	14,029	60,371	4
80.	VANCE-GRANVL CMTY COLLEGE	-7.262	20,413	1,841	22,101	71,372	3
81.	CRAVEN COMMUNITY COLLEGE	-7.272	17,928	1,247	4,839	79,920	4
82.	ROWAN TECHNICAL INSTITUTE	-7.282	20,982	615	10,433	102,950	6
83.	COASTAL CAROLINA CC	-7.294	26,236	627	8,987	121,443	4
84.	STANLY TECHNICAL C	-7.376	16,011	1,196	8,491	77,945	3
85.	MAYLAND TECHNICAL INST	-7.397	13,029	1,677	10,968	55,964	4
86.	SACRED HEART COLLEGE	-7.404	48,047	631	9,225	47,083	4
87.	COLLEGE OF THE ALBEMARLE	-7.460	33,925	1,311	8,409	71,915	4
88.	SHAW UNIVERSITY	-7.551	79,374	1,898	34,638	100,336	5
89.	SAMPSON TECHNICAL C	-7.557	15,690	1,387	15,475	78,930	4
90.	NASH TECHNICAL INSTITUTE	-7.565	18,042	918	7,500	111,826	4

NORTH CAROLINA

(. = MISSING DATA)

STATE RANK	LIBRARY	SCORE	VOLUMES HELD	GROSS VOLUMES ADDED	CIRCULATION	TOTAL EXPENDITURES	TOTAL STAFF
91.	HALIFAX CMTY COLLEGE	-7.593	20,369	2,375	13,703	$81,246	4
92.	PEACE COLLEGE	-7.648	31,850	1,551	11,248	42,146	3
93.	RICHMOND TECHNICAL INST	-7.649	23,013	1,522	8,036	100,256	5
94.	CARTERET TECHNICAL INST	-7.658	17,022	547	6,467	125,068	7
95.	ASHEVL BUNCOMBE TECH C	-7.676	24,775	938	11,758	100,600	6
96.	MARTIN COMMUNITY COLLEGE	-7.779	16,127	1,059	4,585	70,264	3
97.	BLUE RIDGE TECHNICAL C	-7.844	14,552	1,208	7,005	62,521	3
98.	MOUNT OLIVE COLLEGE	-7.871	28,902	1,129	8,668	47,552	3
99.	JAMES SPRUNT INSTITUTE	-7.964	21,531	812	8,240	79,465	4
100.	BARBER-SCOTIA COLLEGE	-8.084	67,526	4,041	3,245	61,488	3
101.	MCDOWELL TECHNICAL INST	-8.119	14,164	867	7,851	41,337	2
102.	SOUTHWESTERN TECH C	-8.147	20,241	1,401	20,624	50,582	3
103.	JOHNSTON TECHNICAL INST	-8.227	12,572	701	8,788	76,656	4
104.	BEAUFORT CO CMTY COLLEGE	-8.330	16,283	1,583	6,274	55,459	4
105.	BLADEN TECHNICAL INST	-8.354	13,782	1,818	3,401	53,405	5
106.	ANSON TECHNICAL COLLEGE	-8.437	12,522	513	5,999	93,138	5
107.	PAMLICO TECHNICAL C	-8.559	10,829	535	4,774	65,727	5
108.	KING'S COLLEGE-RALEIGH	-8.717	11,451	1,129	4,657	47,662	2
109.	MONTGOMERY TECH INSTITUTE	-8.941	8,786	730	2,271	42,238	3
110.	HAMILTON COLLEGE	-10.1	5,976	621	2,223	14,694	1
111.	JOHN WESLEY COLLEGE	-10.44	16,196	863	1,776	10,509	2
112.	WINSALM COLLEGE	-10.95	5,600	90	1,000	9,104	1
113.	ATLANTIC CHRISTIAN C	.	93,130	3,580	30,367	133,403	.
114.	BLANTONS JUNIOR COLLEGE	.	5,266	213	760	.	.
115.	CECILS JUNIOR COLLEGE	.	6,423	219	460	.	2
116.	ISOTHERMAL CMTY COLLEGE	.	27,563	1,479	10,747	.	4
117.	JEFFERSON COLLEGE	.	5,388	0	.	13,070	.
118.	LAFAYETTE COLLEGE	.	5,435	518	.	.	1
119.	LEES-MCRAE COLLEGE	.	.	0	8,297	.	5
120.	PIEDMONT BIBLE COLLEGE	.	39,156	1,942	22,701	74,126	5
121.	ROANOKE BIBLE COLLEGE	.	19,848	2,082	7,453	22,776	.
122.	WAKE TECHNICAL INSTITUTE	.	27,580	1,746	12,626	.	7

NORTH DAKOTA

(. = MISSING DATA)

STATE RANK	LIBRARY	SCORE	VOLUMES HELD	GROSS VOLUMES ADDED	CIRCULATION	TOTAL EXPENDITURES	TOTAL STAFF
1.	U OF ND MAIN CAMPUS	-1.973	524,452	27,455	168,123	$1,312,998	41
2.	ND STATE U MAIN CAMPUS	-2.561	333,187	9,340	50,000	1,141,302	39
3.	MINOT STATE COLLEGE	-4.924	120,229	3,577	35,440	229,685	10
4.	ND STATE SCHOOL SCIENCE	-5.474	56,381	3,999	31,082	214,118	10
5.	VALLEY CITY STATE COLLEGE	-5.941	70,971	4,383	28,095	134,869	5
6.	DICKINSON STATE COLLEGE	-6.339	62,386	2,996	40,643	134,867	5
7.	TRINITY BIBLE INSTITUTE	-6.588	44,231	3,038	77,570	44,901	4
8.	MAYVILLE STATE COLLEGE	-6.671	69,591	2,247	13,561	110,227	4
9.	JAMESTOWN COLLEGE	-6.892	66,027	1,329	19,306	60,593	4
10.	BISMARCK JUNIOR COLLEGE	-6.938	30,717	1,057	16,973	106,427	5
11.	ND STATE U BOTTINEAU BR	-7.299	25,224	933	5,035	68,036	2
12.	MARY COLLEGE	-7.435	38,302	1,570	13,549	54,938	1
13.	U OF ND WILLISTON BRANCH	-9.884	10,454	171	4,134	23,394	1
14.	LAKE REGION JR COLLEGE	.	19,582	295	5,838	28,730	.
15.	NORTHWEST BIBLE COLLEGE	.	26,770	1,720		32,633	1
16.	STANDING ROCK CC	.	5,526	350	1,146	30,150	.

OHIO

(. = MISSING DATA)

STATE RANK	LIBRARY	SCORE	VOLUMES HELD	GROSS VOLUMES ADDED	CIRCULATION	TOTAL EXPENDITURES	TOTAL STAFF
1.	OHIO STATE U MAIN CAMPUS	1.122	3,315,029	103,210	1,590,423	$7,242,273	298
2.	U OF CINCINNATI MAIN CAM	0.086	1,174,705	41,376	524,213	4,273,271	189
3.	CASE WESTERN RESERVE U	-0.351	1,346,464	29,016	259,661	2,977,454	149
4.	KENT STATE U MAIN CAMPUS	-0.690	1,062,895	62,269	415,197	2,189,951	88
5.	U OF AKRON MAIN CAMPUS	-0.750	693,168	37,991	301,743	2,443,979	83
6.	MIAMI UNIV OXFORD CAM	-1.072	925,179	31,230	344,056	2,192,536	83
7.	OHIO U MAIN CAMPUS	-1.152	736,673	21,824	259,170	1,896,312	79
8.	BOWLING GRN ST U MAIN CAM	-1.189	635,484	20,859	365,219	2,457,178	72
9.	CLEVELAND ST UNIVERSITY	-1.230	568,632	28,497	219,199	2,360,071	71
10.	WRIGHT ST U MAIN CAMPUS	-1.273	419,868	21,591	153,431	2,510,450	94
11.	UNIVERSITY OF TOLEDO	-1.443	513,036	32,464	166,787	2,069,665	74
12.	YOUNGSTOWN ST UNIVERSITY	-2.157	417,301	17,727	101,059	1,157,440	42
13.	UNIVERSITY OF DAYTON	-2.522	425,189	13,206	139,035	798,606	43
14.	OHIO NORTHERN UNIVERSITY	-3.337	242,008	13,237	25,665	598,320	25
15.	CAPITAL UNIVERSITY	-3.608	245,315	15,352	58,892	482,147	20
16.	WITTENBERG UNIVERSITY	-3.711	288,618	6,618	59,232	415,112	17
17.	XAVIER UNIVERSITY	-3.715	197,663	11,871	53,706	369,678	13
18.	COLLEGE OF WOOSTER	-3.898	270,591	7,104	64,085	414,775	15
19.	JOHN CARROLL UNIVERSITY	-3.979	349,758	7,403	53,577	289,737	15
20.	CENTRAL STATE UNIVERSITY	-4.026	138,165	4,837	36,826	337,483	20
21.	CUYAHOGA CC DISTRICT	-4.049	146,665	4,812	38,205	644,593	33
22.	MEDL COLLEGE OHIO-TOLEDO	-4.129	74,186	3,394	33,322	448,193	19
23.	HEBREW UNION C MAIN CAM	-4.132	294,820	10,346	12,484	393,128	23
24.	DENISON UNIVERSITY	-4.179	237,889	6,177	47,318	363,751	16
25.	KENYON COLLEGE	-4.203	195,455	7,988	28,065	307,700	12
26.	BALDWIN-WALLACE COLLEGE	-4.238	173,419	5,319	27,192	331,747	19
27.	OHIO WESLEYAN UNIVERSITY	-4.322	378,956	5,885	30,897	375,691	13
28.	SINCLAIR CMTY COLLEGE	-4.550	71,759	7,888	114,611	484,956	15
29.	ASHLAND COLLEGE	-4.606	172,308	6,139	36,140	221,212	14
30.	MARIETTA COLLEGE	-4.628	236,511	4,277	27,470	239,577	12
31.	LORAIN CO CMTY COLLEGE	-4.973	83,230	3,516	49,684	220,005	11
32.	OTTERBEIN COLLEGE	-5.029	117,579	3,581	42,957	194,029	9
33.	NTHESTN OHIO U C MED	-5.154	19,748	7,202	4,105	298,430	10
34.	KETTERING C MEDICAL ARTS	-5.248	45,999	3,722	26,587	186,595	8
35.	HEIDELBERG COLLEGE	-5.262	123,082	2,905	30,759	152,350	7
36.	HIRAM COLLEGE	-5.269	151,899	2,727	29,214	190,217	9
37.	MOUNT UNION COLLEGE	-5.366	185,062	5,037	18,937	176,114	7
38.	FRANKLIN UNIVERSITY	-5.394	43,662	3,086	20,358	244,231	6
39.	MALONE COLLEGE	-5.438	92,015	4,151	32,620	135,884	7
40.	FINDLAY COLLEGE	-5.445	103,660	2,836	25,629	151,795	7
41.	CEDARVILLE COLLEGE	-5.502	75,869	3,900	45,025	167,086	9
42.	WILMINGTON COLLEGE	-5.606	106,406	2,128	15,620	126,106	8
43.	OHIO DOMINICAN COLLEGE	-5.621	91,655	3,299	16,736	162,894	8
44.	MIAMI U MIDDLETOWN CAMPUS	-5.830	65,017	2,206	33,066	140,964	6
45.	KENT ST STARK CO REG CAM	-5.838	61,013	3,669	35,380	139,832	8

OHIO

(. = MISSING DATA)

STATE RANK	LIBRARY	SCORE	VOLUMES HELD	GROSS VOLUMES ADDED	CIRCULATION	TOTAL EXPENDITURES	TOTAL STAFF
46.	OHIO STATE U NEWARK BR	-5.844	40,435	3,030	26,225	$121,702	5
47.	BLUFFTON COLLEGE	-5.863	89,075	2,985	13,946	118,949	5
48.	DEFIANCE COLLEGE	-5.936	83,108	2,085	21,994	141,988	6
49.	COLLEGE OF STEUBENVILLE	-5.981	173,829	12,003	33,544	89,058	4
50.	TRINITY LUTHERAN SEMINARY	-6.051	74,550	2,800	13,506	126,053	7
51.	OHIO STATE U MANSFIELD BR	-6.061	41,117	2,147	22,148	128,884	4
52.	C MT SNT JOS-ON-THE-OHIO	-6.110	105,973	1,827	18,426	109,799	5
53.	KENT ST TRUMBULL REG CAM	-6.119	43,582	4,816	14,458	130,672	5
54.	OHIO U LANCASTER BRANCH	-6.119	47,216	2,658	40,642	132,900	5
55.	MOUNT VERNON NAZARENE C	-6.183	54,071	2,568	18,199	119,350	5
56.	U CINCIN RAYMND WALTERS C	-6.187	30,237	2,637	14,082	245,402	11
57.	RIO GRANDE COLLEGE	-6.195	58,706	2,099	11,313	106,514	6
58.	MICHAEL J OWENS TECH C	-6.244	35,646	1,605	11,295	232,733	6
59.	CLEVELAND INST OF ART	-6.248	33,528	2,000	49,061	81,553	4
60.	UNITED THEOLOGICAL SEM	-6.311	90,840	2,097	13,430	112,361	5
61.	ATHENAEUM OF OHIO	-6.319	105,500	2,500	13,119	83,434	3
62.	KENT ST ASHTABULA REG CAM	-6.338	42,339	1,098	16,602	93,757	4
63.	METHODIST THEOL SCH OHIO	-6.347	71,561	2,799	14,395	115,787	5
64.	LAKE ERIE COLLEGE	-6.355	85,530	1,994	12,189	91,591	6
65.	NOTRE DAME COLLEGE	-6.357	98,541	4,233	17,797	53,529	6
66.	EDGECLIFF COLLEGE	-6.370	71,703	3,585	11,855	87,240	4
67.	WALSH COLLEGE	-6.449	66,951	2,212	5,637	71,190	5
68.	CLARK TECHNICAL COLLEGE	-6.567	23,720	870	13,106	158,902	6
69.	OHIO STATE U LIMA BR	-6.690	51,000	3,560	21,124	159,321	4
70.	PONTIFICAL C JOSEPHINUM	-6.731	92,227	2,771	7,682	71,670	3
71.	CINCINNATI TECH COLLEGE	-6.816	13,972	1,928	5,670	136,356	6
72.	CLEVELAND INST OF MUSIC	-6.848	42,145	1,700	15,597	73,589	4
73.	HEBREW UNION C CAL BRANCH	-6.872	62,750	1,905	4,499	70,737	6
74.	HOCKING TECHNICAL COLLEGE	-6.958	14,548	1,406	7,615	100,707	6
75.	OHIO C PODIATRIC MEDICINE	-6.963	8,479	846	4,153	104,808	5
76.	LAKELAND CMTY COLLEGE	-7.030	66,896	2,401	44,054	147,341	5
77.	OHIO ST U AGRL TECH INST	-7.037	11,863	1,077	12,136	86,134	3
78.	OHIO U CHILLICOTHE BR	-7.065	45,940	1,183	29,861	67,961	4
79.	JEFFERSON TECHNICAL C	-7.182	18,300	800	14,276	94,500	4
80.	TERRA TECHNICAL COLLEGE	-7.210	11,870	1,870	8,000	161,432	9
81.	STHN ST GEN-TECH COLLEGE	-7.298	18,000	3,000	9,000	105,040	7
82.	ART ACADEMY OF CINCINNATI	-7.309	42,802	823	7,643	66,531	5
83.	KENT ST TUSCARAWS REG CAM	-7.484	36,873	1,500	12,710	66,872	2
84.	COLUMBUS C ART AND DESIGN	-7.498	16,620	811	8,276	65,106	4
85.	URBANA COLLEGE	-7.581	52,916	2,065	5,968	86,581	4
86.	OHIO STATE U MARION BR	-7.825	29,299	1,300	13,851	77,886	2
87.	BOWLING GRN ST U FIRELDS	-7.845	30,367	1,303	18,666	82,645	5
88.	OHIO U BELMONT CO BRANCH	-7.990	36,327	610	10,020	44,440	2
89.	OHIO U ZANESVILLE BRANCH	-8.136	54,104	1,441	10,917	106,525	3
90.	SAINT MARY SEMINARY	-8.172	40,058	1,581	2,912	27,493	2

OHIO

(. = MISSING DATA)

STATE RANK	LIBRARY	SCORE	VOLUMES HELD	GROSS VOLUMES ADDED	CIRCULATION	TOTAL EXPENDITURES	TOTAL STAFF
91.	KENT ST E LIVERPL REG CAM	-8.390	28,920	1,321	2,840	$34,870	2
92.	EDISON STATE CMTY COLLEGE	-8.473	16,840	2,137	6,212	40,297	3
93.	NORTHWEST TECH COLLEGE	-8.559	8,800	1,600	2,757	33,765	1
94.	DYKE COLLEGE	-8.662	10,101	446	4,687	58,388	4
95.	U AKRON WAYNE GEN-TECH C	-9.178	18,920	1,000	2,765	34,799	2
96.	WASHINGTON TECH COLLEGE	-9.209	10,450	2,000	2,300	31,899	1
97.	KENT ST U SALEM REG CAM	-9.428	21,659	359	2,470	32,122	1
98.	CHATFIELD COLLEGE	-9.882	17,198	390	1,708	10,752	1
99.	BELMONT TECHNICAL COLLEGE	-10.08	4,497	339	2,139	24,577	1
100.	MIAMI-JACOBS JC BUSINESS	-10.76	1,951	494	2,275	9,836	2
101.	BORROMEO COLLEGE OF OHIO	.	61,597	4,769	4,050	.	2
102.	CIRCLEVILLE BIBLE COLLEGE	.	18,139	754	12,900	.	2
103.	COLUMBUS TECHNICAL INST	.	17,173	738	.	490,069	16
104.	DAVIS JUNIOR COLLEGE	.	3,188	36	236	.	.
105.	LOURDES COLLEGE	.	58,980	2,215	3,775	.	3
106.	MIAMI U HAMILTON CAMPUS	.	55,705	2,834	20,022	170,385	.
107.	OBERLIN COLLEGE	.	802,563	13,305	.	1,036,487	58
108.	OHIO INST UF TECHNOLOGY	.	5,100	200	.	.	1
109.	OHIO U IRONTON BRANCH	.	9,689	0	.	3,047	.
110.	PAYNE THEOLOGICAL SEM	.	16,976	27	5,875	.	1
111.	SHAWNEE ST CMTY COLLEGE	.	61,157	1,439	12,912	99,657	.
112.	TIFFIN UNIVERSITY	.	9,326	239	6,364	.	2
113.	U CINCIN CLERMNT GEN-TECH	.	12,643	1,273	.	92,675	2
114.	URSULINE COLLEGE	.	65,725	3,927	.	62,486	5
115.	WILBERFORCE UNIVERSITY	.	37,963	1,450	4,372	.	6
116.	WRIGHT ST U WSTN OHIO BR	.	20,962	611	6,778	.	2

OKLAHOMA

(. = MISSING DATA)

STATE RANK	LIBRARY	SCORE	VOLUMES HELD	GROSS VOLUMES ADDED	CIRCULATION	TOTAL EXPENDITURES	TOTAL STAFF
1.	U OF OKLAHOMA NORMAN CAM	-0.648	1,562,991	40,490	303,127	$2,410,273	94
2.	OKLA STATE U MAIN CAMPUS	-0.863	1,287,101	30,670	293,863	1,950,607	78
3.	ORAL ROBERTS UNIVERSITY	-1.872	493,910	54,850	183,000	2,006,044	53
4.	UNIVERSITY OF TULSA	-2.209	514,738	37,697	88,722	1,628,440	46
5.	CENTRAL STATE UNIVERSITY	-2.783	267,335	14,634	73,976	1,065,961	48
6.	U OF OKLA HEALTH SCI CTR	-3.347	128,676	4,710	66,026	612,884	29
7.	NORTHEASTERN OKLA STATE U	-3.458	180,567	7,391	51,577	584,353	21
8.	STHWSTN OKLA STATE U	-3.866	196,741	9,215	107,570	403,012	14
9.	EAST CENTRAL OKLA STATE U	-3.913	166,808	15,525	46,593	299,726	12
10.	OKLAHOMA CITY UNIVERSITY	-4.081	212,109	7,068	46,483	334,740	15
11.	CAMERON UNIVERSITY	-4.256	155,827	5,670	71,659	303,658	13
12.	PHILLIPS UNIVERSITY	-4.256	224,183	6,602	73,201	253,828	13
13.	TULSA JUNIOR COLLEGE	-4.563	48,970	6,153	38,650	475,073	21
14.	OSCAR ROSE JUNIOR COLLEGE	-4.644	57,146	5,345	35,000	475,961	26
15.	OKLAHOMA BAPT UNIVERSITY	-4.813	122,310	3,928	88,058	176,865	10
16.	NTHESTN OKLA AGRL-MECH C	-5.045	51,505	3,172	71,707	198,490	12
17.	STHESTN OKLA STATE U	-5.524	123,488	2,596	37,728	144,973	6
18.	NTHWSTN OKLA STATE U	-5.807	114,532	3,020	79,882	110,386	4
19.	BETHANY NAZARENE COLLEGE	-5.854	94,716	2,177	20,250	131,315	7
20.	U OF SCI & ARTS OF OKLA	-5.917	81,427	3,488	28,500	128,185	6
21.	LANGSTON UNIVERSITY	-5.964	131,029	3,418	15,569	100,803	7
22.	SOUTH OKLA CTY JR COLLEGE	-6.244	18,873	2,545	105,614	230,886	10
23.	OKLA PANHANDLE STATE U	-6.341	75,336	3,491	32,199	114,865	2
24.	OKLA CHRISTIAN COLLEGE	-6.433	87,177	2,500	19,783	92,736	5
25.	OKLA C OSTEO MED AND SURG	-6.612	7,334	1,998	8,379	191,475	7
26.	WESTERN OKLAHOMA STATE C	-6.658	30,543	3,001	11,747	87,707	3
27.	EASTERN OKLA ST COLLEGE	-7.038	35,506	997	35,551	77,708	4
28.	NORTHERN OKLAHOMA COLLEGE	-7.044	28,673	1,244	12,684	86,592	4
29.	SEMINOLE JUNIOR COLLEGE	-7.167	20,493	2,351	8,721	72,081	3
30.	MURRAY STATE COLLEGE	-7.212	18,028	1,120	8,000	87,985	7
31.	CLAREMORE JUNIOR COLLEGE	-7.285	22,482	967	14,953	64,629	3
32.	BACONE COLLEGE	-7.292	25,651	1,976	9,652	41,074	3
33.	EL RENO JUNIOR COLLEGE	-7.466	13,276	2,515	10,390	51,688	3
34.	OKLAHOMA CTY STHWSTN C	-7.660	40,820	2,406	7,160	41,168	3
35.	CONNORS STATE COLLEGE	-7.696	30,200	1,824	5,701	111,526	2
36.	BARTLESVILLE WESLEYAN C	-7.990	45,736	1,986	14,324	66,660	2
37.	CARL ALBERT JR COLLEGE	-8.278	12,303	2,100	3,014	57,960	2
38.	OKLA STATE U TECH INST	-8.345	11,954	585	10,200	62,560	4
39.	SAINT GREGORY'S COLLEGE	-8.405	48,863	1,797	3,639	28,992	1
40.	MIDWEST CHRISTIAN COLLEGE	-8.954	18,189	1,147	11,481	22,567	4
41.	SAYRE JUNIOR COLLEGE	-9.729	6,634	956	1,247	23,570	1
42.	HILLSD FREE WILL BAPT C	-10.34	10,293	429	1,430	9,389	1

OREGON

(. = MISSING DATA)

STATE RANK	LIBRARY	SCORE	VOLUMES HELD	GROSS VOLUMES ADDED	CIRCULATION	TOTAL EXPENDITURES	TOTAL STAFF
1.	U OF OREGON MAIN CAMPUS	-0.129	1,424,882	47,846	521,546	$3,522,615	124
2.	OREGON STATE UNIVERSITY	-1.004	844,143	23,889	364,090	2,525,547	80
3.	PORTLAND STATE UNIVERSITY	-1.307	574,477	29,644	183,566	2,217,998	92
4.	LEWIS AND CLARK COLLEGE	-2.818	239,115	15,096	62,022	803,409	25
5.	U OF OREGON HLTH SCI CTR	-3.241	160,579	5,288	55,357	696,720	30
6.	STHN OREGON ST COLLEGE	-3.366	180,834	8,547	78,897	541,423	26
7.	WILLAMETTE UNIVERSITY	-3.529	200,649	6,528	34,118	508,137	21
8.	OREGON COLLEGE OF ED	-4.172	161,869	4,861	86,569	350,599	14
9.	EASTERN OREGON ST COLLEGE	-4.486	86,116	2,600	94,623	344,481	13
10.	PACIFIC UNIVERSITY	-4.686	122,208	4,733	22,043	251,321	15
11.	UNIVERSITY OF PORTLAND	-4.803	179,399	6,619	38,637	241,781	12
12.	LANE COMMUNITY COLLEGE	-4.895	53,265	3,127	109,191	267,297	14
13.	LINN-BENTON CMTY COLLEGE	-5.086	38,430	4,218	25,642	280,402	14
14.	OREGON INST OF TECHNOLOGY	-5.385	52,225	2,993	39,840	191,376	8
15.	CLACKAMAS CMTY COLLEGE	-5.553	41,213	2,777	48,638	168,692	8
16.	LINFIELD COLLEGE	-5.649	97,521	2,355	25,468	149,054	7
17.	MOUNT HOOD CMTY COLLEGE	-6.016	54,008	1,339	65,024	182,537	9
18.	GEORGE FOX COLLEGE	-6.146	65,869	3,111	20,056	100,411	6
19.	CHEMEKETA CMTY COLLEGE	-6.317	44,549	2,841	57,247	229,472	10
20.	WESTERN CONS BAPTIST SEM	-6.354	35,922	1,547	35,775	87,526	6
21.	STHWSTN OREG CMTY COLLEGE	-6.501	47,625	1,872	31,627	229,724	10
22.	UMPQUA COMMUNITY COLLEGE	-6.549	42,860	1,682	30,750	110,784	5
23.	ROGUE COMMUNITY COLLEGE	-6.578	29,019	4,700	12,243	79,917	4
24.	WESTERN BAPTIST COLLEGE	-6.589	40,263	5,015	24,980	60,733	3
25.	CLATSOP COMMUNITY COLLEGE	-6.647	32,739	1,732	16,990	118,795	6
26.	WARNER PACIFIC COLLEGE	-6.675	50,000	2,062	21,822	82,351	3
27.	BLUE MTN CMTY COLLEGE	-6.774	35,479	1,675	13,782	166,268	7
28.	MULTNOMAH SCHOOL OF BIBLE	-6.821	27,062	2,134	31,282	79,298	5
29.	CENTRAL OREG CMTY COLLEGE	-6.850	36,000	873	11,010	73,550	7
30.	MARYLHURST ED CENTER	-6.939	107,800	2,850	17,744	38,837	6
31.	NTHWST CHRISTIAN COLLEGE	-7.075	44,977	1,310	23,422	65,828	4
32.	CONCORDIA COLLEGE	-7.188	40,102	2,334	9,225	61,424	3
33.	OREGON GRADUATE CENTER	-7.686	8,664	1,068	1,300	85,582	2
34.	WSTN EVANGELICAL SEM	-7.722	36,734	1,787	22,534	56,838	4
35.	MUSEUM ART SCHOOL	-7.975	11,044	1,424	5,308	33,111	2
36.	TREASURE VLY CMTY COLLEGE	-8.191	26,830	848	6,215	52,873	3
37.	WSTN STATES CHIRPRCTC C	-8.254	6,992	1,313	16,087	63,979	4
38.	JUDSON BAPTIST COLLEGE	-8.755	25,361	645	2,900	32,231	1
39.	COLUMBIA CHRISTIAN C	-8.806	33,361	1,581	5,656	30,514	2
40.	BASSIST INSTITUTE	-10.48	3,825	402	230	18,061	1
41.	MOUNT ANGEL SEMINARY	.	104,000	3,653	.	.	6
42.	PORTLAND CMTY COLLEGE	.	67,347	3,640	78,268	.	30
43.	REED COLLEGE	.	274,184	7,501	80,617	336,900	.

PENNSYLVANIA

(. = MISSING DATA)

STATE RANK	LIBRARY	SCORE	VOLUMES HELD	GROSS VOLUMES ADDED	CIRCULATION	TOTAL EXPENDITURES	TOTAL STAFF
1.	U OF PENNSYLVANIA	1.013	3,043,428	86,471	509,373	$6,676,372	268
2.	PA STATE U MAIN CAMPUS	0.595	1,556,981	50,320	586,768	5,677,340	266
3.	U OF PITTSBG MAIN CAMPUS	0.583	1,914,422	65,913	629,353	4,961,016	248
4.	TEMPLE UNIVERSITY	0.270	1,637,641	58,419	379,591	4,520,785	215
5.	VILLANOVA UNIVERSITY	-1.828	637,218	20,076	201,194	1,222,393	54
6.	INDIANA U OF PENNSYLVANIA	-2.005	481,303	22,105	212,575	1,416,958	33
7.	LEHIGH UNIVERSITY	-2.033	699,492	25,890	121,583	1,092,544	52
8.	DREXEL UNIVERSITY	-2.038	386,178	13,905	111,970	1,135,328	55
9.	BRYN MAWR COLLEGE	-2.323	548,203	19,773	56,899	1,092,191	38
10.	WEST CHESTER ST COLLEGE	-2.392	370,428	13,187	138,499	1,092,862	31
11.	CARNEGIE-MELLON U	-2.441	465,022	14,940	124,960	844,762	50
12.	SWARTHMORE COLLEGE	-2.447	448,806	13,456	189,165	763,333	38
13.	SLIPPERY ROCK ST COLLEGE	-2.617	408,166	11,908	146,831	937,648	28
14.	BUCKNELL UNIVERSITY	-2.619	395,253	16,211	129,954	841,240	38
15.	DUQUESNE UNIVERSITY	-2.623	473,816	16,673	76,157	774,774	30
16.	EDINBORO STATE COLLEGE	-2.676	337,265	8,714	123,254	931,664	31
17.	CLARION STATE C MAIN CAM	-2.952	299,551	14,999	97,437	827,524	30
18.	MILLERSVILLE ST COLLEGE	-2.953	306,972	13,628	117,890	793,244	27
19.	BLOOMSBURG STATE COLLEGE	-3.045	292,020	12,430	97,825	898,879	24
20.	SHIPPENSBURG ST COLLEGE	-3.184	343,341	7,853	139,368	746,733	31
21.	LA SALLE COLLEGE	-3.232	250,963	10,538	82,100	523,658	26
22.	KUTZTOWN STATE COLLEGE	-3.291	267,470	13,947	75,214	681,930	22
23.	THOMAS JEFF UNIVERSITY	-3.311	117,642	5,927	85,675	636,681	31
24.	EAST STROUDSBG ST COLLEGE	-3.378	304,790	13,941	51,375	675,722	21
25.	LAFAYETTE COLLEGE	-3.389	353,314	11,309	84,151	550,319	25
26.	DICKINSON COLLEGE	-3.417	245,697	8,505	77,478	471,116	21
27.	WIDENER C OF WIDENER U	-3.431	153,830	7,188	462,022	375,904	22
28.	HAVERFORD COLLEGE	-3.525	414,000	7,900	66,806	486,945	23
29.	GETTYSBURG COLLEGE	-3.577	246,687	7,694	74,685	393,235	22
30.	SAINT JOSEPH'S UNIVERSITY	-3.640	181,144	8,125	33,240	442,612	26
31.	FRANKLIN AND MARSHALL C	-3.652	254,709	7,352	70,794	402,142	21
32.	LOCK HAVEN STATE COLLEGE	-3.891	284,579	5,288	64,324	409,449	15
33.	MANSFIELD STATE COLLEGE	-3.918	175,718	3,759	89,829	559,896	23
34.	CALIFORNIA STATE COLLEGE	-3.963	226,734	3,784	83,642	539,100	22
35.	GANNON COLLEGE	-4.045	154,635	7,619	28,925	336,947	17
36.	UNIVERSITY OF SCRANTON	-4.069	189,484	7,068	31,321	336,993	20
37.	CMTY COLLEGE PHILADELPHIA	-4.089	76,307	1,571	85,469	650,526	39
38.	ALLEGHENY COLLEGE	-4.148	263,172	8,867	65,288	289,988	12
39.	MARYWOOD COLLEGE	-4.152	152,771	6,128	98,992	270,410	22
40.	WESTMINSTER COLLEGE	-4.186	186,782	6,955	38,293	304,259	13
41.	WILKES COLLEGE	-4.206	165,307	5,213	38,354	348,292	.17
42.	ROBERT MORRIS COLLEGE	-4.321	84,760	6,495	15,463	441,432	24
43.	BUCKS COUNTY CMTY COLLEGE	-4.351	103,054	8,026	73,061	388,138	21
44.	MUHLENBERG COLLEGE	-4.398	176,669	5,283	33,413	276,985	11
45.	KING'S COLLEGE	-4.440	150,519	4,988	25,819	291,179	17

PENNSYLVANIA

(. = MISSING DATA)

STATE RANK	LIBRARY	SCORE	VOLUMES HELD	GROSS VOLUMES ADDED	CIRCULATION	TOTAL EXPENDITURES	TOTAL STAFF
46.	PA ST U HERSHEY MEDL CTR	-4.510	83,486	2,470	47,988	$338,151	13
47.	YORK COLLEGE PENNSYLVANIA	-4.570	100,942	4,082	32,348	242,348	13
48.	LINCOLN UNIVERSITY	-4.648	136,018	3,600	50,709	263,263	15
49.	ALBRIGHT COLLEGE	-4.662	122,607	4,314	46,244	225,833	11
50.	U OF PITTSBG JOHNSTWN CAM	-4.667	74,197	2,819	27,738	283,726	18
51.	SUSQUEHANNA UNIVERSITY	-4.695	108,088	6,511	19,781	280,103	12
52.	LYCOMING COLLEGE	-4.701	132,221	3,528	28,467	214,258	10
53.	SNT VINCENT C-SEM JT LIB	-4.771	207,732	4,765	18,645	223,011	8
54.	MONTGOMERY CO COMMUNITY C	-4.792	76,618	3,143	52,600	331,598	23
55.	PHILA COLLEGE PHAR & SCI	-4.799	72,462	1,569	7,289	345,846	14
56.	HAHNEMANN MEDL C AND HOSP	-4.800	68,305	2,530	40,428	333,556	17
57.	CC ALLEGHENY CO ALLEG CAM	-4.857	72,812	2,957	32,121	270,841	21
58.	ELIZABETHTOWN COLLEGE	-4.864	127,408	3,669	35,961	222,355	8
59.	HARRISBURG AREA CC	-4.895	86,739	3,903	47,673	338,435	15
60.	MESSIAH COLLEGE	-5.047	95,954	6,874	44,087	187,119	6
61.	SAINT FRANCIS COLLEGE	-5.062	143,794	4,122	13,119	175,322	13
62.	PA STATE U CAPITOL CAMPUS	-5.066	139,651	5,400	31,786	365,431	1
63.	BEAVER COLLEGE	-5.067	118,576	3,847	40,167	176,010	11
64.	WASHINGTON JEFF COLLEGE	-5.128	167,578	4,568	14,044	181,057	9
65.	URSINUS COLLEGE	-5.139	137,787	4,702	22,129	198,146	10
66.	GENEVA COLLEGE	-5.163	119,204	4,071	39,912	192,880	8
67.	PHILA COLLEGE OSTEO MED	-5.177	40,000	2,279	9,446	272,791	10
68.	CEDAR CREST COLLEGE	-5.208	103,245	3,825	29,716	162,289	9
69.	THIEL COLLEGE	-5.219	107,644	3,654	52,644	160,931	7
70.	NORTHAMPTON CO AREA CC	-5.252	51,504	3,991	60,440	229,713	10
71.	SNT CHARLES BORROMEO SEM	-5.295	174,994	5,059	13,619	135,231	11
72.	THE MEDL COLLEGE OF PA	-5.311	30,960	1,911	11,514	245,510	11
73.	PHILA C TEXTILES AND SCI	-5.315	64,626	3,269	17,642	201,450	10
74.	JUNIATA COLLEGE	-5.333	128,928	3,524	11,600	194,926	9
75.	DICKINSON SCHOOL OF LAW	-5.436	92,630	13,733	15,840	256,200	7
76.	ALLNTWN C SNT FRAN DESALS	-5.448	92,774	4,574	29,295	125,458	5
77.	ROSEMONT COLLEGE	-5.519	129,220	3,775	14,881	119,545	7
78.	POINT PARK COLLEGE	-5.642	98,837	2,692	16,073	119,268	7
79.	IMMACULATA COLLEGE	-5.658	115,400	3,267	31,537	77,638	9
80.	LEBANON VALLEY COLLEGE	-5.678	110,539	3,702	11,620	165,285	6
81.	LUTHERAN THEOL SEM PHILA	-5.723	127,230	3,442	12,211	112,977	6
82.	BAPT BIBLE COLLEGE OF PA	-5.730	64,766	3,182	77,240	127,539	8
83.	CHATHAM COLLEGE	-5.767	118,064	2,577	25,261	111,666	6
84.	PHILA COLLEGE OF ART	-5.773	44,966	1,693	45,346	121,177	9
85.	OUR LADY ANGELS COLLEGE	-5.782	65,099	2,534	19,939	83,531	9
86.	LA ROCHE COLLEGE	-5.791	50,000	2,600	23,874	109,552	7
87.	WESTMINSTER THEOL SEM	-5.842	83,500	3,500	12,000	130,600	5
88.	CC ALLEGHENY CO SOUTH CAM	-5.872	42,375	1,743	24,281	170,690	9
89.	DELAWARE VLY C SCI & AGR	-5.891	47,995	1,371	26,635	122,384	9
90.	CHESTNUT HILL COLLEGE	-5.897	92,656	2,645	19,368	91,654	7

-104-

PENNSYLVANIA

(. = MISSING DATA)

STATE RANK	LIBRARY	SCORE	VOLUMES HELD	GROSS VOLUMES ADDED	CIRCULATION	TOTAL EXPENDITURES	TOTAL STAFF
91.	LUTH THEOL SEM GETTYSBURG	-5.925	118,284	2,920	13,126	$117,521	7
92.	MERCYHURST COLLEGE	-5.939	75,835	2,663	17,703	101,580	7
93.	HOLY FAMILY COLLEGE	-6.045	88,443	4,327	21,740	72,547	7
94.	LUZERNE CO CMTY COLLEGE	-6.050	52,027	1,776	17,103	146,600	7
95.	BUTLER CO CMTY COLLEGE	-6.148	38,277	1,917	14,332	120,601	7
96.	CHEYNEY STATE COLLEGE	-6.160	124,700	664	21,487	339,469	17
97.	WILSON COLLEGE	-6.164	151,610	1,289	11,495	106,284	4
98.	PA ST U BEHREND COLLEGE	-6.171	50,772	1,964	21,955	129,689	5
99.	U OF PITTSBG BRADFORD CAM	-6.220	46,945	3,898	5,887	88,044	4
100.	SETON HILL COLLEGE	-6.240	67,592	1,043	29,906	103,119	5
101.	LEHIGH CO CMTY COLLEGE	-6.260	41,870	1,872	18,089	114,265	7
102.	CARLOW COLLEGE	-6.263	102,876	2,119	12,883	101,744	9
103.	GWYNEDD-MERCY COLLEGE	-6.277	58,100	3,000	11,352	86,303	6
104.	WAYNESBURG COLLEGE	-6.341	112,775	2,678	8,950	124,140	4
105.	CMTY COLLEGE DELAWARE CO	-6.374	51,621	2,275	34,980	181,895	9
106.	ALVERNIA COLLEGE	-6.402	52,477	1,934	50,043	47,679	6
107.	ACADEMY OF THE NEW CHURCH	-6.425	98,163	2,764	14,309	79,714	5
108.	LANCASTER THEOLOGICAL SEM	-6.435	122,401	3,071	12,882	86,329	4
109.	EASTERN COLLEGE	-6.460	64,456	1,608	9,545	79,219	5
110.	CC ALLEGHENY CO BOYCE CAM	-6.528	53,589	1,174	46,699	115,361	8
111.	PA STATE U OGONTZ CAMPUS	-6.560	44,211	1,556	17,211	107,281	6
112.	MOORE COLLEGE OF ART	-6.573	31,000	1,087	21,501	96,685	5
113.	CABRINI COLLEGE	-6.680	57,569	1,432	11,726	68,111	4
114.	EASTERN BAPTIST THEOL SEM	-6.689	84,156	1,456	11,395	69,693	4
115.	PA STATE U BERKS CAMPUS	-6.778	30,037	1,689	19,450	89,736	4
116.	WILLIAMSPORT AREA CC	-6.888	42,000	499	9,125	142,449	8
117.	COLLEGE MISERICORDIA	-6.907	102,383	4,383	230	164,986	10
118.	MOUNT ALOYSIUS JR COLLEGE	-6.938	30,222	1,176	11,193	68,989	8
119.	PEIRCE JUNIOR COLLEGE	-7.069	34,906	1,873	42,168	113,155	8
120.	WESTMORELAND COUNTY CC	-7.084	26,816	2,320	7,435	152,164	7
121.	PA ST U WRTHGTN SCRTN CAM	-7.118	29,678	1,976	6,075	69,122	3
122.	PA COLLEGE PODIATRIC MED	-7.130	11,802	732	4,551	85,509	4
123.	THE DROPSIE UNIVERSITY	-7.221	130,000	250	6,000	70,925	3
124.	CC ALLEGHENY CO NORTH CAM	-7.228	11,931	1,641	10,906	149,696	7
125.	U OF PITTSBG GREENSBG CAM	-7.256	46,552	3,138	5,500	84,544	3
126.	PA STATE U MCKEESPORT CAM	-7.277	27,415	790	12,502	62,948	3
127.	VILLA MARIA COLLEGE	-7.297	42,680	2,182	15,966	31,098	3
128.	PA STATE U ALTOONA CAM	-7.314	40,336	2,608	31,338	101,729	5
129.	PA STATE U FAYETTE CAMPUS	-7.336	32,392	1,273	14,408	76,973	4
130.	LACKAWANNA JUNIOR COLLEGE	-7.349	24,000	620	4,678	69,755	4
131.	CLARION ST C VENANGO CAM	-7.351	23,438	1,107	12,323	78,794	3
132.	PA STATE U HAZLETON CAM	-7.363	32,428	1,070	36,295	78,883	4
133.	PA STATE U BEAVER CAMPUS	-7.368	28,891	1,073	25,196	73,473	2
134.	PA STATE U ALLENTOWN CAM	-7.378	23,124	7,267	15,585	60,629	2
135.	PA COLLEGE OF OPTOMETRY	-7.476	14,300	443	9,107	55,377	2

PENNSYLVANIA

(. = MISSING DATA)

STATE RANK	LIBRARY	SCORE	VOLUMES HELD	GROSS VOLUMES ADDED	CIRCULATION	TOTAL EXPENDITURES	TOTAL STAFF
136.	PA ST U NEW KENSINGTN CAM	-7.525	25,039	857	25,283	$70,917	3
137.	ALLIANCE COLLEGE	-7.552	66,499	1,677	2,016	46,278	4
138.	PA STATE U MONT ALTO CAM	-7.578	28,083	1,413	17,312	63,956	3
139.	PA ST U RADNUR CENTER	-7.668	10,216	823	12,599	53,959	1
140.	VALLEY FORGE CHRISTIAN C	-7.719	29,327	1,676	30,905	40,731	3
141.	PA STATE U DU BOIS CAMPUS	-7.855	28,115	1,048	3,192	44,946	2
142.	U OF PITTSBG TITUSVL CAM	-7.881	27,585	1,200	5,152	44,438	2
143.	KEYSTONE JUNIOR COLLEGE	-7.943	33,444	850	9,477	70,605	5
144.	CMTY COLLEGE OF BEAVER CO	-7.961	35,371	1,998	28,913	80,600	4
145.	PA STATE U YORK CAMPUS	-7.965	18,762	995	5,599	51,894	2
146.	PHILA COLLEGE OF BIBLE	-8.067	44,200	1,187	12,974	84,006	4
147.	HARCUM JUNIOR COLLEGE	-8.079	30,380	1,975	19,361	53,261	5
148.	READING AREA CMTY COLLEGE	-8.080	14,554	1,207	4,177	93,984	4
149.	PA STATE U DELAWARE CAM	-8.105	27,034	1,209	9,117	67,759	3
150.	LANCASTER BIBLE COLLEGE	-8.191	26,199	2,027	40,000	51,075	4
151.	CURTIS INSTITUTE OF MUSIC	-8.252	38,300	1,831	5,300	71,372	4
152.	PHILA C PERFORMING ARTS	-8.301	13,981	640	5,562	87,962	5
153.	PA STATE U SCHUYLKILL CAM	-8.374	26,399	1,176	2,869	52,733	2
154.	PA ST U SHENANGO VLY CAM	-8.538	17,143	671	9,713	52,134	3
155.	NORTHEASTERN CHRISTIAN JC	-8.679	25,250	1,318	7,400	51,007	2
156.	VALLEY FORGE MILITARY JC	-8.727	59,214	2,100	2,350	44,776	3
157.	PA ST U WILKES-BARRE CAM	-8.874	15,083	455	8,079	36,870	1
158.	PINEBROOK JUNIOR COLLEGE	-8.976	28,284	11,000	2,561	40,751	1
159.	MANOR JUNIOR COLLEGE	-9.109	21,635	320	4,369	13,681	2
160.	REFORMED PRESB THEOL SEM	-9.566	20,455	617	4,688	14,494	1
161.	THEOL SEM REFORMD EPIS CH	-10.09	20,164	611	810	10,922	1
162.	AMERICAN COLLEGE	.	12,600	1,307	1,345		4
163.	CEN PA BUSINESS SCHOOL	.	3,745	200	2,500	10,797	.
164.	CENTER FOR DEGREE STUDIES	.	2,690	40	400		0
165.	COMBS COLLEGE OF MUSIC	.	12,000	2,000	.	40,665	1
166.	FAITH THEOLOGICAL SEM	.	22,455	151		1,968	0
167.	GRATZ COLLEGE	.	28,000	1,000		44,200	.
168.	GROVE CITY COLLEGE	.	127,148	4,310	23,338		0
169.	MARY IMMACULATE SEMINARY	.	56,650	1,650		28,463	2
170.	MORAVIAN COLLEGE	.	161,189	4,401	45,699	222,746	
171.	NEW SCHOOL OF MUSIC	.	1,531	108		15,645	1
172.	PITTSBURGH THEOL SEMINARY	.	186,721	2,873	27,641	.	6
173.	SPRING GARDEN COLLEGE	.	18,145	742	1,592	.	2
174.	UNITED WESLEYAN COLLEGE	.	28,076	624	8,206	.	1

RHODE ISLAND

(. = MISSING DATA)

STATE RANK	LIBRARY	SCORE	VOLUMES HELD	GROSS VOLUMES ADDED	CIRCULATION	TOTAL EXPENDITURES	TOTAL STAFF
1.	BROWN UNIVERSITY	-0.270	1,636,206	42,632	321,544	$3,168,483	126
2.	U OF RHODE ISLAND	-1.464	869,689	22,488	183,634	1,745,610	66
3.	RHODE ISLAND COLLEGE	-2.809	239,868	13,744	92,865	791,547	28
4.	PROVIDENCE COLLEGE	-3.678	227,508	10,358	40,088	456,430	26
5.	RHODE ISLAND JR COLLEGE	-4.322	72,224	5,185	51,869	465,325	20
6.	ROGER WILLIAMS C MAIN CAM	-5.342	71,120	4,927	14,897	241,684	12
7.	RI SCHOOL OF DESIGN	-5.723	57,004	1,279	114,656	165,085	10
8.	SALVE REGINA-NEWPORT C	-5.782	66,896	3,203	28,117	90,869	7
9.	BRYANT C BUSINESS ADMIN	-6.015	89,023	3,108	34,566	252,726	9
10.	BARRINGTON COLLEGE	-7.302	65,501	1,330	14,347	48,902	2
11.	NEW ENG INST TECHNOLOGY	-10.24	11,110	203	700	18,896	1
12.	JOHNSON & WALES COLLEGE	.	14,500	217	4,026	.	2

SOUTH CAROLINA

(. = MISSING DATA)

STATE RANK	LIBRARY	SCORE	VOLUMES HELD	GROSS VOLUMES ADDED	CIRCULATION	TOTAL EXPENDITURES	TOTA STAF
1.	U OF SC AT COLUMBIA	0.166	1,321,971	79,960	620,425	$3,770,520	160
2.	CLEMSON UNIVERSITY	-1.316	497,793	23,700	202,445	1,855,387	76
3.	MEDICAL UNIVERSITY OF SC	-3.011	128,117	6,602	72,879	832,910	35
4.	WINTHROP COLLEGE	-3.238	271,500	9,760	77,753	675,348	31
5.	COLLEGE OF CHARLESTON	-3.318	197,254	5,949	66,134	563,779	33
6.	FURMAN UNIVERSITY	-3.703	247,502	14,048	58,150	423,977	17
7.	FRANCIS MARION COLLEGE	-3.744	160,487	12,035	37,126	517,965	21
8.	SC STATE COLLEGE	-3.930	214,267	8,958	53,568	398,211	14
9.	LANDER COLLEGE	-4.431	87,248	6,247	57,756	327,482	13
10.	CITADEL MILITARY C OF SC	-4.443	165,206	4,585	34,836	399,000	17
11.	BAPT COLLEGE AT CHASTN	-4.443	94,385	4,409	36,552	338,638	23
12.	BOB JONES UNIVERSITY	-4.669	163,451	5,577	114,608	154,912	19
13.	U OF SC AT AIKEN	-4.715	56,805	7,917	23,845	339,210	10
14.	U OF SC AT SPARTANBURG	-4.855	51,725	4,492	13,244	276,676	11
15.	WOFFORD COLLEGE	-5.020	124,819	6,761	13,403	190,071	10
16.	COLUMBIA COLLEGE	-5.062	101,948	5,493	26,951	184,431	10
17.	U OF SC COASTAL CAROLINA	-5.112	57,165	5,514	47,012	207,604	7
18.	PRESBYTERIAN COLLEGE	-5.255	109,259	8,697	22,899	150,902	7
19.	CONVERSE COLLEGE	-5.300	113,026	3,816	22,482	180,894	10
20.	CLAFLIN COLLEGE	-5.348	116,625	5,457	10,623	230,003	12
21.	TRIDENT TECHNICAL COLLEGE	-5.542	45,464	3,832	29,134	248,884	13
22.	NEWBERRY COLLEGE	-5.707	63,782	5,205	21,425	148,235	8
23.	BENEDICT COLLEGE	-5.798	119,733	86	31,876	264,285	12
24.	COLUMBIA BIBLE COLLEGE	-5.801	49,215	3,460	61,255	119,035	8
25.	GREENVILLE TECH COLLEGE	-5.983	32,664	1,999	26,304	176,561	10
26.	MORRIS COLLEGE	-6.201	61,395	4,296	11,069	119,796	6
27.	TRI-COUNTY TECH COLLEGE	-6.244	30,078	3,054	11,636	116,767	8
28.	MIDLANDS TECH COLLEGE	-6.556	47,914	3,510	16,005	219,913	12
29.	VOORHEES COLLEGE	-6.563	76,873	2,280	5,300	83,258	5
30.	ORANGEBURG CALHOUN TECH C	-6.691	24,524	1,570	11,848	140,857	9
31.	CENTRAL WESLEYAN COLLEGE	-6.698	47,596	2,456	15,986	71,959	5
32.	U OF SC AT BEAUFORT	-6.698	29,338	1,567	7,248	81,170	3
33.	PIEDMONT TECH COLLEGE	-6.777	17,559	847	11,861	111,476	8
34.	ANDERSON COLLEGE	-6.881	27,254	2,149	24,651	73,395	5
35.	ERSKINE C AND SEMINARY	-7.149	110,814	5,849	13,308	113,177	5
36.	COKER COLLEGE	-7.156	60,645	1,235	18,822	63,260	3
37.	SUMTER AREA TECH COLLEGE	-7.206	18,414	987	9,001	70,676	3
38.	U OF SC AT LANCASTER	-7.460	32,308	679	11,406	55,841	3
39.	U OF SC AT SALKEHATCHIE	-7.492	25,504	1,391	16,588	45,909	2
40.	FLORENCE DARLINGTON TECH	-7.733	25,770	1,164	16,740	74,733	4
41.	BEAUFORT TECH COLLEGE	-7.748	12,751	2,150	9,000	85,093	5
42.	U OF SC AT UNION	-7.858	24,730	808	2,788	44,554	2
43.	AIKEN TECHNICAL COLLEGE	-7.951	14,150	1,572	9,257	79,676	7
44.	LIMESTONE COLLEGE	-7.995	52,925	1,525	12,685	54,417	4
45.	WILLIAMSBURG TECH C	-8.361	9,666	1,262	6,540	63,974	4

SOUTH CAROLINA

(. = MISSING DATA)

STATE RANK	LIBRARY	SCORE	VOLUMES HELD	GROSS VOLUMES ADDED	CIRCULATION	TOTAL EXPENDITURES	TOTAL STAFF
46.	HORRY-GEORGETOWN TECH C	-8.365	17,476	965	4,586	$68,801	2
47.	DENMARK TECHNICAL COLLEGE	-8.447	13,554	905	3,468	69,402	4
48.	SPARTANBURG TECH COLLEGE	-8.509	21,616	1,385	7,300	68,414	4
49.	ALLEN UNIVERSITY	-8.623	38,710	2,929	3,025	49,500	2
50.	SPARTANBURG METH COLLEGE	-8.669	26,944	500	7,110	57,273	4
51.	YORK TECHNICAL COLLEGE	-8.705	16,745	715	3,515	54,292	3
52.	FRIENDSHIP COLLEGE	-8.899	9,437	863	1,052	64,984	4
53.	CHESTERFLD-MARLBORO TECH	-9.066	15,335	681	7,722	37,163	2
54.	CLINTON JUNIOR COLLEGE	-11.69	3,000	0	7,200	9,650	2
55.	COLUMBIA JUNIOR C	.	4,194	288	.	.	1
56.	LUTHERAN THEOL STHN SEM	.	68,423	3,170	.	82,574	2
57.	NORTH GREENVILLE COLLEGE	.	33,806	876	6,995	.	4
58.	U OF SC AT SUMTER	.	.	0	62,286	93,065	5

SOUTH DAKOTA

(. = MISSING DATA)

STATE RANK	LIBRARY	SCORE	VOLUMES HELD	GROSS VOLUMES ADDED	CIRCULATION	TOTAL EXPENDITURES	TOTAL STAFF
1.	U OF SD MAIN CAMPUS	-1.923	447,201	19,179	128,822	$1,157,776	51
2.	SD STATE UNIVERSITY	-2.930	308,870	10,248	77,044	757,188	26
3.	AUGUSTANA COLLEGE	-4.340	150,391	5,230	65,133	306,027	11
4.	NORTHERN STATE COLLEGE	-4.799	120,997	5,198	27,008	241,510	9
5.	SD SCH MINES & TECHNOLOGY	-5.184	85,825	2,230	18,653	212,496	9
6.	BLACK HILLS STATE COLLEGE	-5.214	102,784	3,438	28,389	172,985	10
7.	DAKOTA STATE COLLEGE	-5.952	76,775	3,261	11,449	103,660	5
8.	SIOUX FALLS COLLEGE	-6.274	76,327	2,120	13,681	77,070	4
9.	MOUNT MARTY COLLEGE	-6.370	69,078	2,060	17,354	101,474	5
10.	DAKOTA WESLEYAN U	-6.962	68,000	1,400	22,000	65,580	3
11.	NORTH AMERICAN BAPT SEM	-6.977	52,796	2,004	10,721	52,642	3
12.	SINTE GLESKA COLLEGE	-7.180	17,000	2,300	3,653	98,201	5
13.	U OF SD AT SPRINGFIELD	-7.285	79,725	0	24,595	173,193	4
14.	PRESENTATION COLLEGE	-7.391	32,093	1,080	18,559	46,925	3
15.	NATIONAL COLLEGE	-7.490	20,414	1,721	10,975	100,370	4
16.	YANKTON COLLEGE	-7.998	64,655	1,810	4,112	47,473	3
17.	HURON COLLEGE	-8.241	59,941	683	5,100	23,228	2
18.	FREEMAN JUNIOR COLLEGE	-9.068	14,532	543	4,025	25,360	2
19.	OGLALA SIOUX CC	-10.91	11,000	0	1,500	31,900	3

TENNESSEE

(. = MISSING DATA)

STATE RANK	LIBRARY	SCORE	VOLUMES HELD	GROSS VOLUMES ADDED	CIRCULATION	TOTAL EXPENDITURES	TOTAL STAFF
1.	VANDERBILT UNIVERSITY	0.105	1,560,147	53,769	619,224	$3,704,193	149
2.	U OF TENNESSEE KNOXVILLE	-0.218	1,457,351	55,900	743,394	3,969,109	191
3.	MEMPHIS STATE UNIVERSITY	-1.049	867,718	31,636	300,315	2,230,555	112
4.	EAST TENN ST UNIVERSITY	-1.993	559,090	21,935	144,932	1,171,257	45
5.	TENNESSEE ST UNIVERSITY	-2.107	348,582	14,732	1,167,278	887,666	45
6.	MIDDLE TENN ST UNIVERSITY	-2.176	403,795	20,993	165,223	1,018,957	38
7.	U OF TENN CTR HEALTH SCI	-2.905	137,892	21,347	68,511	721,280	35
8.	U OF TENN AT CHATTANOOGA	-2.981	272,177	12,651	56,625	731,294	31
9.	TENNESSEE TECHNOLOGICAL U	-3.073	337,349	12,697	58,533	735,111	28
10.	UNIVERSITY OF THE SOUTH	-3.326	329,017	13,869	56,723	430,667	23
11.	U OF TENNESSEE AT MARTIN	-3.477	206,967	10,536	89,487	540,082	24
12.	AUSTIN PEAY ST UNIVERSITY	-3.685	183,942	8,128	93,612	607,886	26
13.	MEHARRY MEDICAL COLLEGE	-4.538	40,243	892	77,185	508,058	16
14.	SOUTHWESTERN AT MEMPHIS	-4.745	172,831	5,122	46,204	247,228	10
15.	STHN MISSIONARY COLLEGE	-4.765	112,268	4,345	45,189	249,553	16
16.	FREED-HARDEMAN COLLEGE	-4.953	84,256	8,607	70,230	186,646	10
17.	CARSON-NEWMAN COLLEGE	-5.024	137,031	4,401	92,161	147,011	8
18.	DAVID LIPSCOMB COLLEGE	-5.040	106,034	3,713	54,231	228,144	11
19.	LEE COLLEGE	-5.260	83,428	5,167	35,836	163,300	12
20.	CLEVELAND ST CMTY COLLEGE	-5.281	46,876	2,437	19,988	204,891	13
21.	SHELBY STATE CMTY COLLEGE	-5.473	43,842	4,524	29,716	246,920	11
22.	VOLUNTEER ST CMTY COLLEGE	-5.755	31,333	2,234	29,009	141,575	10
23.	JACKSON ST CMTY COLLEGE	-5.811	47,264	1,696	21,217	144,815	8
24.	UNION UNIVERSITY	-5.831	72,909	1,577	29,120	125,950	6
25.	COLUMBIA ST CMTY COLLEGE	-5.883	43,480	1,195	8,511	156,340	7
26.	LAMBUTH COLLEGE	-5.925	78,826	2,369	16,201	94,827	7
27.	TREVECCA NAZARENE COLLEGE	-5.970	73,103	2,661	26,487	96,548	10
28.	TENNESSEE TEMPLE U	-6.013	71,345	6,169	132	215,346	11
29.	MARYVILLE COLLEGE	-6.046	109,761	1,819	37,066	94,526	6
30.	NASHVILLE STATE TECH INST	-6.076	19,659	1,846	7,542	159,194	9
31.	MOTLOW STATE CMTY COLLEGE	-6.112	30,977	1,642	54,430	144,565	7
32.	WALTERS ST CMTY COLLEGE	-6.235	36,416	875	32,792	171,757	11
33.	BELMONT COLLEGE	-6.268	75,386	2,127	12,090	123,065	6
34.	CHATTANOOGA ST TECH CC	-6.369	28,671	3,492	22,458	138,392	5
35.	MEMPHIS THEOLOGICAL SEM	-6.420	67,778	2,910	8,268	73,105	3
36.	TENN WESLEYAN COLLEGE	-6.422	64,501	2,507	11,576	85,386	6
37.	BRYAN COLLEGE	-6.492	60,511	2,353	10,280	76,305	4
38.	LANE COLLEGE	-6.494	80,536	1,581	23,663	107,118	8
39.	STATE TECH INST MEMPHIS	-6.503	29,994	1,712	5,189	159,003	8
40.	MILLIGAN COLLEGE	-6.549	84,776	2,675	16,758	70,914	4
41.	ROANE STATE CMTY COLLEGE	-6.719	28,664	3,725	11,006	169,409	8
42.	CHRISTIAN BROS COLLEGE	-6.735	79,577	2,803	16,188	87,054	6
43.	EMMANUEL SCH OF RELIGION	-6.818	44,090	4,001	7,321	62,021	4
44.	LINCOLN MEM UNIVERSITY	-6.975	55,412	1,175	11,775	66,014	4
45.	LE MOYNE-OWEN COLLEGE	-7.040	79,104	1,375	4,926	76,765	5

TENNESSEE

(. = MISSING DATA)

STATE RANK	LIBRARY	SCORE	VOLUMES HELD	GROSS VOLUMES ADDED	CIRCULATION	TOTAL EXPENDITURES	TOTAL STAFF
46.	SCARRITT COLLEGE	-7.095	52,633	2,248	11,286	$67,600	3
47.	TUSCULUM COLLEGE	-7.135	55,323	1,156	7,991	71,617	4
48.	STHN COLLEGE OF OPTOMETRY	-7.158	14,710	469	5,736	89,316	4
49.	MORRISTOWN COLLEGE	-7.243	22,719	430	6,407	118,753	4
50.	BETHEL COLLEGE	-7.246	67,154	1,136	14,952	58,155	3
51.	KING COLLEGE	-7.722	74,051	1,389	12,580	59,779	3
52.	CUMBERLAND COLLEGE TENN	-7.880	28,547	559	7,500	40,400	2
53.	AQUINAS JUNIOR COLLEGE	-7.897	21,295	525	19,800	35,936	2
54.	MARTIN COLLEGE	-7.964	20,579	1,392	6,516	37,789	2
55.	JOHNSON BIBLE COLLEGE	-8.050	36,349	2,680	15,850	68,916	4
56.	TOMLINSON COLLEGE	-8.159	25,489	1,276	5,054	35,162	3
57.	MEMPHIS ACADEMY OF ARTS	-8.349	16,832	488	7,624	34,050	2
58.	STATE TECH INST KNOXVILLE	-8.799	5,286	1,147	3,428	65,161	3
59.	STEED COLLEGE	-9.769	7,327	380	800	25,515	1
60.	AMER BAPT THEOL SEM	-10.28	16,113	863	2,411	12,743	2
61.	MCKENZIE COLLEGE	-11.13	201	110	305	37,590	2
62.	JOHN A GUPTON COLLEGE	-11.17	4,755	76	215	7,028	1
63.	DRAUGHON'S JR COLLEGE	-11.37	1,448	113	866	10,264	1
64.	BRISTOL COLLEGE	.	2,028	350	1,040	.	0
65.	DRAUGHONS JC BUSINESS	.	2,268	224	1,280	.	.
66.	DYERSBURG ST CMTY COLLEGE	.	27,267	1,650	9,879	78,196	.
67.	EDMONDSON JR COLLEGE	.	1,005	111	446	.	1
68.	FREE WILL BAPTIST BIBLE C	.	30,104	1,571	20,436	.	.
69.	HIWASSEE COLLEGE	.	34,992	493	5,412	51,923	.
70.	KNOXVILLE BUSINESS C	.	3,071	0	500	61,830	1
71.	KNOXVILLE COLLEGE	.	78,455	2,383	17,088	.	8
72.	MID-SOUTH BIBLE COLLEGE	.	19,172	704	.	37,078	2

TEXAS

(. = MISSING DATA)

STATE RANK	LIBRARY	SCORE	VOLUMES HELD	GROSS VOLUMES ADDED	CIRCULATION	TOTAL EXPENDITURES	TOTAL STAFF
1.	U OF TEXAS AT AUSTIN	1.766	3,972,303	214,645	2,642,257	$8,564,666	460
2.	TEXAS A&M U MAIN CAMPUS	0.030	1,222,740	55,951	526,439	3,640,445	154
3.	U OF HOUSTON CEN CAMPUS	-0.123	1,196,071	56,527	272,720	3,561,443	153
4.	TEXAS TECH UNIVERSITY	-0.205	1,151,944	59,046	343,752	3,296,474	127
5.	NORTH TEXAS ST UNIVERSITY	-0.724	818,918	33,323	429,506	2,141,133	98
6.	SOUTHERN METH UNIVERSITY	-1.067	1,103,300	38,045	160,986	2,199,671	70
7.	RICE UNIVERSITY	-1.186	901,953	21,276	176,000	2,081,859	76
8.	U OF TEXAS AT EL PASO	-1.298	475,639	33,138	312,318	1,595,207	66
9.	BAYLOR UNIVERSITY	-1.499	833,305	29,597	228,434	1,574,770	53
10.	U OF TEXAS AT ARLINGTON	-1.780	439,954	31,279	178,165	1,511,904	67
11.	TEXAS CHRISTIAN U	-1.806	849,129	35,722	124,722	1,203,301	44
12.	U OF TEXAS AT DALLAS	-1.960	193,749	32,513	54,460	2,008,496	51
13.	STEPHEN F AUSTIN STATE U	-2.129	333,986	17,500	110,292	1,112,436	47
14.	EAST TEXAS ST UNIVERSITY	-2.130	518,926	23,571	133,618	1,102,042	43
15.	STHWST TEX ST UNIVERSITY	-2.135	365,108	17,963	140,011	1,400,878	54
16.	LAMAR UNIVERSITY	-2.326	377,490	17,674	129,430	1,137,713	47
17.	TEXAS WOMAN'S UNIVERSITY	-2.335	522,091	19,485	237,399	965,069	40
18.	TEXAS MEDL CTR JOINT LIB	-2.401	147,153	8,806	150,898	1,644,574	45
19.	SAN ANTONIO COLLEGE	-2.455	203,289	18,023	77,222	1,727,389	62
20.	U OF TEXAS SAN ANTONIO	-2.480	255,767	38,050	139,477	765,683	39
21.	TEXAS SOUTHERN UNIVERSITY	-2.513	336,616	20,116	61,446	976,532	52
22.	TRINITY UNIVERSITY	-2.591	287,219	13,109	79,231	901,274	50
23.	SAM HOUSTON ST UNIVERSITY	-2.592	590,953	34,106	137,200	1,050,434	31
24.	PAN AMERICAN UNIVERSITY	-2.722	186,818	17,928	131,982	736,591	33
25.	U TEX HLTH SCI SN ANTO	-2.929	112,929	6,486	85,849	895,360	45
26.	WEST TEXAS ST UNIVERSITY	-3.011	247,261	10,944	116,603	596,991	35
27.	U TEX HLTH SCI CTR DALLAS	-3.067	156,792	6,639	45,950	819,610	36
28.	TEXAS A&I UNIVERSITY	-3.273	386,310	15,195	66,559	598,804	20
29.	SNT MARY'S U SAN ANTONIO	-3.315	279,161	8,639	41,892	480,599	35
30.	ABILENE CHRSTN UNIVERSITY	-3.357	235,633	9,090	177,133	419,316	24
31.	TEXAS COLLEGE OSTEO MED	-3.494	36,556	12,496	10,837	1,140,900	25
32.	MIDWESTERN ST UNIVERSITY	-3.574	215,690	11,213	58,952	459,745	14
33.	U HOUSTON CLEAR LAKE CITY	-3.591	218,046	11,168	83,415	449,601	22
34.	U OF TEXAS AT TYLER	-3.653	134,630	11,190	43,157	508,298	17
35.	CORPUS CHRISTI STATE U	-3.699	158,680	11,301	51,276	436,691	15
36.	HAROLD R. YEARY JT LIB	-3.704	121,874	9,770	110,153	522,012	36
37.	HOUSTON COMMUNITY COLLEGE	-3.747	41,217	7,012	17,734	890,578	47
38.	ANGELO STATE UNIVERSITY	-3.748	168,975	9,768	37,655	455,401	18
39.	SUL ROSS STATE UNIVERSITY	-3.813	192,225	12,704	88,722	466,724	14
40.	RICHLAND COLLEGE	-3.838	50,137	5,280	66,509	1,163,567	37
41.	VC UHVC JOINT LIBRARY	-3.950	144,178	5,179	52,052	532,397	21
42.	DEL MAR COLLEGE	-3.982	109,944	5,653	60,444	487,560	21
43.	U OF HOUSTON DOWNTOWN C	-4.003	91,360	16,360	32,269	472,231	28
44.	TARLETON STATE UNIVERSITY	-4.190	144,325	8,218	52,369	415,869	13
45.	EASTFIELD COLLEGE	-4.264	43,845	2,576	89,940	589,944	29

TEXAS

(. = MISSING DATA)

STATE RANK	LIBRARY	SCORE	VOLUMES HELD	GROSS VOLUMES ADDED	CIRCULATION	TOTAL EXPENDITURES	TOTAL STAFF
46.	U OF TEXAS PERMIAN BASIN	-4.376	161,324	4,169	30,650	$289,115	10
47.	TEXAS SOUTHMOST COLLEGE	-4.397	109,868	12,874	107,945	293,500	18
48.	OUR LADY OF LAKE U	-4.438	102,883	3,975	34,404	371,322	20
49.	HARDIN-SIMMONS UNIVERSITY	-4.462	154,276	4,979	38,695	247,031	13
50.	UNIVERSITY OF DALLAS	-4.510	131,846	6,555	70,099	210,206	9
51.	UNIVERSITY OF SNT THOMAS	-4.524	120,925	5,077	33,026	241,228	18
52.	TEX ST TECH INST WACO CAM	-4.657	51,263	3,865	56,787	310,187	15
53.	AUSTIN COMMUNITY COLLEGE	-4.663	26,635	5,993	62,751	559,043	31
54.	INCARNATE WORD COLLEGE	-4.675	119,593	3,968	69,259	237,095	11
55.	AMARILLO COLLEGE	-4.705	64,976	2,942	31,495	343,407	19
56.	TEXAS WESLEYAN COLLEGE	-4.735	126,030	4,726	19,513	234,597	12
57.	SAN JACINTO C CENTRAL CAM	-4.742	103,074	5,655	95,603	232,197	14
58.	AUSTIN COLLEGE	-4.904	127,196	5,335	23,664	197,612	8
59.	MOUNTAIN VIEW COLLEGE	-4.971	36,194	1,194	39,690	452,904	20
60.	EL CENTRO COLLEGE	-5.002	58,022	3,535	18,415	389,297	21
61.	SAINT PHILIP'S COLLEGE	-5.110	55,614	4,790	14,223	344,605	15
62.	ODESSA COLLEGE	-5.146	60,452	2,439	11,669	275,545	14
63.	HOUSTON BAPT UNIVERSITY	-5.160	94,063	5,609	42,566	186,367	11
64.	BROOKHAVEN COLLEGE	-5.233	9,308	4,839	8,566	421,855	16
65.	SOUTHWESTERN UNIVERSITY	-5.236	131,710	4,980	26,442	177,731	11
66.	KILGORE COLLEGE	-5.237	59,067	1,752	17,754	312,762	15
67.	LEE COLLEGE	-5.249	90,641	2,576	14,498	360,745	15
68.	COLLEGE OF THE MAINLAND	-5.257	40,306	2,369	16,967	338,774	9
69.	TEX A&M U AT GALVESTON	-5.298	22,102	5,102	4,954	228,850	9
70.	DALLAS BAPTIST COLLEGE	-5.315	137,296	2,269	20,631	191,329	8
71.	TYLER JUNIOR COLLEGE	-5.354	60,051	2,795	57,011	230,684	10
72.	CENTRAL TEXAS COLLEGE	-5.370	46,016	3,765	25,472	227,907	7
73.	EAST TEXAS BAPT COLLEGE	-5.398	88,824	2,393	34,590	137,736	14
74.	WHARTON CO JR COLLEGE	-5.487	51,478	1,834	25,850	205,940	9
75.	SOUTH TEXAS COLLEGE LAW	-5.494	80,960	7,712	12,250	295,237	6
76.	BAYLOR COLLEGE DENTISTRY	-5.496	51,060	4,505	26,070	126,725	6
77.	GALVESTON COLLEGE	-5.515	34,197	2,100	15,388	238,196	12
78.	MCMURRY COLLEGE	-5.560	136,056	3,613	20,050	130,367	7
79.	SAINT EDWARD'S UNIVERSITY	-5.576	83,795	6,422	17,579	132,245	7
80.	LETOURNEAU COLLEGE	-5.625	96,742	5,450	19,340	145,112	7
81.	EL PASO CO CMTY COLLEGE	-5.675	41,300	6,295	23,582	350,084	21
82.	BLINN COLLEGE	-5.687	64,347	5,241	25,321	203,491	4
83.	BRAZOSPORT COLLEGE	-5.689	42,877	2,155	22,521	155,202	7
84.	STHWSTN ADVENTIST COLLEGE	-5.769	95,889	3,589	50,231	131,045	4
85.	GRAYSON CO JUNIOR COLLEGE	-5.778	48,579	3,577	17,134	191,716	8
86.	NORTH LAKE COLLEGE	-5.784	15,250	5,100	12,406	238,423	5
87.	JARVIS CHRISTIAN COLLEGE	-5.791	55,376	3,887	52,878	113,034	8
88.	TEXAS LUTHERAN COLLEGE	-5.827	89,635	3,054	35,874	116,249	8
89.	HOWARD PAYNE UNIVERSITY	-5.868	119,779	3,400	13,200	150,626	6
90.	NORTH HARRIS CO COLLEGE	-5.909	23,003	2,643	17,772	271,748	11

TEXAS

(. = MISSING DATA)

STATE RANK	LIBRARY	SCORE	VOLUMES HELD	GROSS VOLUMES ADDED	CIRCULATION	TOTAL EXPENDITURES	TOTAL STAFF
91.	MCLENNAN CMTY COLLEGE	-5.975	66,913	3,373	22,176	$165,111	9
92.	BEE COUNTY COLLEGE	-6.319	34,516	2,222	11,084	129,460	6
93.	TEXARKANA CMTY COLLEGE	-6.328	30,333	789	16,771	115,677	7
94.	U OF MARY HARDIN-BAYLOR	-6.364	84,191	844	19,103	87,538	6
95.	SOUTHWEST TEX JR COLLEGE	-6.383	32,705	1,760	11,222	119,734	7
96.	WEATHERFORD COLLEGE	-6.388	46,550	2,171	16,000	95,303	5
97.	WAYLAND BAPTIST COLLEGE	-6.407	77,883	2,479	16,021	101,296	3
98.	MIDLAND COLLEGE	-6.433	20,995	2,810	5,782	143,056	9
99.	HUSTON-TILLOTSON COLLEGE	-6.484	60,867	1,941	8,028	115,872	6
100.	SAN JACINTO C NORTH CAM	-6.487	29,703	6,473	14,398	99,476	5
101.	ALVIN COMMUNITY COLLEGE	-6.531	34,120	2,123	12,831	106,383	6
102.	LUBBOCK CHRISTIAN COLLEGE	-6.569	67,194	2,729	19,230	101,052	6
103.	AUSTIN PRESB THEOL SEM	-6.602	109,232	1,855	15,301	83,763	4
104.	EPIS THEOL SEM SOUTHWEST	-6.608	79,823	18,930	9,401	59,090	4
105.	CISCO JUNIOR COLLEGE	-6.638	26,931	786	50,124	60,123	5
106.	TEXAS COLLEGE	-6.780	100,246	1,332	19,960	68,146	6
107.	TEX ST TECH-HARLINGEN CAM	-6.881	13,650	1,195	8,765	96,661	6
108.	GULF COAST BIBLE COLLEGE	-6.912	35,044	3,033	11,742	73,510	5
109.	SOUTHWESTERN ASSEMB GOD C	-6.936	56,309	2,091	31,666	49,878	4
110.	NAVARRO COLLEGE	-6.943	33,248	1,015	24,133	66,726	4
111.	ANGELINA COLLEGE	-7.019	28,780	1,483	13,000	91,715	5
112.	COOKE COUNTY COLLEGE	-7.112	34,256	1,786	5,984	105,053	2
113.	VERNON REG JUNIOR COLLEGE	-7.155	20,153	1,103	6,802	83,694	4
114.	TEMPLE JUNIOR COLLEGE	-7.217	29,935	1,465	10,612	82,336	3
115.	WESTERN TEXAS COLLEGE	-7.336	33,034	2,855	8,112	95,341	8
116.	HOWARD C AT BIG SPRING	-7.419	31,023	1,165	12,926	55,399	4
117.	HILL JUNIOR COLLEGE	-7.547	24,891	1,077	10,500	51,000	2
118.	AMERICAN TECHNOLOGICAL U	-7.628	13,845	3,065	6,133	55,181	2
119.	PANOLA JUNIOR COLLEGE	-7.653	25,073	1,069	7,532	47,093	3
120.	PARIS JUNIOR COLLEGE	-7.748	26,174	1,830	73	173,834	7
121.	RANGER JUNIOR COLLEGE	-7.903	20,958	620	5,478	40,354	2
122.	STHWSTN CHRISTIAN COLLEGE	-7.953	19,581	1,574	2,025	52,315	2
123.	SCHREINER COLLEGE	-7.994	15,787	979	4,251	41,485	2
124.	HENDERSON CO JR COLLEGE	-8.059	28,000	1,000	5,836	98,098	3
125.	DALLAS BIBLE COLLEGE	-8.126	28,869	2,772	5,098	28,383	2
126.	TEX ST TECH AMARILLO CAM	-8.178	11,115	1,242	6,348	85,715	4
127.	LON MORRIS COLLEGE	-8.310	21,136	814	1,700	59,075	2
128.	JACKSONVILLE COLLEGE	-8.393	18,797	526	3,891	28,921	2
129.	CLARENDON COLLEGE	-8.426	20,282	1,518	4,743	39,320	2
130.	WILEY COLLEGE	-8.543	57,825	152	4,228	82,125	6
131.	PAUL QUINN COLLEGE	-8.597	88,883	3,463	5,251	43,837	4
132.	OBLATE COLLEGE OF STHWST	-8.654	37,241	534	1,875	21,954	2
133.	CONCORDIA LUTH COLLEGE	-8.896	22,156	1,804	3,134	51,394	2
134.	TEXAS CHIROPRACTIC C	-9.289	3,000	288	3,056	37,186	2
135.	BISHOP COLLEGE	.	167,500	1,500	.	.	6

TEXAS

(. = MISSING DATA)

STATE RANK	LIBRARY	SCORE	VOLUMES HELD	GROSS VOLUMES ADDED	CIRCULATION	TOTAL EXPENDITURES	TOTAL STAFF
136.	CEDAR VALLEY COLLEGE	.	13,023	4,290	12,198	.	10
137.	DALLAS CHRISTIAN COLLEGE	.	24,135	2,503	13,819	31,113	.
138.	FRANK PHILLIPS COLLEGE	.	28,918	1,672	6,000	60,610	.
139.	SOUTH PLAINS COLLEGE	.	47,571	2,226	13,491	.	5
140.	SOUTHERN BIBLE COLLEGE	.	18,076	1,036	.	.	1
141.	TARRANT CO JUNIOR COLLEGE	.	128,725	7,885	.	1,550,394	82
142.	U TEX MEDL BR GALVESTON	.	234,728	14,861	39,194	.	67

UTAH

(. = MISSING DATA)

STATE RANK	LIBRARY	SCORE	VOLUMES HELD	GROSS VOLUMES ADDED	CIRCULATION	TOTAL EXPENDITURES	TOTAL STAFF
1.	UNIVERSITY OF UTAH	0.664	2,119,959	127,824	494,702	$4,724,848	241
2.	UTAH STATE UNIVERSITY	-2.092	312,144	12,570	151,200	1,351,974	58
3.	WEBER STATE COLLEGE	-2.769	233,595	17,611	89,983	1,112,670	31
4.	SOUTHERN UTAH ST COLLEGE	-4.666	137,146	11,660	40,343	348,992	10
5.	WESTMINSTER COLLEGE	-6.621	56,302	1,947	11,625	73,560	4
6.	DIXIE COLLEGE	-6.796	48,005	1,946	10,042	67,598	5
7.	UTAH TECH COLLEGE SALT LK	-7.346	17,100	2,176	9,190	134,444	5
8.	LATTER-DAY SAINTS BUS C	-11.23	3,820	0	5,144	19,232	1
9.	BRIGHAM YOUNG U MAIN CAM	.	1,437,439	60,672	1,001,566	.	280
10.	BRIGHAM YOUNG U-HAWA CAM	.	96,249	5,318	75,089	.	44
11.	COLLEGE OF EASTERN UTAH	.	24,793	552	74	77,021	3
12.	SNOW COLLEGE	.	28,762	323	.	.	4
13.	STEVENS HENAGER COLLEGE	.	2,243	69	1,019	.	0
14.	UTAH TECH COLLEGE PROVO	.	.	2,705	.	138,899	11

-118-

VERMONT

(. = MISSING DATA)

STATE RANK	LIBRARY	SCORE	VOLUMES HELD	GROSS VOLUMES ADDED	CIRCULATION	TOTAL EXPENDITURES	TOTAL STAFF
1.	U VT & STATE AGRL COLLEGE	-0.961	699,690	36,997	314,985	$1,967,481	82
2.	MIDDLEBURY COLLEGE	-2.856	275,869	13,731	95,179	669,992	30
3.	SAINT MICHAEL'S COLLEGE	-4.752	102,897	3,983	29,687	231,979	14
4.	NORWICH U MAIN CAM	-5.139	120,000	4,693	20,962	232,036	9
5.	CASTLETON STATE COLLEGE	-5.517	64,869	1,340	23,201	170,735	7
6.	VERMONT LAW SCHOOL	-5.692	55,769	7,678	787	202,565	7
7.	BENNINGTON COLLEGE	-5.748	80,811	2,396	25,025	163,775	8
8.	JOHNSON STATE COLLEGE	-5.850	82,170	3,085	41,742	158,963	6
9.	LYNDON STATE COLLEGE	-6.126	54,447	2,360	24,606	120,372	7
10.	GODDARD COLLEGE	-6.178	70,680	2,637	12,601	136,842	10
11.	TRINITY COLLEGE	-6.559	52,438	2,591	9,822	92,855	6
12.	VERMONT TECHNICAL COLLEGE	-6.756	41,998	1,411	15,965	99,016	5
13.	MARLBORO COLLEGE	-7.456	42,586	1,500	5,535	49,882	2
14.	VERMONT COLLEGE	-7.530	27,988	1,071	9,649	54,368	4
15.	GREEN MOUNTAIN COLLEGE	-7.596	63,721	3,236	15,543	96,236	7
16.	SCH FOR INTRNATL TRAINING	-7.889	23,447	1,064	4,050	42,702	3
17.	CHAMPLAIN COLLEGE	-8.247	26,700	1,925	13,950	53,895	3
18.	SOUTHERN VERMONT COLLEGE	-8.910	15,000	1,612	2,940	32,590	1
19.	C SNT JOSEPH THE PROVIDER	-9.230	20,204	386	7,623	16,892	2

VIRGINIA

(. = MISSING DATA)

STATE RANK	LIBRARY	SCORE	VOLUMES HELD	GROSS VOLUMES ADDED	CIRCULATION	TOTAL EXPENDITURES	TOTAL STAFF
1.	U OF VIRGINIA MAIN CAMPUS	1.035	2,313,336	106,416	747,340	$6,666,911	272
2.	VA POLY INST AND STATE U	0.304	1,157,590	83,150	579,975	4,296,090	161
3.	C OF WILLIAM AND MARY	-1.436	820,778	38,181	136,837	1,681,243	68
4.	OLD DOMINION UNIVERSITY	-1.517	443,467	26,585	207,912	1,470,232	63
5.	NORTHERN VA CMTY COLLEGE	-2.043	199,517	12,602	150,431	4,050,825	104
6.	GEORGE MASON UNIVERSITY	-2.330	177,854	18,480	124,984	1,013,841	41
7.	JAMES MADISON UNIVERSITY	-2.616	273,857	11,856	149,139	787,780	37
8.	UNIVERSITY OF RICHMOND	-3.281	282,428	13,940	60,842	722,153	32
9.	VIRGINIA STATE UNIV	-3.565	197,357	6,189	38,952	570,940	25
10.	WASHINGTON AND LEE U	-3.585	256,768	9,436	36,329	486,416	17
11.	TIDEWATER CMTY COLLEGE	-3.591	105,758	5,478	78,167	707,228	43
12.	MARY WASHINGTON COLLEGE	-3.696	254,756	7,028	80,381	435,371	18
13.	RADFORD UNIVERSITY	-3.698	189,404	11,942	84,655	590,521	23
14.	LONGWOOD COLLEGE	-3.845	179,313	8,854	66,196	338,713	22
15.	HAMPTON INSTITUTE	-4.033	244,030	5,847	65,109	384,289	25
16.	VIRGINIA MILITARY INST	-4.156	244,666	6,343	30,033	401,299	19
17.	CHRISTOPHER NEWPORT C	-4.250	129,620	5,589	44,469	404,042	15
18.	UNION THEOL SEM JOINT LIB	-4.345	207,155	6,366	60,095	301,467	19
19.	NORFOLK STATE UNIVERSITY	-4.345	241,924	13,542	100,868	632,909	36
20.	LYNCHBURG COLLEGE	-4.446	108,918	5,470	52,043	256,863	12
21.	HOLLINS COLLEGE	-4.504	144,489	4,292	33,490	275,292	12
22.	EASTERN VA MEDL SCHOOL	-4.617	28,011	3,540	24,035	317,685	13
23.	J SARGEANT REYNOLDS CC	-4.751	42,834	8,375	32,481	399,951	16
24.	U VA CLINCH VLY COLLEGE	-4.931	82,052	5,172	17,794	231,808	11
25.	LIBERTY BAPTIST COLLEGE	-4.961	80,285	4,901	23,664	294,657	19
26.	FERRUM COLLEGE	-5.194	64,117	5,023	24,175	196,751	8
27.	ROANOKE COLLEGE	-5.271	129,226	5,573	15,650	186,573	8
28.	ESTN MENNONITE C AND SEM	-5.335	92,169	4,284	19,742	209,797	8
29.	SWEET BRIAR COLLEGE	-5.364	174,545	3,444	23,074	209,783	13
30.	RANDOLPH-MACON WOMAN'S C	-5.410	138,243	3,462	28,283	193,503	12
31.	EMORY AND HENRY COLLEGE	-5.434	94,242	4,301	21,284	149,554	9
32.	MARYMOUNT COLLEGE OF VA	-5.481	52,677	4,130	17,755	200,161	12
33.	HAMPDEN-SYDNEY COLLEGE	-5.505	118,511	4,267	14,101	156,736	7
34.	THOMAS NELSN CMTY COLLEGE	-5.527	46,340	3,184	42,810	231,396	14
35.	BRIDGEWATER COLLEGE	-5.538	106,382	4,650	15,022	152,624	6
36.	VIRGINIA UNION UNIVERSITY	-5.555	123,267	1,853	18,325	165,894	9
37.	VA WESTERN CMTY COLLEGE	-5.563	42,415	2,066	24,213	189,170	9
38.	NEW RIVER CMTY COLLEGE	-5.583	23,266	1,803	35,669	222,769	11
39.	AVERETT COLLEGE	-5.587	59,289	4,954	29,821	131,318	6
40.	RANDOLPH-MACON COLLEGE	-5.597	109,221	3,213	15,684	139,513	6
41.	VIRGINIA WESLEYAN COLLEGE	-5.614	65,697	2,853	14,531	143,107	7
42.	MARY BALDWIN COLLEGE	-5.619	120,533	3,326	12,281	151,098	7
43.	DANVILLE CMTY COLLEGE	-5.835	36,607	1,623	41,484	205,122	9
44.	SHENANDOAH C-CONSV MUSIC	-5.995	56,050	5,900	120	202,536	9
45.	PROT EPIS THEOL SEM IN VA	-6.130	100,000	3,338	8,336	177,176	5

VIRGINIA

(. = MISSING DATA)

STATE RANK	LIBRARY	SCORE	VOLUMES HELD	GROSS VOLUMES ADDED	CIRCULATION	TOTAL EXPENDITURES	TOTAL STAFF
46.	VA INTERMONT COLLEGE	-6.168	55,979	2,763	17,700	$104,377	5
47.	LORD FAIRFAX CMTY COLLEGE	-6.494	29,351	2,211	30,802	178,059	9
48.	BLUE RIDGE CMTY COLLEGE	-6.517	36,362	2,275	19,505	101,561	5
49.	PIEDMONT VA CMTY COLLEGE	-6.531	18,889	1,459	26,903	152,043	9
50.	RICHARD BLAND C WM & MARY	-6.663	46,954	1,735	8,804	80,881	4
51.	MTN EMPIRE CMTY COLLEGE	-6.838	19,934	1,245	6,170	110,243	6
52.	DABNEY S LANCASTER CC	-6.856	32,150	998	25,152	92,407	7
53.	SOUTHSIDE VA CMTY COLLEGE	-6.877	27,001	977	10,645	92,054	6
54.	SAINT PAUL'S COLLEGE	-7.101	38,785	704	6,005	104,342	4
55.	JOHN TYLER CMTY COLLEGE	-7.117	27,375	1,009	24,573	113,128	6
56.	WYTHEVILLE CMTY COLLEGE	-7.140	29,375	996	17,067	72,700	4
57.	PAUL D CAMP CMTY COLLEGE	-7.228	19,708	1,341	13,846	123,218	7
58.	CENTRAL VA CMTY COLLEGE	-7.330	37,590	1,645	27,828	93,189	5
59.	SOUTHWEST VA CMTY COLLEGE	-7.376	33,551	2,126	23,118	86,011	5
60.	BLUEFIELD COLLEGE	-7.380	47,982	1,582	10,797	40,954	4
61.	RAPPAHANNOCK CMTY COLLEGE	-7.524	39,800	2,573	21,851	82,059	6
62.	VA HIGHLANDS CMTY COLLEGE	-7.548	23,599	968	15,935	95,155	5
63.	PATRICK HENRY CC	-7.600	28,413	996	9,668	105,868	6
64.	GERMANNA CMTY COLLEGE	-7.615	20,096	1,668	10,348	51,277	3
65.	ESTN SHORE CMTY COLLEGE	-8.245	18,795	1,902	5,475	53,653	3
66.	NATIONAL BUSINESS COLLEGE	-10.46	5,600	433	719	16,766	2
67.	SOUTHERN SEM JR COLLEGE	.	33,496	2,790	6,932	.	2
68.	VIRGINIA COMMONWEALTH U	.	540,586	45,603	.	2,738,347	113

WASHINGTON

(. = MISSING DATA)

STATE RANK	LIBRARY	SCORE	VOLUMES HELD	GROSS VOLUMES ADDED	CIRCULATION	TOTAL EXPENDITURES	TOTAL STAFF
1.	UNIVERSITY OF WASHINGTON	1.614	2,903,685	122,449	2,986,202	$9,256,277	328
2.	WASHINGTON ST UNIVERSITY	0.167	1,189,899	48,477	743,394	4,250,300	168
3.	CENTRAL WASH UNIVERSITY	-2.015	302,380	14,060	126,313	1,525,694	58
4.	WESTERN WASH UNIVERSITY	-2.154	374,111	21,347	270,438	1,569,313	56
5.	EASTERN WASH UNIVERSITY	-2.293	313,848	15,433	125,744	1,199,577	48
6.	UNIVERSITY OF PUGET SOUND	-2.492	326,341	16,764	116,570	849,362	33
7.	EVERGREEN STATE COLLEGE	-2.816	135,496	8,455	153,263	1,051,296	35
8.	GONZAGA UNIVERSITY	-3.031	316,688	9,259	73,703	654,366	26
9.	PACIFIC LUTH UNIVERSITY	-3.575	206,032	10,680	114,688	441,512	15
10.	SEATTLE UNIVERSITY	-4.096	182,513	4,490	60,935	379,284	21
11.	WHITMAN COLLEGE	-4.460	158,614	5,719	23,420	331,119	12
12.	SEATTLE PACIFIC U	-4.610	115,735	4,208	82,730	242,979	11
13.	SPOKANE FLS CMTY COLLEGE	-4.749	38,606	2,809	38,922	552,182	18
14.	WALLA WALLA COLLEGE	-5.015	138,157	4,152	44,015	248,033	13
15.	WHITWORTH COLLEGE	-5.101	73,784	2,730	37,893	209,438	7
16.	EVERETT CMTY COLLEGE	-5.135	46,417	2,234	29,619	348,490	14
17.	COLUMBIA BASIN CC	-5.148	36,436	1,718	113,259	225,326	11
18.	NORTH SEATTLE CC	-5.226	33,091	2,896	23,566	383,570	13
19.	SKAGIT VALLEY COLLEGE	-5.248	58,724	2,791	24,997	239,505	11
20.	HIGHLINE CMTY COLLEGE	-5.322	64,562	2,624	33,136	280,963	16
21.	SHORELINE CMTY COLLEGE	-5.715	68,086	2,924	99,572	440,360	19
22.	BELLEVUE CMTY COLLEGE	-5.791	38,264	1,475	81,604	388,820	18
23.	SEATTLE CC CENTRAL CAMPUS	-5.793	55,000	1,598	51,443	353,453	17
24.	SEATTLE CC SOUTH CAMPUS	-5.944	16,164	910	18,308	234,728	12
25.	SPOKANE COMMUNITY COLLEGE	-6.040	26,525	4,083	29,055	332,176	12
26.	TACOMA COMMUNITY COLLEGE	-6.078	68,932	2,162	25,952	236,539	14
27.	LOWER COLUMBIA COLLEGE	-6.091	25,800	1,415	18,087	155,560	8
28.	FORT STEILACOOM CC	-6.164	31,148	2,857	39,346	316,624	16
29.	OLYMPIC COLLEGE	-6.276	48,363	1,922	37,043	264,230	12
30.	EDMONDS COMMUNITY COLLEGE	-6.314	30,086	1,994	46,322	250,748	14
31.	YAKIMA VALLEY CC	-6.344	37,782	1,161	15,207	155,455	9
32.	PENINSULA COLLEGE	-6.391	32,264	1,495	21,729	134,639	6
33.	WALLA WALLA CMTY COLLEGE	-6.420	32,207	1,483	26,443	316,506	14
34.	GRAYS HARBOR COLLEGE	-6.465	40,598	790	13,593	130,958	5
35.	GREEN RIVER CMTY COLLEGE	-6.495	35,000	1,809	17,299	227,095	14
36.	WENATCHEE VALLEY COLLEGE	-6.591	25,585	1,193	21,426	208,090	9
37.	CENTRALIA COLLEGE	-6.668	30,235	1,069	16,486	131,528	5
38.	BIG BEND CMTY COLLEGE	-6.686	36,137	1,537	6,769	119,850	5
39.	NTHWST C ASSEMBLIES GOD	-7.197	47,853	1,220	26,190	62,477	3
40.	SAINT MARTIN'S COLLEGE	-7.728	88,956	1,363	7,300	73,386	5
41.	WHATCOM CMTY COLLEGE	-7.780	9,756	768	17,479	104,619	6
42.	OLYMPIA TECH CMTY COLLEGE	-7.878	6,888	1,642	6,886	106,274	3
43.	FORT WRIGHT C HOLY NAMES	-8.111	70,810	1,797	9,751	42,506	3
44.	PUGET SOUND C OF BIBLE	-8.254	21,501	2,399	8,010	29,909	2
45.	LUTH BIBLE INST SEATTLE	-8.941	20,000	1,500	6,000	33,245	2

WASHINGTON

(. = MISSING DATA)

STATE RANK	LIBRARY	SCORE	VOLUMES HELD	GROSS VOLUMES ADDED	CIRCULATION	TOTAL EXPENDITURES	TOTAL STAFF
46.	CLARK COLLEGE	.	.	1,403	52,762	$140,527	7
47.	CORNISH INSTITUTE	.	3,630	630	.	30,900	2

WEST VIRGINIA

(. = MISSING DATA)

STATE RANK	LIBRARY	SCORE	VOLUMES HELD	GROSS VOLUMES ADDED	CIRCULATION	TOTAL EXPENDITURES	TOTAL STAFF
1.	WEST VIRGINIA UNIVERSITY	-1.287	778,176	29,936	195,488	$1,875,076	98
2.	MARSHALL UNIVERSITY	-2.631	334,780	8,924	102,631	1,006,978	42
3.	WEST VA INST TECHNOLOGY	-4.334	130,982	5,168	19,634	299,120	19
4.	FAIRMONT STATE COLLEGE	-4.499	156,822	4,661	48,255	324,053	16
5.	CONCORD COLLEGE	-4.526	121,185	4,701	39,646	254,877	12
6.	W VA STATE COLLEGE	-4.668	161,982	4,760	33,721	333,778	16
7.	GLENVILLE STATE COLLEGE	-4.940	96,480	2,364	24,157	212,431	9
8.	BETHANY COLLEGE	-5.126	132,940	1,895	42,039	210,723	8
9.	WEST VA WESLEYAN COLLEGE	-5.187	123,228	4,339	51,789	179,773	11
10.	W VA COLLEGE GRAD STUDIES	-5.221	47,759	2,231	12,157	237,497	13
11.	BLUEFIELD STATE COLLEGE	-5.284	109,369	3,450	19,151	157,717	7
12.	SHEPHERD COLLEGE	-5.703	123,380	4,670	56,976	260,997	13
13.	PARKERSBURG CMTY COLLEGE	-5.724	39,693	2,240	7,750	436,599	17
14.	U OF CHARLESTON	-5.751	85,389	2,078	10,528	159,032	9
15.	SALEM COLLEGE MAIN CAMPUS	-5.792	96,000	6,000	60,000	90,585	6
16.	ALDERSON BROADDUS COLLEGE	-5.857	77,946	3,293	27,091	148,551	7
17.	WHEELING COLLEGE	-6.007	104,105	3,755	15,988	122,516	6
18.	POTOMAC STATE COLLEGE	-6.538	38,054	946	15,654	96,080	5
19.	WEST LIBERTY ST COLLEGE	-6.816	171,913	0	17,500	243,871	14
20.	DAVIS AND ELKINS COLLEGE	-6.946	81,529	5,345	30,000	94,065	7
21.	W VA SCH OSTEOPATHIC MED	-7.075	8,000	1,500	3,234	128,270	5
22.	WEST VIRGINIA NORTHERN CC	-7.435	28,112	3,286	4,534	111,650	9
23.	STHN W VA CC-LOGAN CAM	-7.703	25,344	1,395	10,592	72,180	4
24.	STHN W VA CC-WILLIAMSON	-8.028	22,918	1,015	8,857	70,356	4
25.	BECKLEY COLLEGE	-9.051	11,633	390	7,069	37,161	2
26.	SALEM COLLEGE CLARKSBURG	-10.64	19,000	400	3,500	5,850	1
27.	APPALACHIAN BIBLE COLLEGE	.	26,923	1,673	.	25,145	3
28.	OHIO VALLEY COLLEGE	.	18,985	665	24,747	.	2

WISCONSIN

(. = MISSING DATA)

STATE RANK	LIBRARY	SCORE	VOLUMES HELD	GROSS VOLUMES ADDED	CIRCULATION	TOTAL EXPENDITURES	TOTAL STAFF
1.	U OF WISCONSIN MADISON	1.613	3,501,402	129,271	1,501,569	$8,652,165	335
2.	U OF WISCONSIN MILWAUKEE	-0.415	1,169,444	56,509	504,348	3,627,621	86
3.	MARQUETTE UNIVERSITY	-1.196	639,325	24,741	374,410	1,775,116	68
4.	U OF WISCONSIN OSHKOSH	-2.261	306,063	15,669	144,011	1,118,778	41
5.	U OF WISCONSIN STEVNS PNT	-2.277	260,392	14,183	287,889	1,023,159	46
6.	U OF WISCONSIN WHITEWATER	-2.482	304,453	11,109	107,000	1,038,885	39
7.	U OF WISCONSIN EAU CLAIRE	-2.635	405,753	21,491	288,370	861,918	30
8.	U OF WISCONSIN LA CROSSE	-2.639	318,055	14,004	288,370	799,170	25
9.	U OF WISCONSIN CTR SYS	-2.917	408,283	11,359	139,777	914,911	40
10.	U OF WISCONSIN PARKSIDE	-3.303	284,456	9,977	62,037	766,222	26
11.	U OF WISCONSIN PLATTEVL	-3.356	188,810	9,022	73,251	713,332	24
12.	U OF WISCONSIN RIVER FLS	-3.381	187,844	9,244	94,130	561,972	22
13.	U OF WISCONSIN STOUT	-3.444	172,012	13,036	127,918	620,592	25
14.	MEDICAL COLLEGE OF WIS	-3.972	95,702	5,754	45,222	423,843	19
15.	U OF WISCONSIN SUPERIOR	-4.127	211,200	5,682	127,626	308,860	11
16.	LAWRENCE UNIVERSITY	-4.161	224,218	6,627	33,729	370,624	11
17.	SAINT NORBERT COLLEGE	-4.549	125,717	5,068	32,567	275,212	13
18.	ALVERNO COLLEGE	-4.770	73,109	3,093	52,560	198,593	13
19.	CARTHAGE COLLEGE	-4.796	110,816	3,690	34,518	198,416	11
20.	RIPON COLLEGE	-5.093	109,341	3,626	23,834	186,530	7
21.	BELOIT COLLEGE	-5.199	225,000	4,250	41,647	175,230	7
22.	MADISON AREA TECH COLLEGE	-5.348	52,000	3,700	50,672	283,170	11
23.	MILWAUKEE AREA TECH C	-5.525	49,455	4,734	58,551	264,646	15
24.	MOUNT MARY COLLEGE	-5.717	106,541	2,969	34,608	80,601	6
25.	NICOLET COLLEGE-TECH INST	-5.899	29,738	2,200	15,720	179,850	8
26.	DISTRICT ONE TECH INST	-6.193	39,650	2,800	63,489	170,691	8
27.	CARDINAL STRITCH COLLEGE	-6.309	69,509	3,298	23,921	44,353	6
28.	MORAINE PARK TECH INST	-6.438	24,000	6,000	15,000	105,350	6
29.	MOUNT SENARIO COLLEGE	-6.524	39,140	1,849	17,546	90,903	5
30.	NORTHLAND COLLEGE	-6.628	67,051	2,774	9,334	67,040	4
31.	VITERBO COLLEGE	-6.656	66,937	2,034	38,291	33,241	5
32.	GATEWAY TECH INST-KENOSHA	-6.843	28,471	1,037	83,847	141,564	9
33.	INSTITUTE PAPER CHEMISTRY	-6.865	39,000	801	2,667	102,330	6
34.	MARIAN C OF FOND DU LAC	-7.121	72,000	4,500	87,000	48,599	5
35.	LAKELAND COLLEGE	-7.180	48,110	3,137	15,075	79,724	4
36.	SILVER LAKE COLLEGE	-7.233	60,071	1,740	22,955	28,530	5
37.	MILWAUKEE SCH ENGINEERING	-7.244	29,150	1,801	3,845	87,450	3
38.	NORTH CENTRAL TECH INST	-7.284	27,677	2,816	33,733	114,116	6
39.	MID-STATE TECHNICAL INST	-7.404	26,992	2,112	18,622	80,105	8
40.	FOX VALLEY TECH INST	-7.502	27,173	3,500	20,402	105,990	3
41.	EDGEWOOD COLLEGE	-7.572	59,728	1,173	9,830	48,491	2
42.	WAUKESHA COUNTY TECH INST	-7.579	19,750	2,011	34,030	83,488	5
43.	LAKESHORE TECHNICAL INST	-7.733	22,375	2,560	16,354	74,597	4
44.	CONCORDIA COLLEGE	-7.751	41,846	1,272	7,860	59,384	3
45.	GATEWAY TECH INST-RACINE	-7.939	13,261	654	21,185	70,245	4

WISCONSIN

(. = MISSING DATA)

STATE RANK	LIBRARY	SCORE	VOLUMES HELD	GROSS VOLUMES ADDED	CIRCULATION	TOTAL EXPENDITURES	TOTAL STAFF
46.	BLACKHAWK TECHNICAL INST	-8.053	13,000	600	3,471	$116,430	5
47.	SACRED HEART SCH THEOLOGY	-8.123	48,554	1,573	4,334	31,072	2
48.	HOLY REDEEMER COLLEGE	-8.236	31,929	1,612	2,458	19,212	2
49.	WISCONSIN LUTHERAN C	-8.497	7,500	4,000	622	27,079	1
50.	MILTON COLLEGE	-9.435	62,595	0	9,477	64,738	2
51.	CARROLL COLLEGE	.	155,955	4,610	35,771	173,697	.
52.	MADISON BUSINESS COLLEGE	.	7,446	352	1,744	.	1
53.	NASHOTAH HOUSE	.	57,769	2,609	.	83,549	5
54.	NORTHEAST WIS TECH INST	.	12,982	1,032	9,096	.	10
55.	SNT FRAN SEM PSTL MINSTRY	.	57,504	2,294	5,000	.	2
56.	SNT FRANCIS DE SALES C	.	28,015	782	.	.	1
57.	U OF WISCONSIN GREEN BAY	.	281,800	20,000	.	661,738	25
58.	WESTERN WIS TECH INST	.	24,315	2,352	28,362	.	5

AMERICAN SAMOA

(. = MISSING DATA)

STATE RANK	LIBRARY	SCORE	VOLUMES HELD	GROSS VOLUMES ADDED	CIRCULATION	TOTAL EXPENDITURES	TOTAL STAFF
1.	AMER SAMOA CMTY COLLEGE	-8.222	18,000	1,050	4,000	$62,914	5

CANAL ZONE

(. = MISSING DATA)

STATE RANK	LIBRARY	SCORE	VOLUMES HELD	GROSS VOLUMES ADDED	CIRCULATION	TOTAL EXPENDITURES	TOTAL STAFF
1.	PANAMA CANAL COLLEGE	-7.557	34,082	0	102,630	$150,670	3

GUAM

(. = MISSING DATA)

STATE RANK	LIBRARY	SCORE	VOLUMES HELD	GROSS VOLUMES ADDED	CIRCULATION	TOTAL EXPENDITURES	TOTAL STAFF
1.	UNIVERSITY OF GUAM	-5.618	90,000	5,763	22,790	$377,225	21

PUERTO RICO

(. = MISSING DATA)

STATE RANK	LIBRARY	SCORE	VOLUMES HELD	GROSS VOLUMES ADDED	CIRCULATION	TOTAL EXPENDITURES	TOTAL STAFF
1.	U OF PR RIO PIEDRAS	-0.792	1,076,005	32,157	848,651	$2,850,210	217
2.	U OF PR MAYAGUEZ	-3.174	200,031	3,489	107,324	821,668	59
3.	U PR REG COLLEGES ADMIN	-3.207	124,291	7,410	99,004	898,891	57
4.	INTER AMER U METRO CAM	-3.359	89,877	10,235	110,649	560,834	45
5.	U PR HUMACAO U COLLEGE	-4.503	48,640	3,082	102,634	344,745	21
6.	U OF PR MEDICAL SCIENCES	-4.520	43,592	2,404	14,445	430,386	27
7.	INTER AMER SAN GERMAN CAM	-4.816	90,916	1,761	21,095	296,364	27
8.	U PR CAYEY UNIVERSITY C	-4.853	76,158	3,135	18,095	326,466	27
9.	COLEGIO U DEL TURABO	-5.165	34,827	1,741	53,079	310,834	28
10.	PUERTO RICO JR COLLEGE	-5.269	35,276	1,215	24,635	359,275	33
11.	BAYAMON CEN UNIVERSITY	-5.510	34,458	8,544	24,045	359,276	29
12.	U OF THE SACRED HEART	-5.615	70,929	3,631	44,013	257,441	22
13.	INTER AMER J AGUADILLA BR	-5.869	33,154	4,665	17,670	148,640	11
14.	INTER AMER U ARECIBO BR	-6.062	28,517	2,245	22,697	116,720	10
15.	INTRATL INST WORLD U	-6.087	70,795	6,447	21,925	360,100	22
16.	INTER AMER U GUAYAMA BR	-6.667	17,415	2,897	8,111	75,220	7
17.	INTER AMER U PONCE BR	-6.685	15,802	1,419	7,949	89,630	9
18.	INTER AMER U BARNQUITS BR	-7.266	19,548	382	14,388	72,960	6
19.	UNIVERSIDAD DE PONCE	-9.049	5,299	455	1,358	29,400	2
20.	AMERICAN C PUERTU RICO	.	11,000	1,000	.	73,300	5
21.	ANTILLIAN COLLEGE	.	29,445	4,493	63,690	.	8
22.	CAGUAS CITY COLLEGE	.	4,210	1,803	58	.	.
23.	CARIBBEAN U COLLEGE	.	10,500	3,850	.	.	6
24.	CATHOLIC U PUERTO RICO	.	294,707	14,278	139,306	.	57
25.	CONSERVATORY OF MUSIC PR	.	14,826	2,436	15,746	.	2
26.	EDP C OF PUERTO RICO	.	1,980	959	350	.	3
27.	INST COMERCIAL DE PR JC	.	6,200	600	7,219	48,050	.
28.	INST TECNICO COMERCIAL JC	.	2,725	725	.	.	.
29.	INTER AMER U FAJARDO BR	.	18,848	3,797	6,978	.	10
30.	RAMIREZ C BUS AND TECHN	.	2,891	157	613	.	1
31.	SAN JUAN TECHNOLOGICAL CC	.	3,310	432	2,996	.	5
32.	UNIV POLITECNICA DE PR	.	1,500	200	700	.	1

TRUST TERRITORY PACIFIC ISLANDS

(. = MISSING DATA)

STATE RANK	LIBRARY	SCORE	VOLUMES HELD	GROSS VOLUMES ADDED	CIRCULATION	TOTAL EXPENDITURES	TOTAL STAFF
1.	CMTY COLLEGE MICRONESIA	-9.185	9,000	540	4,120	$32,287	3

VIRGIN ISLANDS

(. = MISSING DATA)

STATE RANK	LIBRARY	SCORE	VOLUMES HELD	GROSS VOLUMES ADDED	CIRCULATION	TOTAL EXPENDITURES	TOTAL STAFF
1.	COLLEGE OF VIRGIN ISLANDS	-4.793	71,009	6,622	21,543	$252,965	8

NOTES

1. William Kruskal, "Statistics in Society: Problems Unsolved and Unformulated," Journal of the American Statistical Association, 76 (Sept. 1981), 511. For valuable suggestions and guidance throughout the preparation of this report I am grateful to Mr. Richard Beazley and Mr. Samuel Peng of the National Center for Education Statistics.

2. Library Statistics: A Handbook of Concepts, Definitions, and Terminology (Chicago: American Library Association, 1966), p. 141. A draft revision of this handbook (Library Data Collection Handbook, ed. Mary Jo Lynch [Chicago: American Library Association, 1981]) does not include a definition of research libraries. A useful summary of other definitions appears in an unpublished report by Boyd Ladd and Robert Ladd, Initial Report on Criteria for Defining a Universe of Research Libraries for NCES (Washington, 1982).

3. For other concerns about the data on microforms see Richard M. Beazley, Library Statistics of Colleges and Universities, 1979 Institutional Data (Washington: NCES, 1981), p. 15.

4. Carnegie Council on Policy Studies in Higher Education, A Classification of Institutions of Higher Education, rev. ed. (Berkeley: The Council, 1976), pp. xv, 1 - 7.

5. In these variables Total microforms equal physical units of microforms of books, periodicals, and other. Expenditures for library materials include expenditures for books plus periodicals plus microforms plus audiovisual.

6. A useful introduction to cluster analysis is Brian Everitt, Cluster Analysis, 2nd ed. (New York: Halsted, 1980).

7. William Klecka, Discriminant Analysis (Beverly Hills: Sage, 1980) is one of the best introductions to discriminant analysis.

8. For a useful, recent summary of factor analysis, see John C. B. Cooper, "Factor Analysis: An Overview," The American Statistician, 37 (May 1983), 141 - 147. In carrying out the principal component analysis, we use natural logarithms of

the raw data because of the data's lognormal tendencies. The use of logarithms ensures that the distribution of the scores resulting from the analysis is approximately normal.

9. In Castaneda v. Partida the Court implied that a hypothesis of no discrimination should be rejected at a significance level of .05. For commentary see David Kaye, "Statistical Evidence of Discrimination," Journal of the American Statistical Association, 77 (Dec. 1982), 773 - 783.

10. It may be of interest to note that the 181 libraries of Table 1 are located in 45 states, as well as the District of Columbia and Puerto Rico. The five states not represented in the list are Alaska, Idaho, Maine, North Dakota, and South Dakota. The states represented by the largest numbers of libraries are California, 22; New York, 15; Illinois, 11; Ohio, 11; and Texas, 9.

11. Of the 2,943 libraries listed in the Appendix 290 lack component scores because they did not report data for one or more of the twelve variables from which the scores are computed. Over half of the libraries reported zeros for one or more variables, especially microforms; total reference, directional, and group transactions; interlibrary borrowing; expenditures for binding; or other operating expenditures. The component score formula involves logarithms of the variables, and the logarithm of 0 is an undefined value. The libraries reporting 0 for one or more variables would thus also lack scores; and altogether over half of the potential 2,943 scores would be missing. In order to avoid such a large number of missing scores, we substituted 1's for 0's. Thus, it became possible to estimate scores for the libraries with zeros for some variables. Note, however, that the scores for these libraries are deflated somewhat. An example early in the list is U of Arkansas Pine Bluff, with a score of -5.042. From its data on volumes, volumes added, and staff, one would expect Pine Bluff to rank higher than 10th in the Arkansas list; but its score is deflated because it reports 0 for expenditures for binding. If it had reported even $200 for binding, say, its score would have been -4.317, and it would have been ranked 7th instead of 10th.

12. The 14 non-research libraries exhibit component scores ranging from -1.694 to -2.455. That is, most of these 14 libraries come very close to falling within the range of research libraries.